GALILEO'S LAWYER

Courtroom Battles in Alternative Health, Complementary Medicine and Experimental Treatments

Richard A. Jaffe, Esq.

Thumbs UP Press
3200 Southwest Frwy.
Suite 3200
Houston, TX 77027
832-615-7355
877-515-2777

Published in the United States of America
First edition, Second printing.

Layout and cover design by Sonja D. Fulbright

To the memory of Thomas Navarro, Sue Spenceley, Jimmy Hagen, Fran Hoggatt, Ed Gochenour, and the others who died;

And to Mary Jo, Dustin, Paul, and the rest who lived.

They all had to fight their government before they could fight their disease.

CONTENTS

Introduction

All truth passes through three stages. First, it is ridiculed. Second, it is violently opposed. Third, it is accepted as being self evident.

–Arthur Schopenhauer

I defend medical mavericks. Many of my clients have invented new treatments. Those that haven't, use the latest or greatest complementary and alternative health remedies in the field that is now called "integrative medicine."

These mavericks are adored by most of their patients, and ridiculed and reviled by their detractors. Supporters believe that alternative remedies are natural, non-toxic, holistic, groundbreaking and life saving. Opponents claim that the very same remedies are unproven, dangerous, life threatening and fraudulent.

Galileo fought the prevailing scientific theory of his time—that the sun revolved around the earth—and was forced to defend his beliefs before the ruling authority, the church. Many of my clients have been forced to defend their treatments in modern day versions of the inquisition, that being licensing proceedings before the state medical boards, malpractice actions and criminal prosecutions. These medical mavericks are like Galileo fighting the medical inquisition, or they are quacks and charlatans like the Russian faith healer and con-man Rasputin.

That makes me Galileo's lawyer, or Rasputin's mouthpiece, depending on your perspective. This book tells the stories of medical mavericks and their legal battles against the government and the church of medical orthodoxy.

Why Is Any of This Interesting or Important?
Whatever your perspective, alternative health is a big business and a hot topic. The supplement industry alone generates more than twenty billion dollars annually. Studies show that almost half of all Americans use alternative or unconventional remedies, such as supplements, herbs, chiropractic, acupuncture, or other forms of natural healing.

Almost every week there is a major story about some unconventional, unapproved, or alternative treatment, or a study about the beneficial effect or uselessness of a well-known vitamin or nutritional supplement. And of course, books about health and diet are frequent occupants of the best-seller lists.

Why are so many Americans looking beyond traditional doctors for relief from everything from back pain to terminal cancer? For starters, baby boomers are not as accepting of growing old and infirm as earlier generations. We expect to live longer and healthier, and we are willing to spend time, effort, and money to realize our expectations.

But the main reason people seek out alternative remedies is that modern medicine cannot effectively treat most types of chronic illnesses, like Parkinson's disease, many forms of advanced cancer, multiple sclerosis, fibromyalgia, autism, Alzheimer's, Lou Gehrig's disease, and the list goes on and on.

We want cures. If conventional medicine doesn't have them, then many of us will go to unconventional practitioners. Think about it: why are there no popular alternative remedies for conditions like syphilis? The reason is simple: conventional medicine has an effective and reasonably priced treatment with no side effects. But there are dozens of alternative cancer clinics around the world, and the supplement industry sells billions of dollars of supplements to prevent heart disease, cancer, and other major illnesses. Many Americans are obviously dissatisfied with the modern, conventional treatments—and rightly so.

Cancer is one of the main battlegrounds in health care, as it is one of the leading causes of death. Each year almost 1.5 million Americans are diagnosed, and each year 550,000 die of the disease. Most of these 550,000 people were treated by aggressive, conventional cancer therapies. True, some people are cured of cancer. But as a general rule, the cured had their cancers detected at an early stage.

Cancer experts agree that most forms of end-stage, widely metastatic cancer is incurable, despite the tens of billions of dollars spent in the last few decades to find cures. As an Italian physician has stated, "Only the beginning of a cancer admits a cure, but when 'tis settled and confirmed, 'tis incurable and [the patient] dies under a cold sweat."

This lyrical summary of the state of the art of cancer treatment is unremarkable, except for the fact that the Italian was actually the renowned Roman physician Celsus, and he gave this summary of the efficacy of cancer treatment in the first century AD.[1] His two-thousand-year-old state-of-the-art analysis still basically applies today.[2] With over half a million treatment failures each year, is it any wonder that people seek alternatives to conventional cancer therapies?

Heart disease is another battleground and the other leading cause of death in Americans. Conventional medicine has statins, other drugs, and procedures such as angioplasty and bypass surgery. But more people are starting to worry about the long-term side effects of these drugs. Statins can adversely

---

1   Patterson, James, *The Dread Disease: Cancer and Modern American Culture* (Cambridge: Harvard University Press, 1989) page 13.
2   Recently there has been news that cancer death rates are down, which I believe is largely due to early detection, a decline in smoking, and fewer women taking carcinogenic hormone replacement therapy. Also in fairness, modern cancer research has come up with some extremely successful treatments for some forms of cancer like childhood leukemia. However, early detection is still probably the most important part of cancer treatment, as it was two thousand years ago.

affect memory, cause muscle problems, and who knows what else. Bypass surgery and angioplasty frequently must be repeated. Many people are suspicious of drug companies and the FDA, so they are turning to unconventional remedies for heart disease.

There are similar issues in other chronic conditions, like back pain. The popular conventional modality is surgery. But these heroic, highly invasive, and expensive interventions often do not provide satisfactory results, so more people are choosing chiropractic, which has been documented to be more effective than some forms of back surgery, or they are utilizing other forms of manipulation or acupuncture that deal with concepts foreign to conventional medicine, like meridians and Chi.

Many are also seeking out complementary practitioners to guide them to a healthy lifestyle and the proper use of nutritional supplements. They do this because conventional doctors and dietitians usually will not recommend an herb or supplement unless it has been proven effective by randomized, controlled clinical trials. But the explosive growth of the supplement industry in the past twenty years has demonstrated that many Americans are not buying conventional medicine's message about diet and supplements. Many Americans are taking back health care from conventional doctors and turning to unconventional practitioners for guidance.

Throughout history, many medical innovations were initially rejected by the medical establishment. Physicians ignored and then ridiculed Semmelweis for recommending that surgeons and physicians wash their hands before patient contact. But obviously, not all novel ideas pan out. In fact, most do not.

If our society were run entirely on principles of *caveat emptor*, "let the buyer beware," the practitioners of the two camps would be fighting these battles exclusively in the marketplace. Theoretically, under capitalist principles, whoever has the most effective treatment at the best price captures the market.

But markets are not perfect. Before the advent of the modern food and drug laws in the early twentieth century, we lived in a world where the snake-oil salesman could put anything into a patent remedy or elixir and claim it cured any disease.[3] And before the twentieth century, in many parts of the country, barbers sidelined as doctors and dentists, and anyone, regardless of training, could treat any person for any disease. Those days are long gone.

The Regulators Step In

Our government has taken on the job of protecting the public in the health care field. This task is accomplished by the licensure of health care practitioners and the regulation of drugs and medical devices.

In a free and open society, a balance must be struck between protecting the public from dangerous or worthless treatments and allowing patients the freedom to make their own health care choices. But many argue there is too much regulation and not enough freedom, especially for the terminally ill, who have nothing to lose.[4]

Under the current state of government regulation, only drugs and medical devices that have been approved by the federal government for some condition are legally available in this country.

Supplements are, for the most part, freely available. However, supplement manufacturers cannot make any claims that their products help any disease or medical condition unless they can first convince the government by way of extremely expensive clinical trials that the claims are true. As a result, few disease claims about supplements are legally made.

As to health care practitioners, the medical profession "owns" the diagnosing and treatment of diseases or medical conditions, because they

---

3   A very good book about some of the worst offenders who took advantage of the lack of any drug regulation and the evolving FDA laws is James Harvey Young's, *The Medical Messiahs: A Social History of Quackery in Twentieth-Century America* (Princeton: Princeton University Press, 1967).

4   One well regarded American thinker has said "If people let the government decide what foods they eat and what medicines they take, their bodies will soon be in as sorry a state as are the souls who live under tyranny." That American was Thomas Jefferson and for better and worse, things have changed since his time. Health oriented people should look up to Jefferson for another reason. Not only did he grow his own vegetables, he may have been the first president (and last) who was mostly a vegetarian. He ate meat rarely and mostly as a condiment for his meals. See http://www.pbs.org/jefferson/archives/interviews/Hatch. htm.

have convinced the legislators of every state that only a trained and licensed medical doctor can safely diagnose and treat diseases. In many states, only a licensed dietitian can give nutritional advice for a fee, even though most dietitians work in food production or in institutions such as hospitals, schools, and prisons.

But despite the government's efforts to regulate and control the heath care field, in a free and open society there is one certain market force: demand. If there is a strong demand for some good or service, people will surface to fill that demand. Thus enters the complementary, alternative, or integrative health care practitioner.

To navigate the complex federal and state regulatory jungle, these practitioners have developed a variety of self-preservation skills. Many unlicensed practitioners are accomplished in verbal acrobatics. These folks do not treat diseases, because they are not licensed medical doctors, but they help build the immune system or provide nutritional support to help the body heal itself. Their supplements do not cure medical conditions like benign prostate disease. Rather, they support urinary health and good flow. (For an explanation of how healthcare is regulated, see the appendix, "Healthcare Law 101," on page 267.)

In Defense of Medical Mavericks and Health Freedom

Intentionally or unawares, some of these folks cross the regulatory line, or so the regulators charge. They are medical doctors who provide unapproved treatments that put patients at risk (or so it is claimed), they "practice medicine" without a medical license, or they are supplement or device manufacturers who go too far in promoting their wares.

Sometimes the policy considerations in these cases are complicated. Many medical mavericks care more about treating patients than compliance with arcane governmental regulations. Sometimes these practitioners are on the wrong side of the law, or so it would appear at first blush. (I said I was a defense lawyer.)

Many terminally ill patients have a strong desire to receive unconventional and unapproved treatments despite the legal technicalities and the belief system of the over-regulators. As some of the following stories demonstrate, the government sometimes frustrates these desires in its attempt to protect the "Public," oftentimes to the detriment of actual patients.

In short, because modern medicine is unable to effectively treat so many deadly diseases, gravely ill people and their family members seek out unconventional remedies. When the medical mavericks who have invented or use these novel, unconventional and unproven remedies are attacked by the government, that's where I come in. I am Galileo's lawyer. Welcome to my world.

CHAPTER ONE

Emanuel Revici:
Genius, Quack or Medicine Man?

Medical malpractice is defined as a departure from the accepted medical standard of care. The medical community decides what constitutes accepted medical care. In cancer, the standard treatments are surgery, radiation, and chemotherapy, or "cut, burn, and poison" as they are affectionately referred to in the alternative medical community. Any treatment not within the accepted standard of care (or which is not given in an FDA-approved clinical trial) is technically a departure from the standard of care and is considered medical malpractice and negligence.

But suppose a patient doesn't want to take one of these accepted treatments. Can a doctor provide something else? Can he or she provide an experimental, unproven treatment outside of an FDA-approved clinical trial without the fear of facing a malpractice action from the patient if things don't go well? The answer to this question changed, at least in New York, as a result of two cases involving Dr. Emanuel Revici.

Introduction

Emanuel Revici was born in Bucharest, Romania, at the end of the nineteenth century. He was drafted out of medical school, commissioned a lieutenant, and placed in command of a medical brigade in the Romanian army during World War I. After the war, Revici completed his medical training at the University of Bucharest medical school. He then taught at the university and practiced medicine outside the university. (Revici was Jewish and Jews were not allowed to practice in Romanian universities.)

In the late 1930s, he moved to Paris where he did clinical research. In 1941, the French Underground arranged for his wartime stay in Mexico City, as the Nazis were after him in Vichy, France for his clandestine work with the Underground.

Revici opened up the original Institute of Applied Biology in Mexico. In 1947, he moved the institute to Brooklyn, New York, at the invitation of prominent local doctors, community leaders, and businessmen. In 1955, his fund-raising foundation purchased a small hospital on Manhattan's Upper East Side, renaming it Trafalgar Hospital. Trafalgar was a general community hospital. The oncology section, which Revici directed, was devoted to the clinical use of his method and therapies.

Revici died in 1998 at the age of 101. My joke to him was that he himself was his best advertisement since he took his own medicine.

During his entire medical career, Revici worked on his biological theory of disease and treated patients with medicines he produced. Revici's big picture idea was that life worked by the interaction of two opposite forces, the anabolic—or building phase, and the catabolic—the tearing down phase.

Revici thought cancer was caused by a biochemical imbalance of two classes of lipids: fatty acids and sterols. Lipids are fats stored in the body that are used for energy production. He believed that lipids like cholesterol, triglycerides, fatty acids and sterols were indispensable to the body's defense system. He was one of the first medical researchers to focus on these substances in the context of cancer.

In 1961, he published his *magnum opus, Research in Physiopathology as a Basis of Guided Chemotherapy with Special Application to Cancer.* It was not a best seller,[5] and even medically trained readers thought it dense and difficult to read. He used common concepts in odd and new ways. Some who managed to trudge through a chunk of the book found that it had novel and ingenious insights and theories.

Revici had been the subject of criticism and adverse medical publicity almost since he first came to the United States. By 1961, he landed on the American Cancer Society's "Unproven Methods" list. Being on this list surely didn't help in the sale of his book, or acceptance of his theories.

In 1965, JAMA (the *Journal of the American Medical Association*) published a short summary of a "Clinical Appraisal Group" which consisted of nine doctors. They reported that supposedly none of the thirty-three patients followed showed any benefit from Revici's treatment. However, a few of the patients were kicked out of the study because they appeared to have benefited from the treatment. (Of course that was not the reason given by the appraisal group.)

Revici had a dedicated group of supporters, many of whom were his successfully treated cancer patients and their families. Revici never used the word "cure" because he didn't think it was possible to ever prove a cure for cancer. He also had a number of medical doctors and researchers who became strong advocates after seeing the results of his work.

Like many alternative doctors, Revici's supporters helped him immensely. They raised the money to buy him his hospital and funded his legal defense (and may the Lord bless and keep them for that noble act). They wrote letters and articles disputing the negative reports. They helped counter the negative press and TV media by putting faces to the idea that he was helping people. And I suppose on a psychological level, life can be good when you are surrounded by grateful people who think you can work miracles.

Since the late 1970s, Revici had worked out of a four story brownstone in Manhattan's Upper East Side. Revici and his staff made most of the medicine he used on the third floor of his brownstone. The medicine, mostly selenium and other trace mineral elements, would be given to patients in little dark bottles,

---

5   Revici maintained that the American Cancer Society paid the publisher to burn the unsold copies of his book.

with a dropper on the top to measure the number of drops the patient was advised to take. Revici sometimes told people to put the drops of medicine on a piece of bread and then eat it, though some of his medications were given via injection.

Revici primarily treated advanced cancer patients, and like many old-time unconventional practitioners with novel treatments, his medical charting was terrible. You had to know his method and substances to understand his medical notes. To a conventional doctor, his notes were gibberish.

Given his age and thick Romanian accent, he was very hard to understand. Despite living in the United States for fifty years, he never learned the English word "and." For him it was always "uuund." Sometimes it was simply impossible to understand him. I suspect that people did a lot of nodding when he spoke to give him the impression they actually understood what he was talking about. I know I did.

By the time I first met him, he was close to ninety years old, and not surprisingly, he seemed well past his prime. He was frail and stooped over. His niece, Elena Avram, ministered to him and acted as his business manager. She took very good care of him. But past his prime or not, somehow, with those little dark dropper-topped bottles, he managed to cure some folks who were given death sentences by conventional doctors. And I mean cure, like being alive, disease-free five, ten or even thirty years later. (Of course, Revici would never call these folks cured.)

When It Rains, It Pours

One day, my law partner, Sam Abady, got a call from a private investigator acquaintance of his who was hooked into the Revici support group. Sam went to meet with Revici and some of his supporters.

Revici and his supporters were worried. Three malpractice cases had been filed against him, and he was in the middle of an administrative licensing (or de-licensing) proceeding before the New York Office of Professional Medical Conduct. All the proceedings were related.

The three lawsuits were filed by the same law firm, Pegalis & Wachsman. The main attorney was Harvey Wachsman. Harvey was a medical doctor who liked being called "Doctor" by the judges. He had been a neurosurgeon, but sometime around age forty, he quit medicine and went to law school. Harvey became one of the most prominent and successful plaintiff malpractice attorneys in New York. He made a ton of money for his clients and himself, or so he said. Harvey was not tall, but he was a big guy, maybe three hundred pounds.

He also had a big ego and a bigger mouth, which he often used to regale me or anyone who would listen with tales about how important and successful he was. He was a member of the prestigious Cosmos Club in Washington, D.C. He had cases around the country, and he gave lectures around the world. His greatness was universally acknowledged and appreciated by all, at least according to him.

I guess that made us just like him. Founded in 1983 (two years before we met Revici), Abady & Jaffe had one associate and a part-time first-year law student helping us out. I was the most senior attorney, having graduated law school four years earlier. My partner, Sam Abady, had all of two years experience when we formed the firm. Between the two of us, we had left or been fired from four top New York law firms. The main thing we had going for us was that we were hungry, very hungry; plus Sam was a good talker. He had been the international college debating champion, and the title was well deserved.

Our firm spent the first six months working out of my two-bedroom apartment near Lincoln Center. But by the time we got the Revici case, we had moved to the top floor of an office building in midtown on Fifth Avenue. It was Flo Ziegfeld's (of *Ziegfeld's Follies* fame) old penthouse. (If the walls could talk…) To get there, we had to take two elevators and walk up a fight of stairs.

The plaintiffs in the three malpractice cases were also the subject patients in the licensing cases. Although the identity of a complainant in a licensing proceeding is confidential, it was clear that Wachsman was behind the complaints. He was playing hardball, but it was a good tactic. The hope was that the board would yank Revici's license; then Wachsman could use the license revocation to prove malpractice in the civil cases.[6]

Unfortunately, Revici was in an even tougher position because a default had been entered against him in one of the federal civil malpractice actions. Revici had been represented by Henry Rothblatt, who was one of the country's premier litigators and health care attorneys. Rothblatt had a sort of partnership with F. Lee Bailey, and together they wrote many legal textbooks. So it was hard to understand how he had allowed Revici to get into this mess. Regrettably, there was no asking Henry, since he had recently died of melanoma (and no, he was not a patient of Revici's).

Sam returned from the meeting with the file. His then live-in girlfriend (and later wife) was a medical doctor. Sam loved talking about medicine, and he knew a great deal about the subject for a layman.

Me, I was the administrative partner. I was just interested in paying the rent and staff, with the hope that there would be enough left over at the end of the month for Sam and me to take a small salary.

Up until then, I had been doing commercial litigation, mostly representing businessmen being sued by banks—deadbeats, if you will. But I wasn't particular: I drafted contracts, represented real estate developers—whatever paid the bills.

I had no inclination for medicine, other than the inclination to pass out at the sight of blood. However, I did have some exposure to alternative health treatments—at least if you consider having a father who blindly used alternative remedies like trying to heal his hernia by putting cabbage leaves on it as exposure to the field. My father also used to drag me to macrobiotic restaurants, mostly Father Divine's in downtown Philadelphia. All the brown rice and cooked-to-hell cabbage and collard greens you could eat for $2.50. I didn't eat much.

Getting Un-defaulted

But before we could get into the whole alternative medicine thing, we had a more immediate problem. Because of the default, there would be no jury trial,

---

6   There may have been one flaw in Wachsman's plan. Revici did not carry malpractice insurance, which normally would be enough to make a grown malpractice attorney cry.

no defense, no nothing. The only thing scheduled was an inquest in which the judge herself would determine how much money the plaintiff would be awarded. Not a great way to enter a case.

How did Revici get into this pickle? All three cases were proceeding normally through the discovery process. Revici had been deposed in one of the federal cases. The attorneys had argued continuously, and the deposition was adjourned.

The federal district judge, Chief Judge Constance Baker Motley of the United States District Court for the Southern District of New York got involved and ordered the deposition to continue. Rothblatt refused to produce Revici.

Unfortunately, Rothblatt never informed Revici about his clever strategy. The federal judge retaliated (as they are wont to do when lawyers ignore their orders) and entered a default against Revici. And then, inconsiderately, Henry Rothblatt died of cancer, and Abady & Jaffe entered the picture.

Sam handled the inquest. There was not much he could do. The patient told about her hardships—and she had plenty, resulting from her bi-lateral mastectomy—and her shortened life expectancy due to Revici's mistreatment. Sam did his best, but Judge Motley was not listening.

The judge took it under advisement and said she would issue a written decision at some future time. We figured we had a month or two to come up with a plan and implement it. Sam moved on to other cases; it was left to me to figure out what to do.

It was obvious that we had to get rid of the default. The Federal Rules of Civil Procedure provide a mechanism for doing just that—Federal Rule 60 (b). A court can vacate a default for the "excusable neglect" of an attorney. However, Henry's actions were not neglectful. They were intentional.

There is a catch-all rule to vacate a default for "exceptional circumstances." Getting angry at a judge and being stupid may not be all that uncommon, but it was not what the drafters of the rule had in mind.

I started thinking about Rothblatt's cancer. He had melanoma, and that form of cancer commonly spreads to the brain. I got some information about his medical history, and sure enough, his melanoma had spread to his brain.

Medical research revealed that brain metastases could cause impaired judgment. So that was it. Rothblatt's judgment might have been impaired by his cancer.

Was it? Who knows? What we did know was that Henry had screwed up and exhibited bad judgment. That was enough for me. I put together a good set of motion papers. We even had an affidavit from a neurologist attesting to the judgment impairment theory. Revici said that he was never informed by Rothblatt about the rescheduled deposition.

It looked like a pretty good argument. Pegalis & Wachsman objected, of course, but the motion was a winner. Maybe the judge thought it would be easier trying the case than writing up a decision and determining a damage award. Whatever the reason, the judge vacated the default, and we were back in business.

We finished up the discovery on the case, and before we knew it, the case was set for trial.

Bad Decisions All Around

The more we looked at the case, the more difficult it looked under New York law. The plaintiff, Edith Schneider, had been diagnosed with stage I breast cancer. She had a very small cancerous lump in one breast with no other involvement. Her family doctor recommended a mastectomy. But Mrs. Schneider wanted to go "the natural way." She did not want to have surgery. So she went to three additional doctors, two surgeons and an oncologist, and they all recommend a mastectomy. But she still refused.

She then found her way to Revici, and he foolishly agreed to treat her with his own medications even though she would not do the lumpectomy he says he recommended to her. (Schneider denied Revici said anything about surgery.)

Schneider signed Revici's standard consent form that informs patients his treatment is experimental and not FDA-approved but that the medications have been "thoroughly tested" (by whom, the form didn't say).

Revici's treatment did not help her. Eventually she developed large masses in both her breasts and had lymph node involvement. She had a bilateral mastectomy, and of course, her prognosis became much worse than it was when she first saw Revici.

She then sued Revici for medical malpractice, lack of informed consent, and fraud. We thought we could win on the fraud and lack of informed consent claims. The patient had known Revici's treatment was experimental and unproven, and four doctors had told her she needed surgery. These two facts seemed to negate any claim that Revici defrauded her or that she did not have informed consent before she undertook Revici's treatment.

But the medical malpractice claim had us worried. Clearly Revici's treatment was a departure from the accepted standard of care for stage I breast cancer, which was surgery. By some estimates, surgery has a 96 percent cure rate for a small breast tumor characterized as stage I.

Revici's treatment was completely unproven, and it had never been tested in an FDA-approved clinical trial. Although he had patients who said they were cured by his treatment, the medical and scientific community considers this "anecdotal" evidence worthless.

No doctor in his right mind would recommend or even sanction a patient taking Revici's treatment instead of curative surgery. Therefore, Revici's treatment was clearly a departure from the accepted standard of care. As a result, the law considered his treatment to be negligent or malpractice, pure and simple.

Schneider's cancer progressed despite Revici's treatment, and she was obviously injured. Thus, Revici's technically negligent care "proximately caused" (as lawyers say) Mrs. Schneider harm or injury. And that's all it takes to obtain a damage award for medical malpractice. All a jury has to do is figure out how much to award the plaintiff.

Of course, it was Mrs. Schneider's decision not to have surgery. But Revici still agreed to treat her stage I breast cancer, which in retrospect was a mistake. In part because of the imbalance of information between a doctor and a patient, New York law did not recognize "assumption of risk" as a complete bar to recovery. Patients cannot legally assume the risk of treatment that is negligent or does not meet the standard of care.

But the physician's liability for negligence can be reduced if the patient had contributed to her own injuries, and that is called contributory or comparative negligence. In New York, a plaintiff's negligent conduct did not stop a recovery of money from the negligent defendant; it just reduced the damage award by the percentage of the plaintiff's contributory or comparative negligence. Usually, the most you could get from the jury was a 50 percent reduction of the award, and usually the reduction was much less. Juries tend to blame the doctors if they are negligent. We were looking for something better than a reduction of the damage award.

We Come Up with a Bright Idea, Maybe

Cathy Helwig was a first-year law student who worked for us part time. One day she mentioned that they had discussed in her torts class a recent New York case. (Torts deal with injuries to people and suing to recover damages.) A teacher had sued the school board for negligence. The school had sponsored a race. But the teachers would not be running; they would be riding donkeys. As can be expected, some jackass fell off the donkey, got hurt, and sued the school board for creating a dangerous activity.

The New York Court of Appeals (the highest court in New York State) made a distinction between implied and express assumption of risk. If the plaintiffs knew about the risk and implicitly assumed the risk of the activity, the award could be reduced by the percentage of the plaintiff's negligence, just like in any comparative negligence case. The court called that implied assumption of risk.

If, on the other hand, two parties explicitly agree in advance that the defendant need not exercise reasonable care, then the agreement is an enforceable contract and there could be no recovery against the negligent defendant. That was called express assumption of risk, which would be a complete bar to recovery.

The donkey case got us thinking. Maybe it was time for the New York courts to acknowledge that a patient could expressly assume the risk of technically negligent medical treatment. Revici's case seemed like an excellent vehicle to establish the doctrine. The patient had repeatedly been told by her doctors that she needed surgery even before she met Revici, but she rejected that advice. Although Revici's treatment was certainly a departure from the "accepted standard of care," and hence technically malpractice, it was unconventional therapy, not really negligent treatment as most people would understand the term. It was the patient's choice to seek out and obtain this "negligent" therapy.

We also thought the case could be framed as a freedom of choice and personal responsibility issue. Patients should have the right to seek unconventional treatment. But if they do, maybe they should not be able to complain about the result, so long as they were properly warned. Seemed reasonable to us, but there was no authority for it, and we knew it would be difficult to sell it to a federal district court, since federal district judges are never excited about making new state law.

So we wrote a jury charge on an "express assumption of risk" affirmative defense that would be a complete defense to the case. (A jury charge is an instruction on a point of law to the jury. The judge decides what jury charges to give to the jury based on input from the attorneys). We also put one in for comparative negligence (implied assumption of risk) in case the judge would not give the express assumption of risk charge.

A New and Magical World

As we were in the final preparation for the trial, a new and magical world appeared before me—a world that would become one of the most valuable weapons in all of my future battles. It was a world with its own rules and governed by its own logic. This new world had some similarities to the world I inhabited, but only on the surface. I am speaking of the media.

Early on in the case, Revici had been hammered by the media. Wachsman was a virtuoso at manipulating the media. Somehow, he and his PR firm, Howard Rubenstein, had gotten a national ABC TV show to cover the funeral of one of Revici's patients, and the piece just also happened to cover Revici getting sued by the executor of the patient's estate. "Quack, charlatan, murderer" were all terms used to describe Revici and also some really bad stuff.

We were getting indications that there would be a repeat of the media attacks for the trial. But we were starting to feel our way in this strange new world. Turns out, Gabe Pressman, one of the most venerable New York TV newsmen, was interested in Revici and the controversy surrounding him.

Gabe Pressman was an old-time newspaper reporter who made the move to TV journalism in the 1960s. He is a terrific guy and much deeper and insightful than most of the modern crop of TV "gotcha journalists."

Over the years, I got to know Gabe pretty well. Alternative health fascinated him. A decade later, he would become interested in the whole Burzynski saga,[7] and I often spoke to him and appeared on several of his shows on cancer.

Gabe and his NBC affiliate were working on a multi-part series on *The Politics of Cancer*. They ended up featuring Revici in one of the segments right before the Schneider trial. Though the piece presented both sides, the mere acknowledgment that there were politics surrounding Revici's treatment was a good thing.

NBC's *The Politics of Cancer* series received so much local attention that on *voir dire*, or jury selection, Wachsman requested the judge to ask prospective jurors if they had seen the piece and if so, what they thought of it. Wachsman was getting a taste of his own medicine, and that suited us just fine.

However, throughout the Revici saga, the media was a mixed bag. Because of the malpractice and licensing cases, and in general because for so long he was considered a quack by conventional medicine, Revici received more negative press than positive.

I defended Revici on two prominent TV talk shows: the *Morton Downey Jr. Show* and *Geraldo*. The Downey show was a zoo. The format was like the Coliseum in Rome: the guests were the Christians, and Mort was the lion. The show tended to take on simple issues with a clear villain, which caused a lot of yelling and booing.

But the Revici issue was complicated and nuanced. To my great surprise and relief, Mort was a perfect gentleman to me, and he didn't go on the attack

---

7   The next chapter in this book entitled "The Burzynski Wars" relates the story of this medical pioneer.

the way he did with most of his guests. I only recently learned that Downey's producer was in our corner and that's the reason the show went well.

I had no such luck on *Geraldo*. Producers of these types of shows have a standard trick (which I didn't know at the time). They lie to you about the name of the segment. You think I would have agreed to appear if they had told me the name of the segment was "Doctors Who Maim Their Patients"?

They really sucker-punched me on that one. There were six guests. I sat next to a woman whose face had been butchered by a cosmetic surgeon who had let his chauffeur do the surgery. Her lawyer sat on the other side of her. There was a father whose son was killed by a surgeon who let an unlicensed person perform the surgery. His lawyer sat next to him. Harvey was there representing his three clients who supposedly were killed or maimed by Revici. And I was there representing Revici. When discussing Revici in the opening, Geraldo reluctantly admitted that Revici wasn't as bad as the other doctors mentioned in the show. (Yeah, and he was a whole lot better than the Nazi doctor Josef Mengele and Genghis Kahn too!)

Despite the ups and downs with the media, Sam and I were excited about this malpractice case. It was interesting. It was important. For better or worse, it was in the media, and we were going against one of the top lawyers in the field (according to him, anyway). So far, we were going toe-to-toe with Harvey. Well, at least we had vacated the default. But good things often end suddenly.

Things Go Bad Right at the Beginning

We had ended the first trial day by picking the jury. Around ten o'clock that night, I got a call from Sam. He said that I was not going to believe what had just happened to him. I told him, "Sure I'll believe it." He insisted I wouldn't believe it. We went back and forth about whether I would believe him.

Finally, after he was convinced I would really believe him, he told me that he was working on the opening argument in his apartment when he got a call from a woman. She had gone to summer camp with Sam's sister and supposedly, she was trying to track her down. She had seen Sam several times when he went to see his sister at camp. Sam had no idea who she was, but he chatted amiably with the woman about his sister, the camp, and the good old days in general.

They talked about what she was currently doing, and she mentioned that she was living in New York City. He told her he was a lawyer, and that he was working on a big case.

Then she dropped the bombshell. "I know. I am juror number six." For the first time in his life, Sam Abady, the former world debating champion, was speechless.

In the old days of English common law, a jury consisted literally of people who knew the parties to the suit. Hence when they said "jury of your peers," they really meant it. But in the American legal system, jurors cannot know nor have any contact with the parties or their attorneys. The process of jury selection, or *voir dire*, includes making sure there is no connection whatsoever between a juror and the parties or their attorneys.

One of the main things a judge will explain after the jury is sworn in is that the jurors can have no contact with any of the parties or their counsel. Judges routinely explain that attorneys will look away when a juror passes by so as not to even make eye contact.

So after hearing this from the judge a few hours before, this moron decides to call up Sam just to talk about the good old days. Sam explained to her that what she had done was totally improper and that he would have to tell the judge in the morning and hung up. Then he called me.

This was bad. Judge Motley already didn't like Revici or either of his lawyers. Whenever we would appear, she would call Harvey "Dr. Wachsman." She seemed to think Revici was the scum of the earth, and we were just a half step up in the food chain. Now, we were looking at improper jury contact.

We talked it through, though more for the psychological reasons than for the planning. We had no choice. So the next morning, we went to see the judge. She was justifiably incensed.

She did not believe Sam just happened to get the call out of the blue. Unfortunately, she had chided Sam during his questioning during jury selection that he was being overfriendly with the prospective jurors, especially the female ones. So she blamed him.

She started talking about throwing him off the case and making me try the whole thing myself. I told her I was not prepared to try the whole case. "I'm just the motion man," I said. I was plenty worried, since I had not planned to do the opening.

Judge Motley then excused us and said she was going to interview the moron juror. Sam and I even had this crazy idea that she had been planted by Wachsman to shake us up. Well if he did, it had worked. We were plenty shaken up. My mind started racing as I began feverishly preparing some sort of opening. Also, for all we knew, the moron would lie and say Sam had called her.

We were called back to chambers after the judge finished with the juror. The soon to be ex-juror had told the truth and admitted she had called Sam. But the judge was feeling smugly prescient since she had warned Sam the day before about his conduct toward the female jurors.

She told us she was referring the matter to the U. S. Marshals Service and possibly the U. S. attorneys office and that there would be a full investigation. She allowed Sam to continue. Of course, the juror was thrown off the case, and one of the alternates took her place. Not the best way to start a big federal trial.

Showtime

Judge Motley brought the jury in, and we were ready to try the case. Sam and I must have looked like the guys on the Smith Brothers' cough drops box. We both had full beards. Sam was around five feet nine inches tall, dark complexion, and carried an extra forty pounds in his midsection.

Me, I was six feet and in decent shape, since I was a regular at the New York Health and Racquet Club. Because of my red hair and red beard, people said I looked like the Viking "Eric the Red." But with a suit and my black fedora hat, I could also have passed for an orthodox rabbi from Brooklyn.

On the other side was Dr. Harvey Wachsman; he was heavy, had thinning grey hair, had a shrill voice with a heavy Brooklyn accent, and was arrogant in the way that many medical doctors or lawyers can be (and he was both). Assisting him was one of his associates, Alice Collopy, who was in her midthirties, short, attractive, and very stiff and formal. She was smart enough to be a good lawyer, competent, and much more detail-oriented than Harvey. She was a decent person. Harvey treated her like a lackey.

Wachsman as the plaintiff's counsel spoke first. To me, it was over the top and too aggressive. Since he was so good on his feet and because he had more trial experience than I did, Sam did the opening. He was terrific.

The plaintiff presents first in a civil trial and Harvey and Alice presented a well-organized case. Of course, they had Mr. and Mrs. Schneider testify. They also called two experts and one of the treating doctors. It was very solid, at least on the direct examination. They also called Revici as a hostile witness. Regrettably, he was probably their best witness.

We decided I would do the cross-examination of all of the plaintiff's witnesses, and Sam would handle Revici, our expert, and the closing. That played to Sam's strengths. Sam was excellent on his feet. But how do you cross-examine a woman who lost both her breasts and had a short life expectancy? What do you say to her husband?

A Light Touch

I gave this much thought. Attacking them was out of the question. They obviously had gone through a difficult time. To avoid creating more sympathy for her, a light touch was needed.

So I did not ask her any questions about her dealings with Revici. Instead, I just had her go over her conversations with the four doctors who recommended surgery. We had all the medical records, and I had her explain each reference in every doctor's note that advised her to have surgery. She could not get too emotional about all this stuff. By the end of this back and forth, the jury understood that she had known the risks of not undergoing surgery before she ever stepped foot in Revici's office. That was about all I could do with her, and I was happy with that.

For the husband, I had something else in mind. After establishing that he had gone with his wife to most of the appointments with the other doctors, I only asked him one question. "Mr. Schneider, having heard these doctors tell your wife that she needed surgery and the risks she faced if she didn't have it, as her husband, I ask you, why didn't you drag her to the operating room and make her get this life-saving surgery?" With noticeable resignation in his voice, he quietly said it was her choice, and she chose not to do it. I thanked him and sat down.

The treating doctor confirmed that Mrs. Schneider was advised to have surgery, and she knew what the risks were in not having it. This physician had excellent notes about her interactions with Mrs. Schneider. I just had her go over word-for-word what she told Mrs. Schneider and what Mrs. Schneider told her. By the end of the doctor's testimony, it was crystal clear that Mrs. Schneider knew that without the surgery she might die.

We Have Some Fun

Wachsman called two experts. The first was from Harvard's physics department. His job was to establish that selenium was a dangerous chemical. I think they called him because he worked at Harvard. He was not a medical doctor, let alone an oncologist, and he didn't seem to know much about selenium. I thought about trying to strike him as a witness or challenge his credentials, but instead, I decided to have some fun with him.

We did some medical research and pulled up every article about selenium published in the past twenty years, and every article about a couple of other medications. Those were the days of dot-matrix, continuous-feed printer paper. When we printed up the lists of articles, it was a lot of pages, maybe fifty or a hundred pages of just the names and citations of the scientific articles (and some other lists).

So on cross, I just started reading the names of the articles and where they were published (and most were published in reputable journals, at least as far as I and the jury knew). One by one I read them.

In order to discuss an article with an expert, you have to first ask the expert if he is familiar with the article. If he says he is, you can ask him questions about the article. But if he isn't, you can't ask him about the article. This Harvard professor was not familiar with the first article on selenium, so I moved to the second. Nope, he didn't know that one either. I went down my list, quoting the title of each article about selenium and where it was published. He was not familiar with a single one of them.

All of these articles had titles like "The Use of Selenium to Prevent and Treat Tumors." So he didn't look so much like an expert on selenium since he had not heard of any of these articles. And the jury was hearing about all these wonderful articles about the magical anti-cancer properties of selenium.

After going through about a dozen such articles, the jury was seeing me appear to get frustrated, since I was not able to discuss any of these articles with him. Actually, I was hoping he had not read any of the articles, because that made two of us. I hadn't read a single one of them either. All I had were the names of the articles.

I then asked the judge for a moment to look through all the pages of the articles. At that point the fifty attached pages somehow started to unfold and fall to the floor like an expanding accordion, page after attached page. I clumsily tried to stop the pages from unraveling. (The clumsy part was no act.) I eventually retrieved all the attached papers from the floor, but it took some time, as I was having some trouble putting them back together. All this time, everyone was waiting for me to continue. As I finished putting the pages back together, I told the judge I had no further questions. I think the point was made.

It's Hard to Argue with a Guy Who Is Right

I had a much tougher time with the second expert. Dr. Robert Taub was a highly trained and very articulate oncologist who worked at Columbia Presbyterian Hospital. His job in the case was to establish that the standard of care for stage I breast cancer was surgery and that it was a completely curable disease. He also opined that faced with a patient with this diagnosis, it was the physician's job to convince the patient to undergo surgery and that there was no other rational choice. If a patient would not follow the advice, then the doctor should turn the patient away rather than give experimental treatment. I worked hard crossing him but got nowhere. The problem was that he just made too much sense. I thought Revici was incredibly arrogant to treat the patient with his brown dropper-topped bottles given how curable the disease was and given the fact that the chances of cure dramatically diminishes the more the tumor is allowed to grow. But what if the patient simply refuses and insists on unconventional treatment, I asked Taub over and over again. Suppose the patient goes to four doctors or ten and she still refuses? And Taub kept coming back to his statement, "The doctor's job is to ensure that the patient gets the best treatment possible." But what if the doctor also recommends surgery, but agrees to treat the patient with medications and maybe tries to talk her into to surgery later on? "No, that's not enough. She needs surgery. Giving her anything else is malpractice." I'm not sure what the jury thought about all this, but I felt that I did not neutralize his testimony.

Revici Takes the Stand

The only other witness Wachsman called was Revici, and that didn't go well. We had tried to prepare Revici, but that proved to be impossible.

By that time, Revici was close to ninety. Despite fifty years in the United States, his English was very poor. Also, maybe because he was so old or so fixed in his ideas, it did not matter what question he was asked, he would answer the question he wanted to answer. (Politicians do that also, so maybe it was not his age that caused him to behave this way.)

During most of his answers, the judge had to instruct Revici to answer the question and not give soliloquies irrelevant to the question or to the lawsuit. He would turn and look at her and say, "Of course, of course." Then he would do the exact same thing on the very next question. But it did not matter, since most of what he said was unintelligible to the jury and everyone else in the courtroom.

Sam's future mother-in-law was watching the trial. She was married to one of England's most prominent physicians. After listening to Revici on the stand for a few hours, she commented to us, "I wouldn't let that guy treat my dog." I guess the disaster that was Revici's examination had a silver lining. What kind of idiot would allow this guy to treat a patient for stage I breast cancer, and how can anybody think that this doddering old fool could have a cure for cancer? That was not the impression we were trying to make on the jury, but those were the cards we were dealt. Sam tried to revive Revici by calling him as our witness in the defense case. But it did not help. Revici gave Sam as hard a time in answering questions as he had given Wachsman. I think everyone in the courtroom was relieved when Revici left the stand the second and final time.

Sam did the direct examination of our expert, Gerhard Schrauzer. Dr. Schrauzer was very professional, and you could see he was one of the world's experts on selenium. Schrauzer testified extensively about all of the research showing the benefits of selenium on cancer. The contrast between him and the Harvard physicist was not lost on the jury. After Dr. Schrauzer testified, we rested.

And that was it, or so we thought. All in all, it had not gone too badly for Revici. Only Taub (and Revici himself) had done us any real harm. Up close, Wachsman was surely a very competent attorney, but he was no Clarence Darrow. He was loud and abrasive. I thought it would be hard for a jury to like him. His assistant, Alice, handled some of the witnesses, and to us, she seemed more effective and certainly more likeable.

More importantly, they didn't present an overpowering case. All of their witnesses agreed that Mrs. Schneider was repeatedly told she needed surgery, but she refused, despite the pleas from all her doctors and her husband. So we were feeling good and maybe even confident.

But Wachsman still had something up his sleeve. He announced that he had a rebuttal witness. Rebuttal witnesses are witnesses presented by the plaintiff after the close of the defendant's case. The advantage of this tactic is that there is no pre-trial discovery of rebuttal witnesses. That is because they are supposed to be used only to rebut matters brought out in the defense case that could not have been reasonably anticipated.

Harvey was not going to rebut anything. He just made a tactical decision to put part of his case-in-chief as rebuttal evidence. This quickly became clear once we figured out who the rebuttal witness was and what he was going to say.

Enter the Quack-Busters

The world of alternative health has always been polarizing. Proponents are adamant supporters. Now, the big players in the alternative health field are people like Andrew Weil, Deepak Chopra, Gary Null, and Kevin Trudeau. Some of these folks have been around for twenty or thirty years, but they did not have the following they do now. The alternative health community back then was small, unsophisticated, unorganized, and not well funded. That was not the case with the opposition.

Then and now, there are many opponents to anything alternative, simply because these remedies have not been proven by controlled clinical trials to be safe and effective. Well, duh, that's why they're called "alternative." If a remedy is proven, then it is not alternative or unconventional.

The opponents seemed to be organized and very well funded. They called themselves the "quack-busters." Their stated goal was to debunk alternative remedies and attack alternative health practitioners.

The quack-busters developed a not-so-secret list of the country's hundred biggest medical "quacks." They rated the practitioners by using a "ding dong" index. "Ding dongs" were like star ratings for restaurants or hotels. The more "ding dongs," the bigger the quack.

The core group of quack-busters included (the late) John Renner, Stephen Barrett, William Jarvis, and Grace Powers Monaco.

But by far the most rabid quack-buster of them all was Victor Herbert. The first time I heard his name was when Harvey Wachsman announced that Dr. Victor Herbert would be his sole rebuttal witness. We protested to the judge and argued that he was not a true rebuttal witness.

By this time, the judge was even more hostile toward Revici and his lawyers. She would do anything she could to see that Revici would be found liable, and allowing Wachsman to call the premier quack-buster would greatly help the cause. However, with imperial-like magnanimity, she did allow us a short break after his direct examination to prepare his cross.

Wachsman had given us a copy of Herbert's *curriculum vitae* (C. V.) right after he announced he would be calling him. It was an amazing document. It was hard to believe that one person could have done all he claimed to have done in only one lifetime. He was a medical doctor, of course, and had taught at many top universities. He worked for the government, published dozens and hundreds of papers and books, lectured around the world, and was an adviser to numerous companies and industries. He was a lieutenant colonel in the Green Berets. And he was an attorney licensed in several jurisdictions.

But he came to court because he was a self-proclaimed quack-buster extraordinaire. According to Herbert, he went around the country doing what he could to protect the public from quacks like Revici. He felt bad for all the people who Revici and his ilk duped, defrauded, and maimed.

According to Herbert, Revici was one of the cruelest killers in the world, and those were the words he used. Herbert said that Revici's treatments had been thoroughly refuted, debunked, and rejected twenty or thirty years ago. He claimed that Revici knew they did not work and still continued to dupe people into taking his worthless treatments.

This guy was killing us. He was smug, arrogant, but very straightforward. His legal training was evident. Sam raised numerous objections, most of which were overruled by Motley. It was brutal.

I spent the break calling a couple of the alternative health advocates to see what I could find out about Herbert. Apparently, he was a consultant to the sugar lobby and received money from "big pharma" (i.e., the pharmaceutical industry) and other conventional health institutions. He was also vehemently opposed to vitamins and nutritional supplements that were being sold to consumers. I did not come up with much.

Sam did what he could in cross-examining Herbert. They argued a lot, and the best thing Sam did was to show that Herbert was an arrogant, argumentative, self-assured jerk. Between the direct and cross-examination, we hoped that the jury would understand that Herbert was just a biased medical hit man.

As Herbert was leaving the stand, he and Wachsman exchanged self-satisfied, congratulatory grins. They had sunk Revici, or so they thought. That little exchange really ticked me off. Looking at them look at each other, I decided I was going to get both of them (and eventually, I did).

Finally It's Over, but We're Not Finished

After Herbert testified, the case was ready for summations. We were given a little time to prepare. Sam didn't do any overt preparation. We just sat around and talked about the case, and I guess Sam cogitated unconsciously. He had been working on the case for several weeks and like some talented lawyers, he worked best unconsciously.

By this time, we had what is called a charging conference, which is when the lawyers get together with the judge to discuss the jury charges. Judge Motley had rejected our request to give an express assumption of risk charge. As much as I disliked her and felt that she was prejudiced against Revici and us, I couldn't fault her for not issuing the jury charge. New York law did not recognize the affirmative defense of express assumption of risk to a malpractice action. As a federal district judge, she did not want to create this defense and certainly not for a doctor like Revici.

We did get the comparative negligence or implied assumption of risk charge. We thought the jury understood that Mrs. Schneider knew and appreciated the risk of forgoing surgery, so we thought we had a good chance of having the damage award reduced. We also thought we had thoroughly discredited Wachsman's fraud and lack of informed consent claims.

Wachsman did a good job closing. He was still annoying (at least to me), but he had good points and made them very effectively. Sam was excellent. He spoke without any notes. He talked about freedom of choice, the right of patients to make even bad decisions, and how important it was that people be allowed to choose unconventional therapies. After he finished his closing, Motley appeared annoyed. I think she was concerned that Sam might have convinced the jury to find in Revici's favor.

After the summations and the reading of the jury charges, the jury retired to deliberate. They were out some time, but eventually they came back with a verdict.

The jury was given a special interrogatory form that asked them specific questions. We won outright on fraud and lack of informed consent. The first question on the malpractice claim was whether Revici's treatment was a departure from the accepted standard of medical care. We basically conceded that his experimental treatment for a curable cancer was a departure from the accepted standard care. The jury saw it that way.

The jury also found that Revici's departure was the proximate cause of injuries sustained by Mrs. Schneider. As to damages, the jury awarded her $1,050,000.

The next interrogatory was on our comparative negligence or implied assumption of risk charge. Was Mrs. Schneider's conduct partially responsible for her injuries, and if so, what percentage was she responsible? The jury found that she was fifty percent responsible, which was basically as much fault as they could assess against her.

So the bottom line was that Wachsman had obtained a verdict for $525,000. It could have been worse, and Wachsman was probably expecting more. So ended the first Revici trial, but we were far from finished.

The Schneider Appeal

We felt strongly that, in light of the donkey case, New York was ready to adopt an express assumption of risk defense to medical malpractice, regardless of whether a federal district court judge would give the instruction. So everyone was clear that we would take the case up on appeal to the Second Circuit Court of Appeals.

We agreed on a reasonable fee with Revici's supporters and we started preparing the necessary paperwork. Revici did not have a lot of cash back then, and he also did not have any free assets, as we had taken a lien on his brownstone to secure our attorney's fees and also for some protection against the possible judgment.

The filing of an appeal does not automatically stop collection efforts on the judgment. Therefore, the losing defendant usually posts an appeals bond that acts to stop the victorious plaintiff from attempting to collect on the judgment. Revici did not have the cash or securities to post a bond to secure a half-million-dollar judgment. But interestingly, throughout the duration of appeal, Wachsman never seriously attempted to collect on the judgment.

Appeals usually take at least a year. The trial transcript has to be prepared, corrected, and sent to the parties. Then the record or paperwork of the case has to be prepared and transmitted to the appellate court. In this case, it did not have to travel far since the Second Circuit Court of Appeals was in the same building as the district court, in downtown New York at Foley Square.

Then the parties write briefs in support of the appeal. The appellant, the party filing the appeal, writes the first brief. The appellee then responds. And finally, the appellant is given an opportunity to submit a reply brief. In most appeals of civil trials, the judges call for oral argument, and the judges requested it in our case.

Sam was busy with other things and could not spend any significant time on the appeal. By that time, one of Sam's good friends, an extremely able attorney named Matt Dineen, was working with us, and Cathy Helwig was still helping out. Matt, Cathy, and I did the briefs. We argued all kinds of issues like evidentiary errors and the Victor Herbert trick. However, the main thrust was the jury charge and, in particular, the judge's failure to give the express assumption of risk defense.

Sam did the oral argument and it went smoothly, for us anyway. The judges seemed swayed by the fact that Mrs. Schneider voluntarily chose to forgo surgery and instead chose to undergo Revici's questionable treatment. They gave Alice Collopy, who argued the appeal for Mrs. Schneider, a hard time.

In a few months, we received the decision. The Second Circuit overturned the jury verdict, holding that the trial judge committed reversible error by not giving the express assumption of risk defense as a complete bar to recovery. As the Second Circuit stated, "While a patient should be encouraged to exercise care for his own safety, we believe that an informed decision to avoid surgery and conventional chemotherapy is within the patient's right 'to determine what shall be done with his own body.'"[8]

It was a complete victory. Back then, there were not many legal victories in the alternative health community, so news of the Second Circuit's decision spread throughout the country. Sam, and to some extent our firm, was heralded as the great white hope amongst alternative health practitioners. Sam was invited to speak at conferences, and we ended up landing a number of other clients in the field, including the ever-increasingly popular diet doctor, Robert Atkins.

---

8   For the legally interested, *Schneider v. Revici* is reported at 817 F.2d 987 (2nd Cir. 1987).

The Second Circuit had an unwritten rule that if a case was overturned on appeal, it would be reassigned to another district court judge. That was excellent news from our perspective, since Judge Motley was horribly biased against us. It was not just her rulings. She engaged in the most outrageous behavior I have ever seen from a judge—very clever but thoroughly despicable.

Throughout the trial, when one of Wachsman's witnesses was on the stand, she would hold an exaggerated pose of rapt attention. She would stare at the witness with hands folded underneath her chin, with a furrowed brow, like she was mesmerized. When Revici and Schrauzer testified, or during my cross of their witnesses, she wore an exaggerated expression of boredom. She would literally stick out her hand, turn it palm up, make a half-fist, and look at her fingernails. She actually started filing or brushing her nails with an emery board—but up high so the jury could see that she was not paying attention to our witnesses.

It was a clever way to send a message to the jury. I thought about standing up and making a comment about her conduct on the record. But it was her court, and I figured it would just make her more rabid against us. That was the only time I ever saw a judge use this tactic. We were mighty happy to be rid of her, and I am certain the feeling was mutual.

Round Two: It's Payback Time

The case was reassigned to District Judge John Sprizzo. He called us down to his courtroom for a conference to discuss the retrial. (Sam was busy on other cases, so I took the case over.) At this point, Mike Carlucci, another of Harvey's associates, was handling the case. Mike was tall, good looking, and affable; a very good guy and easier to deal with than Alice Collopy.[9]

The only thing I wanted from Sprizzo was the chance to depose Victor Herbert, since we had not had the opportunity pretrial. It seemed reasonable, so he granted the request.

---

9   I would later learn that they were seeing each other and would eventually marry. They are still married and practicing law together. Good for them!

Herbert's office was at the Bronx VA (Veteran's Administration) Medical Center, and we arranged for me to depose him there for his convenience. By this time, I knew quite a bit about Dr. Herbert. He really was the nastiest, most rabid quack-busting anti-alternative health person out there. Because of his personality and legal training, he was constantly mixing it up with alternative health practitioners and their lawyers. He had been involved in numerous lawsuits, as a testifying witness and as a party.

I discovered one extremely interesting fact about Herbert. He was actually written up in some book about medical pioneers who advanced medical knowledge by engaging in self-experimentation. Herbert's early claim to fame rested on his research on the body's need for folic acid.

He proved this need in part by devising an experiment whereby he would deprive himself of all folic acid. He did this by double boiling meat and vegetables, thereby removing the folic acid. Apparently, he became weak and disoriented as a result of his self-deprivation. And the book heralded him for his noble sacrifice. Hmm, disorientation…. And then I knew what I was going to do to him.

Herbert's office was suitably crowded and overflowing with medical textbooks and books about alternative health. He had a picture of himself with Louis J. Sullivan, who at the time was the U. S. Secretary of Health and Human Services. Apparently, Sullivan was a student of his, and Herbert had been Sullivan's best man or something like that.

I spent about an hour and a half deposing him, just eliciting his background and accomplishments. He was only too happy to relate the many, varied, and important things he had done in his life, sprinkled with references to all the very important people he had helped or who thought highly of him. Carlucci was just letting him ramble on, and both of them were having a good old time while Herbert established his expertise on a wide variety of health topics.

Who's a Nut Job?

Just before I was ready to puke, I asked him quietly, "Dr. Herbert, have you ever been treated for a mental disease or disorder?" Carlucci woke up from his blissful stupor. Herbert just sat there with his mouth open.

"Objection! Objection!" Carlucci bellowed. "I request that you state for the record the good-faith basis of this question."

I was ready for that. I mentioned Herbert's self-experimentation with folic acid, which he referred to during the deposition. I explained that there had been studies that showed that people who were folic-acid deprived could experience long-term cognitive problems and mental disorders.

I mentioned one other basis. I had heard about some psychiatric or health clinic in Princeton, New Jersey, called the Brain-Bio Institute or something of the sort. I didn't know much about it, but what I did know was that the doctor in charge was an MD/PhD by the name of Russell Jaffe. I had never met or heard of Dr. Jaffe, and he was not a relative.

I had heard some rumor that Herbert was treated there or had some connection to the place. So I told Carlucci and Herbert that we had reason to believe that Herbert had been treated at the Brain-Bio Institute at Princeton for a mental disorder and otherwise implied that I had seen Herbert's psychiatric records. I then mentioned that the medical director was Dr. Russell Jaffe.

Carlucci went ballistic, and Herbert became apoplectic. Carlucci instructed Herbert not to answer the question. Carlucci then said that if I had illegally obtained Dr. Herbert's medical records from a relative of mine, both Dr. Jaffe and I would face charges. Carlucci wouldn't let me ask any more questions, terminated the deposition, and threw me out of Herbert's office. But I wasn't finished with Herbert yet, not by a long shot.

I had a smile on my face all the way back to my office. It got me thinking. They both had such an intense reaction, maybe there was something to this mental disorder idea. Herbert seemed like a nut job to me. Maybe he really was certifiable.

We Get Some Help from the Judge

When a witness is instructed by his attorney not to answer a question during a deposition, the remedy is to go to court and seek an order from the judge compelling the answer. And that is exactly what I did. I got a copy of the transcript of the deposition, and I put together a set of papers. Nothing fancy.

I simply explained that in light of Dr. Herbert's self-experimentation and the documented scientific fact of possible long-term cognitive impairment, we were entitled to inquire whether Dr. Herbert was mentally competent to give testimony in this *or any other trial* as an expert witness. Carlucci submitted papers in opposition to the motion. The judge called us down for oral argument.

It was late November or early December, and the judge had a number of cases before he was to hear our matter. One of those was a criminal case involving an older black man who was being sentenced by Judge Sprizzo.

The defendant had pled guilty to some crime, and it was his third conviction. None of the crimes were that horrible, but the defendant looked worried. He also looked like he had been beaten down by the system.

Sprizzo looked at him and shuffled through his papers. He explained that normally a crime such as the defendant had committed would warrant several years in prison, but Sprizzo said that he had looked at the defendant's past criminal history and felt the prison time he had received on these prior offenses had been excessive (and in both cases, he had been sentenced someplace in the deep South).

So Sprizzo said to balance things out, he was going to give the defendant an early Christmas present and not give him any jail time. The old black guy was stunned, quietly thanked Sprizzo, and left the courtroom. I liked that judge! He knew how to dispense justice.

Eventually our turn came. I explained what I wanted and why. No embellishments. But I did quote a couple of Herbert's most outrageous statements from his trial testimony, just to set the proper mood for the judge. I think that did the trick. Carlucci talked about what an esteemed scientist Dr. Herbert was, but the wind was blowing against him.

The judge went my way and then some. I had not asked for anything special in terms of the continued deposition, but Sprizzo took it upon himself to order that the continuation of Herbert's deposition take place before a federal magistrate. At the end of the deposition, the magistrate would determine whether Herbert was mentally competent to testify at this or any other trial. This time, I was laughing all the way back to the office. People on the subway must have thought that I was just another crazy New Yorker.

The Green Beret Is Called Up (Yeah, Right), and It's Over

I sent Carlucci a note suggesting a couple of possible deposition dates. It took him some time to respond, which he did by letter. I knew that Herbert was a reserve officer in the Green Berets, but I didn't know how important he was. Carlucci informed me that Herbert was being called up for some reason, for some exercise or war preparation or something. Even though he would not be deployed for months, unfortunately, Herbert did not have the time to finish the deposition. As a result, they were withdrawing Herbert's name as a witness for the retrial. I had put Herbert in his place and it felt good.

It felt even better when a few weeks later, and shortly before the scheduled retrial, Wachsman's firm notified us that they were not going forward with the retrial; they were walking away from their $525,000 judgment against Revici. And so ended *Schneider v. Revici*.

Next Up: Boyle v. Revici

It was good news for Revici and his supporters, but Revici was still in the thick of it with Wachsman's firm. After the end of the Schneider trial, but before Wachsman had given up his verdict, we had to start dealing with the second federal malpractice trial Wachsman had filed against Revici.

Revici had seen Cecelia Zyjewski around the same time he had treated Mrs. Schneider. Cecelia was an older woman who lived in New Britain, Connecticut. She had never married and lived with her brother, Skip. She had been diagnosed with stage I colorectal cancer. Her tumor was at the edge of her anal canal. The tumor was not big, and she had no other evidence of cancer. Her cancer was treatable by surgery and by all accounts was completely curable. There was some risk, however, that she would need a colostomy, which, of course, no one would look forward to.

Like Mrs. Schneider, Cecelia Zyjewski went to several physicians, all of whom strongly advised her that she needed to have the tumor removed. And like Mrs. Schneider, she refused.

Cecelia found her way to Dr. Revici, and he agreed to treat her with his medications. Nothing he did helped her. Her condition deteriorated and her cancer spread. She continued to refuse to have any kind of surgery until the end when the doctors had to perform an emergency colostomy to save her life. By that time, the cancer had ravaged her body. In fact, the cancer ate through the wall between her vaginal cavity and her anal canal, a gruesome fact Harvey would repeat over and over again during the trial.

Cecelia eventually died. But even before she died, her nephew, Arthur Boyle, was appointed as her guardian. Boyle was angry that Revici agreed to treat her and contacted Harvey Wachsman. It was Cecelia's funeral that the ABC news crew had filmed. After Cecelia died, Wachsman filed a malpractice suit with Arthur Boyle, the executor of the estate, as the plaintiff.

This case proceeded more slowly. It had been kicked around between several federal judges. Judge Whitman Knapp (of the Knapp commission) out of White Plains, New York, had the case on his docket for awhile. There were a variety of legal issues that came up, and we went back and forth with Harvey and his firm for some time. But we were both mainly focused on the Schneider case. After Schneider's trial, both law firms started focusing on this case: *Boyle v. Revici.*

By the time the Boyle case was ready for trial, the Second Circuit had issued its landmark decision in the Schneider case. So we knew we could argue assumption of risk as a complete defense to the medical malpractice case. Or at least we thought we could. The only problem we had was that Revici could not find the signed informed consent form.

The good news was that three of Cecelia's relatives had been involved in her treatment with Revici, and they were supportive of him. The bad news was that one of them, Cecelia's brother Skip, had died before the trial and before he could be deposed. That left only Carol Palumbo, Cecelia's niece (and the sister of the plaintiff Arthur Boyle), and Carol's husband, Dominic. Fortunately, Carol and Dominic had taken Cecelia to Dr. Revici's office and sometimes even sat with her during the visit.

Perhaps because of Knapp's busy docket, the case was transferred back to Manhattan to the court of District Judge Mary Johnson Lowe. From the very beginning, Sam rubbed Judge Lowe the wrong way. It was not hard to do. Judge Lowe had a well-deserved inferiority complex. The publication *American Lawyer* consistently found her to be one of the most reversed judges in the Southern District of New York.

Of course, the facts of the case did not help us. Despite some positive press, Revici was still viewed by most mainstream people as a quack. Lowe knew that Motley had been reversed on appeal. We had a hard time with Lowe throughout her tenure on the case.

Based on his early dealings with Judge Lowe, we decided that Sam should not be involved in the case. I had plenty of other things to do. So Matt Dineen and Cathy Helwig did most of the work. I was to lend a hand when needed.

This Looks Like an Easy Case

Despite having an irascible judge, it didn't seem like a hard case after the Schneider appellate victory. We could prove through the testimony of Dominic and Carol Palumbo that Cecelia knew the treatment was experimental and not FDA-approved. We could also prove from the medical records that she was advised she should have surgery. That made it basically the same as the Schneider case. So we were not expecting any problems.

But as is often the case, stuff happens. Matt was a super-smart and exceptionally competent attorney, but he was very shy and did not have much trial experience. And of course, Judge Lowe did not like anybody associated with Revici. She made no pretense of being fair and took every opportunity to rule against us.

So the case proceeded to trial: Harvey and Alice for the plaintiffs, Matt and Cathy for Revici. Things did not go well. After the first day, I got several calls from Revici's supporters complaining that Matt was getting hammered by Wachsman. Matt was not happy either. He had had enough of Judge Lowe and Revici. Sam was tied up and otherwise did not want any part of the trial. So that left it up to me, by default.

Ready or not, Here I Come

I went down the next day and took over as lead counsel. I had not prepared the case, but I had read all the motions and was generally familiar with the facts. And of course, I had been deeply involved in the Schneider case. Most importantly, I had no choice.

Judge Lowe didn't like me any better than Sam or Matt. She continued to rule against us any time she could. She limited what we could ask on cross-examination and would not let me pursue Boyle's evasive answers. Robert Taub testified again, and once again, he was adamant that Revici should never have treated the patient. I did what I could with him, but it wasn't much.

I ate with Revici at one of the lunch breaks. It was just the two of us. We were discussing the case and the causation issue. He was pretty lucid—for him, anyway. He admitted that if Cecelia had had the surgery, she would be alive today. So I asked him, if that was the case, why he had agreed to treat her. He said it was her choice. I appreciated Revici's candor, but frankly, I agreed with Taub. Revici should never have treated her. I held my tongue. I had a job to do.

We did not have much of a defense, other than calling both Carol and Dominic Palumbo to testify that Cecelia knew Revici's treatment was experimental, and she also was fully aware that her doctors strongly recommended that she have surgery. Basically, it looked like a repeat of the Schneider trial. But as usual, when you least expect it....

We had our charging conference with Judge Lowe. We submitted both the express assumption of risk and a comparative negligence/implied assumption of risk charge to the judge and cited *Schneider v. Revici.* To us it was a slam dunk. True, there was no signed informed consent form, but we had the testimony of Dominic and Carol Palumbo that Revici explained to Cecelia that the treatment was experimental and not FDA approved. They even said she had signed the consent form. The form just could not be produced from Revici's records. There was no logical reason why a signed document was a prerequisite for asserting the express assumption of risk defense, and the Second Circuit never said it was.

Wachsman and Alice argued the opposite. Then Judge Lowe said something amazing. She said if she gave the assumption of risk charge, she would have to enter a directed verdict (i.e., judgment) in favor of Revici, since the Palumbos had established that Cecelia had assumed the risk and there was no evidence to the contrary.

Here We Go Again

If I had not been trying the case before her for the last several days, I would have been shocked. First of all, it was the smartest thing I ever heard come out of her mouth. She knew and acknowledged that we won the case without even going to the jury.

But then she did something even more amazing. She ruled that she would not give the express assumption of risk defense, because there was no written informed consent form. Matt and I were flabbergasted but not surprised. Lowe was biased, and that's what a biased judge does. Matt and I looked at each other. Here we go again. Like Motley, Lowe agreed to give the comparative negligence charge.

We finished up the case. Wachsman and I did the closings and the case went to the jury. The jury's verdict was no surprise.

This time we had stipulated that the treatment was technically a departure from the accepted standard of care. We thought it might limit Wachsman's efforts to put on the gory details of Cecelia's medical problems. It didn't.

My First Million-Dollar Verdict!

The jury found that the treatment caused injuries, and awarded damages of $1.5 million. The jury found that Cecelia was 5–10 percent negligent and the verdict was reduced to $1.35 million.

As I would often later joke, this was my first million-dollar verdict. Too bad I represented the defendant. But we had an excellent case on appeal, and we were certain that the court of appeals would reverse the judgment because the judge failed to give the express assumption of risk defense.

Sam and Cathy handled the appeal because by that point, I had dissolved the law firm and moved my practice to Houston. As everyone expected, the Second Circuit reversed Judge Lowe and specifically stated that the express assumption of risk defense does not require a written informed consent form or any particular form of evidence. Testimonial evidence was just as good as a written consent form. So once again, Wachsman's judgment was reversed, and once again the case was sent back for retrial. This time, there would only be one issue at the retrial: whether the patient had expressly assumed the risk of the so-called "negligent" treatment.

I ended up handling the Boyle case on remand. Because of the Second Circuit's rule on reassignments after reversals, we got rid of Judge Lowe (and she got rid of us).

Dr. Harvey Exits the Case and the Ho Hum Retrial

The case was reassigned to District Judge John Martin. Martin had been the United States Attorney for the Southern District of New York. He was a very smart, no-nonsense judge. As fate would have it, Harvey immediately didn't hit it off with Martin. He would not call Harvey "Doctor," which appeared to annoy Harvey. Martin was not nearly as deferential to Wachsman as Judges Motley and Lowe had been. And worst of all, Martin acted just like a judge should act: fair and impartial to both sides. This was a completely new experience for Harvey in these Revici cases, and I am sure he did not like it.

The main problem for us on the retrial was that the case had created animosity between our star witness, Carol Palumbo, and her brother, Arthur Boyle, the plaintiff. Between the end of the trial and its reassignment to Judge Martin, the family had reconciled. Part of the reconciliation was that neither Carol nor Dominic Palumbo would testify at any retrial. Because they lived out of state and more than one hundred miles away from the courthouse, we could not subpoena them and force them to testify.

I told the judge that I intended to prove our case by reading the trial and/ or deposition testimony of the Palumbos. Harvey went crazy. He ranted and raved. But John Martin was the wrong judge to pull that stuff on, and he gave Harvey an earful. After Martin ruled that he would allow us to read the prior testimony at the trial, Harvey stormed out of the courtroom in a huff, and that was the last I saw of the great Dr. Harvey Wachsman.

Alice Collopy and Mike Carlucci, who were by that time married, took over the case. We did some minor preliminary work. They tried to have some other medical doctor testify at the retrial. I deposed him, but he didn't know anything about the only issue in the case, which was whether the patient assumed the risk of Revici's treatment, so I moved to preclude their witness from testifying. Martin saw it my way and struck their witness from the case.

The day of the trial came and it was anti-climactic. We picked the jury. We did openings. Arthur Boyle testified, but he did not have much to say; he couldn't say whether Cecelia did or did not assume the risk.

As to our defense, Marcus Cohen, the unofficial spokesman for Revici's patients, read the part of Dominic Palumbo. A very beautiful blond cancer patient cured by Revici read Carol Palumbo's testimony. And that was all she wrote. We did summations, and the case was sent to the jury.

Of course, Judge Martin gave the express assumption of risk defense. The jury came back in maybe three quarters of an hour and found in Revici's favor. And so went Harvey Wachsman's second judgment against Revici.

The Operation Is a Success but the Patient Dies

After the verdict, I went to Revici's offices to tell him and Elena the good news. They were pleased. This was the third and last of the civil malpractice cases filed by Wachsman, and Revici had prevailed in all of them.[10]

However, it was bittersweet for them. By then, Revici's medical license had been revoked by the New York medical licensing board, the Office of Professional Medical Conduct (OPMC). Abady & Jaffe had worked on the licensing case briefly when we first took over the malpractice cases, but we had long since been replaced by an attorney who supposedly had political connections. The licensing case went back and forth and up and down the administrative system. At first Revici's license was suspended, but eventually, OPMC revoked it.

Elena brought in several doctors to try to run the clinic. Revici still had an office at the clinic and acted as a "consultant." The problem with Revici's treatment was that it was more of an art than a science. He was more medicine man than disciplined clinician. He had no standard reproducible protocols, and it was exceedingly difficult for other physicians to understand why he would give some medications at one time and others at other times. Eventually, the practice just faded away of natural causes.

---

10   Wachsman had previously voluntarily dismissed his third case against Revici.

When Revici turned one hundred, his supporters threw him a big birthday party. Several hundred of his supporters and former patients attended. Later that year, because of the work of his politically connected patients and supporters, Revici's medical license was returned to him. He was very gratified by that.

Revici passed away shortly after his 101st birthday. Although a few doctors still use some of his formulations, his art of treating cancer patients has largely passed with him. However, I believe that his work on lipids will eventually be rediscovered and validated.[11]

Lessons Learned

And so ended my introduction into the world of alternative health. I had become an advocate but not a blind supporter. Revici surely helped many people, but I don't think he should have treated Schneider, Zyjewski, or any other such patient with early-stage cancer that is curable by conventional means.

Admittedly, it is a complex issue. Almost all curative treatments for early-stage solid tumor cancers involve disfiguring surgery. It is easy to say that someone else should have her breast cut off or have her anal canal resected and face a possible permanent colostomy. It is much harder for some patients to accept that fate without question and without first trying an unproven, unconventional treatment.

I confess to some personal experience with these issues. During the 1970s, my grandfather was diagnosed with mid-stage colon cancer. He had numerous unsuccessful and very painful operations to try to arrest the spread of the cancer. He died a horrible death. That experience made me skeptical of conventional cancer treatment.

---

11   That process has already started. For example, one medical author has recently stated: "Another critical component of lipid metabolism warranting discussion is that of eicosanoids popularized by Barry Sears, PhD in his book, *The Zone*. Emmanuel Revici, MD provided the early conceptual model for this entire field of fat metabolism." See http://www.drkaslow.com/html/cholesterol.htm, which is an except from *Cardiovascular Efficiency vs. Nutritional Deficiency*, by Dr. Jeremy E. Kaslow.

But as fate would have it, while we were litigating the Boyle case, my father was diagnosed with stage I colon cancer, the same disease as Cecelia Zyjewski. Although he was an alternative health nut and thought about exploring some alternatives for his cancer, he decided (with my strong recommendation) to have the surgery and seek unconventional care afterwards. The surgery cured him, and he lived the last twenty years of his life cancer free. Based on these two experiences, I can understand the desire of Mrs. Schneider and Cecelia Zyjewski to avoid surgery, as well as the anger their families had when Revici's treatment didn't work.

But more important than personal experiences is the danger of medical board action. Medical boards believe it is unreasonable to give an unproven therapy to a patient with a curable early-stage cancer. A licensing action would surely result if the patient's cancer progressed and the medical board found out about it.

The Revici cases created some protection against malpractice actions for doctors who provide unconventional treatments to patients. But despite this legal precedent, I have advised unconventional cancer doctors to limit their treatment of early-stage cancers when there is a relatively safe and proven conventional alternative, because of potential medical board action. Most of my clients have followed this advice and have avoided the problems Revici faced. In the alternative health field, it is said that the pioneers are the ones with the arrows in their backs. Emanuel Revici was surely proof of that.

CHAPTER TWO

The Burzynski Wars

The Burzynski wars started in a small lab in communist Poland circa 1967. Stanislaw Burzynski (Stash, or Stan, as he is known to his friends) was a medical student. During a routine lab project, Stash made a simple observation. He noticed that the blood of cancer patients lacked certain types of amino acids and peptides, which are normally found in healthy patients.

Interesting, he thought, and perhaps important. He had no idea at the time that this single small finding would consume the next forty years of his life, put him in harm's way of numerous governmental entities, and lead him on a collision course with the scientific establishment and the church of the medical orthodoxy.

First, a Fable

During the Middle Ages, there was a king who had a Jewish court jester named Mendel. Unfortunately, Mendel had a roving eye and had an affair with the queen. The king found out, summoned Mendel, and ordered his execution.

As they were taking him away, Mendel turned and yelled out, "King, King, you can't execute me; I have a wonderful and unique talent that will make you famous throughout the world."

"And what, pray tell, is that talent?" asked the king.

Mendel replied, "King, I can teach your horse to fly."

The king started to laugh and waved him off.

The jester said, "No, verily, I can teach your horse to fly, and you will be the most famous king in the world if you allow me to do it."

The king was intrigued and asked the jester, "What do you need to make my horse fly?"

Mendel said that he needed a paddock, a house, an assistant, and a woman to keep him company.

The king asked him why he needed all that.

The jester said it was a hard job, and these things would help him concentrate because it would take him two years to teach the king's horse to fly.

"Two years," the king said. "That seems like a very long time."

Mendel then said, "Look, your kingship, I've done this before, and I'm telling you, it takes two years."

The king thought about it for awhile and said, "Okay, Mr. Jester. I'm going to give you everything you asked for, but at the end of the two years, if my horse isn't flying, I will torture you mercilessly, and you will wish that you had been put to death today."

As the king's guards took Mendel away to find his new woman and locate a house, Yankel, the assistant jester, came up to Mendel and said, "Mendel, what in God's name have you done? You know you can't teach the king's horse to fly. In two years, the king will surely do what he says and put you to a horrible death."

Mendel gave Yankel a grin and said, "You know, Yankel, a lot can happen in two years. The king could die of natural causes. I could die of natural causes. The horse could die of natural causes, or I might teach the horse to fly. For now, we'll let the future take care of itself. See you at six for dinner at my new house."

Introduction

Medium height, with thick hazel-brown hair, his pronounced nose and small, blue, penetrating eyes gave Stash Burzynski an almost hawk-like visage. Some people just looked smart. Stash looked really smart but more clever than an absent-minded physics genius smart. This was mostly because of the eyes; they seemed to move very quickly, darting around and scanning everything in his environment. You could feel his penetrating gaze bore right into you.

Stash Burzynski studied at the Medical Academy of Lublin in the mid-1960s. He had a special interest in biochemistry. He graduated first in his class at age twenty-four. The next year he received a PhD in biochemistry, the youngest person ever to have received an MD and PhD in the history of the school.

But Stash had a problem. He was not a member of the communist party, and he was not overly enthusiastic about the communist Polish regime. In Poland back then, nonparty medical school graduates ended up in the army. But Stash wanted to continue his research, so he decided to immigrate to the United States. In 1970, he came to America with twenty bucks in his pocket and no job.

He stayed with an uncle in the Bronx. He heard about a lab position at the Baylor College of Medicine in Houston. The director of the department of anesthesiology, Professor Ungar, had actually heard about Stash's work on peptides. Stash flew down to Houston to interview and hoped for the best.

Life at Baylor

He got the job. He would be an assistant professor in Ungar's department. Stash would have minimum teaching responsibilities and would continue his peptide research.

He stayed at Baylor for seven years. The first six years were quiet, productive, and free of controversy. He tested his peptides *in vitro* (in test tubes) and on animals. During these years, he refined his ideas. He was convinced he had discovered something big.

He met a female polish émigrée, Barbara Sadlej. She was blond, buxom, and also a medical doctor, an attractive combination for the young researcher.

Barbara had two small daughters from a previous marriage. Stash and Barbara married, and he had an instant family. Life was good for Stash during these years.

By that time, medical science had mapped out the cellular immune system, which consists of specialized cells, such as white blood cells, killer cells, T lymphocytes, and macrophages. Based on his research, Stash thought the body had an additional defense system on a much smaller scale than cells. He was looking at midsized peptides and amino acids, which were the building blocks of more complicated structures, such as cells. He termed these compounds "antineoplastons." ("Neoplasm" means "cancer" or "malignancy.")

Based on his scientific research, Stash thought his antineoplastons acted on cancer cells in a fundamentally different way than the body's cellular defense mechanisms. He thought his antineoplastons could be a more effective and less toxic treatment than chemotherapy, which basically works by interfering with a cancer cell's ability to divide and reproduce.

All of this was interesting and possibly even groundbreaking, but it had nothing whatsoever to do with anesthesiology, the department paying his salary. But Professor Ungar liked Stash and appreciated his work, so he protected him and basically gave him a home to do his research.

In 1976, Professor Ungar left Baylor for the University of Tennessee. The new Baylor department chairman was not as broad-minded as Professor Ungar and made it clear that there was no place for Stash in his department.

By that time, Stash was well respected at Baylor. He had been receiving grants from the National Cancer Institute for several years. Stash approached Baylor's oncology department about moving. They were highly interested, but there was a hitch. They wanted Stash to assign all his patents to the school and file all subsequent patents in Baylor's name.

Stash had discovered these peptides while in Poland and had been working on these discoveries on his own. Stash's mother did not raise her son to be a fool, and he wasn't about to turn over to Baylor the fruits of his work, even if he did some of the research and testing there. So there would be no move to the Baylor oncology department.

But he had another, bigger problem brewing at Baylor. Stash received his Texas medical license and started working in a small private internal medicine practice in 1973. In 1976, quietly, he started giving antineoplastons to advanced cancer patients in his private practice.

To find more patients for his treatment, he contacted Baylor's Institutional Review Board[12] for permission to use his medicine on some of Baylor's advanced cancer patients. They turned him down because he did not have approval from the Food and Drug Administration to test his drug, which is obtained by filing an Investigational New Drug (IND) application.

Once Baylor found out what he was doing, they ordered him to stop. Stash's position was that Baylor could not dictate to him how he conducted his private medical practice outside of Baylor. He was just a researcher at Baylor and did not have any clinical medical privileges or patient responsibilities at the school.

Stash might have been technically correct, but Baylor was still his employer. Between this problem and the fact that his work was not related to his position in the anesthesiology department, by July 1977, Stanislaw Burzynski would be out of Baylor. Sometimes there are life-altering choices. Stash was now facing one.

He was absolutely committed to pursuing his antineoplastons research. He had two options: Through Professor Ungar, Stash had been offered a job as an associate professor of biochemistry and oncology at the University of Tennessee. This was the safe choice. But Stash wanted to try his medicine on a large number of patients.

Notwithstanding Professor Ungar's anticipated support, Stash worried that he would face the same impediments from University of Tennessee bureaucrats as he had at Baylor.

His other option was to go out on his own and try to support himself by treating cancer patients with antineoplastons. He decided to go it alone, if he could legally give the medicine to his patients. If he couldn't, then he would take the University of Tennessee's offer and hope for the best.

---

12   An institutional review board (IRB) is a group of doctors, scientists, and laymen who oversee the testing of new drugs and devices in humans during FDA-approved clinical trials.

Stash hired a law firm to advise him. This was a good (albeit belated) idea since he was already treating patients with antineoplastons. The lawyers told him that as long as he made the medicine in his own lab and gave it to his own patients, it was legal under FDA law.

They felt the prerequisite for the FDA to assert jurisdiction was interstate commerce. If Stash's practice did not involve interstate commerce, then the FDA could not bother him, or so he was advised.

Stash was going to personally administer his medicine to his patients either at Twelve Oaks Hospital or some other location in Houston. Back then, he was not thinking about giving his medicine to patients and having them travel back to other states for self-administration in their homes. So the attorneys felt he could make and inject patients with the medicine without approval from the FDA.

The lawyers also looked at Texas state law. Some states have what is called a "mini-FDA act" whereby only FDA-approved drugs can be given to patients, regardless of whether there is interstate commerce. In 1977, Texas didn't exactly have a mini-FDA act, but there was a provision of the *Texas Food, Drug, and Cosmetics Act* that prohibited physicians from using any drug not approved by either the federal or state government, unless the drug was used for scientific or investigational purposes. For better and worse (and it was for better for Burzynski), the statute did not define what constituted scientific or investigational use.

Perhaps because of the ambiguity of the statute, his attorneys called the Texas Department of Health and the medical board and were told that as long he was making the medicine in his own lab and only giving it to his own patients, it would be legal under state law.

Stash Burzynski Goes into the Cancer Treatment Business

Since his attorneys gave him the green light, in 1977, Stanislaw R. Burzynski, MD, PhD, opened the Burzynski Research Laboratories in a small office in southwest Houston. Though he probably did not realize it at the time, with this act, Stash Burzynski had crossed over from mainstream medical research to the uncertain and dangerous world of alternative medicine. He would suffer the consequences of this act emotionally, scientifically, and financially for the next thirty years, and we are still counting.

But before he could treat a large volume of patients, he had to solve a supply problem. The antineoplastons Burzynski discovered are produced by the body in large quantities and can be found in blood, saliva, and urine.

During the testing period and his small practice, his need for material was quite small. For the previous few years, he had been obtaining antineoplastons from human blood in an unusual way. He got his raw material from the blood of his friends and acquaintances. He would go to parties and public gatherings with IV lines and bottles and beg and cajole his friends and colleagues to donate blood for his research.

After awhile, he noticed he was getting fewer and fewer invitations to parties, and when his friends would see him on campus or the street, they would turn and walk away quickly, pretending they didn't see him.

Given his diminishing supply of friends and his increased needs, Burzynski decided that the only feasible way of obtaining these peptides was from urine. Many drugs are made from disgusting starting products. In fact, there are a number of drugs already made from urine, such as Premarin, which is made from the urine of pregnant mares. Because he was a biochemist, he knew that through chromatography and other biochemical techniques, he could isolate and purify the needed compounds from urine.

In the years to come, his use of urine as the raw material for his drug caused many people to call him the "Urine Doctor." In the early years, when they did TV shows about him, they would usually start the piece with a flushing toilet. Where do you find huge quantities of urine? Many places. He installed urine collectors in public parks. His most controversial collection source was the Texas state penitentiary system. For a long time, he had urine collectors in Gilley's Bar, which was made famous in the film *Urban Cowboy*. Little did all those weekend cowboys know that their beer drinking was furthering modern cancer research.

The Quiet Early Years at the Burzynski Research Lab

The first few years at the Burzynski Research Laboratories were relatively quiet. From the beginning, Burzynski's operation became a haven for Polish expatriates. To this day, a large percentage of the clinic's employees are Polish. They had brilliant Polish scientists and total misfits (sometimes in the same person). Aside from the Poles, most of the technical workers were foreign. They had a number of very talented Chinese and Pakistani PhD's. For some reason, few technical employees were native Texans or Americans, at least in the early days.

Stash's wife Barbara worked in the pharmacy department. His brother Tadeusz, an engineer, was head of the production department. When his stepdaughters came of age, they too started working at the clinic, as did his son. It was truly a "mom and pop" operation (or "momushka and poposka").

Stash wrote all of the treatment protocols, and he put patients into categories by disease and stage. Because of his academic background, Burzynski collected data about the results of his treatment. As the money situation improved, he hired more and more researchers to assist with the basic science research.

The most important thing Burzynski and his researchers did in those early years was to isolate the active ingredients from the urine that caused the anticancer effects. Once isolated, he was able to produce these compounds synthetically from chemicals rather than from urine. Over the following ten years, he relied less and less on the natural version of antineoplastons (medicine derived from urine). It was much harder and more expensive to make the natural medicine, and he did not like the "urine doctor" moniker that followed him. It was too bad, since the naturally derived medicine was actually more potent than the earliest versions of the synthetic medicine.

Burzynski always had big plans for antineoplastons. He built a large, sophisticated plant. He and the other researchers went to many cancer conferences around the world to present their data in poster presentations and lectures. Because he was not affiliated with a major cancer institution, he was mostly shut out of the large, mainstream conferences in the United States.

So in the 1970s and early 1980s, he treated patients, wrote up and published his results, and gave presentations in whatever international chemotherapy and oncology conferences he could attend. In those early years, the presentations were not well attended. Oftentimes, it would be mostly the Burzynski researchers at his lectures. One researcher would ask the others scientific questions, with just a few non-Burzynski affiliated scientists listening in.

During these early years, the clinic had some amazing success stories. Most of his patients had exhausted all conventional treatment. That means most of his patients were dying or had incurable diseases. Many had been severely debilitated by radiation and chemotherapy. A substantial percentage of patients (then and now) come to him in wheelchairs.

His patient population created some difficulties in assessing the effect of his treatment. Many of his patients came to him shortly after being told that the conventional therapy had failed. Because Burzynski's goal was to help these patients rather than amass the most scientifically valid data, he would treat these people immediately. Later on, if their tumors decreased or went away, conventional doctors would claim that it was the prior treatment that actually helped or cured the patient rather than Burzynski's treatment.

He faced this problem for many years. I used to joke that even if Burzynski's treatment didn't work, people should still go to him, because he was the luckiest cancer doctor in the world. He managed to treat all the cancer patients who had miraculous delayed effects from prior conventional therapy. "Lucky Burzynski," that's what they should have called him.

Burzynski's biggest problem was that the treatment was very expensive, upwards of ten thousand dollars a month. And the treatment lasted for months or years. Some patients paid for a few months and then couldn't pay anymore. Burzynski wasn't the kind of doctor to cut people off from treatment just because they were out of money.

The operation had a huge nut. There were usually 120 employees to run the large medical clinic and the complete drug manufacturing plant. But most of the time Burzynski only treated anywhere from 80 to 250 patients, so the economies of scale were not good.

The FDA Knocks on Burzynski's Door and He Meets the First Grand Jury
But more ominous things started happening. In the early 1980s, the Harris County Medical Society received a couple complaints against Burzynski and

started looking at him. The society contacted the Texas Medical Board and the Food and Drug Administration. (Burzynski believes it was doctors at M. D. Anderson who reported him to the FDA.)

After a series of back-and-forth letters, the FDA notified Burzynski that he was in violation of federal law by introducing into interstate commerce an unapproved new drug and ordered him to stop. Burzynski took the position that he was treating everyone in Texas and that he was permitted to do so under Texas law. By this time, he was giving his medicine to patients to take back with them to their homes.

This issue came to a head in 1983. The FDA filed a civil injunction action against Burzynski seeking to close his clinic because of his use of an unapproved drug.

The FDA caught a bad break at the outset because the case had been assigned to Judge Gabrielle McDonald, who was the first black female federal judge appointed in Texas. She had been a civil rights attorney and had made quite a name for herself defending civil rights.

Worse for the FDA, two years previously, Judge McDonald had another high-profile alternative health case, that one involving the Texas Medical Board's attempt to regulate acupuncture. She had written a strong decision holding that the board's regulations of acupuncture violated the United States Constitution. She more or less held that people have some rights to alternative treatment, and the Texas Medical Board had not respected those rights. She was the judge you wanted to decide the Burzynski injunction case, unless you were the FDA.

But Burzynski was having his own troubles as a result of the civil injunction proceeding. Creditors started descending on him like vultures. Eighteen creditor lawsuits were filed shortly after the FDA filed its injunction action. There were threats of bankruptcy flying back and forth. Vendors wanted their equipment back. The clinic was in bad financial shape before, but the injunction action made things much worse.

Burzynski didn't have the money to pay payroll taxes, so the IRS was also coming after him hard and threatened to close him down. He was forced to sell his house just to pay off the IRS payroll tax lien. These were tough times for Burzynski and his clinic.

But the main problem was the FDA and its request for an injunction to close the clinic down. The hearing lasted several days, but ultimately the main factual points were not disputed. Burzynski's drug was not approved by the FDA. He had not even applied for an IND which would have allowed him to test the drug on humans. Patients were in fact coming from outside of Texas to take the treatment. Patients were then returning to their home states with the medicine. Indeed there was testimony that the clinic was shipping the medicine to patients in other states.

Those were some tough facts for Burzynski. It surely looked like he was violating federal law. But this was Gabrielle McDonald, and some habits are hard to break, like the habit of protecting people from government. She wrote a decision that was wonderfully if excruciatingly vague. She ordered Burzynski to stop shipping his medicine to patients out of state or otherwise to refrain from "introducing into interstate commerce" his medicine. But she also said that he could keep the clinic open and give his medicine to patients as long as his activities were "wholly intrastate" (i.e., within the state of Texas). What about patients coming into Texas and going home with medicine? That was not addressed in the decision, which Burzynski took to mean he could do it since she did not specifically prohibit it. Clever judge and good for Burzynski and his patients. Burzynski had dodged the FDA's first bullet and continued to treat his patients.[13]

The result did create some headaches for patients (and the clinic) because most of them came from out of state. They only needed to come to the clinic a couple times a year, but patients were only given a month or two supply of medicine. The patients and others came up with clever artifices to have medicine sent to them in their home states.

---

13   As part of her decision, Judge McDonald ordered Burzynski to file an IND to test his drugs. He did that, but the FDA put the IND on clinical hold. The clinical hold lasted six years, until 1989. The original filed IND covered breast cancer. But by 1989, Burzynski realized there were other forms of cancer, like brain tumors, which were much more responsive to antineoplastons than breast cancer, so Burzynski never did the clinical study for breast cancer under his original IND.

In 1985, two bad things happened (for Burzynski at least): First, Texas adopted a mini-FDA act. Under the new law, doctors could only use drugs approved by the FDA. I am sure that Burzynski's prior victory against the FDA was one of the reasons Texas passed that law.[14]

So the loophole that had allowed Burzynski to treat patients more or less legally in Texas was now closed. Thus, irrespective of federal law, it was now illegal for him to treat patients in Texas with his drug, or so it appeared. That change in the law would cause Burzynski considerable grief in the future.

Still hurting from its defeat or lack of complete victory in 1983, the FDA went after Burzynski again in 1985. They opened up a grand jury investigation to determine whether Burzynski had been violating Judge McDonald's 1983 injunction order by shipping his medicine across state lines.

During the 1983 civil injunction action, some of Burzynski's patients hired Houston attorney John Johnson to intervene or join the case on Burzynski's side. Johnson was one tough Texan. He was a partner in a medium-sized firm and specialized in suing insurance companies. He was very good at his work.

So when the FDA came back in 1985, the patients hired Johnson to challenge the FDA's right to regulate their life-saving treatment. They also sued because the FDA had taken the patients' medical records without the patients' permission. The case went nowhere—nowhere good anyway. The lawsuit was dismissed. Johnson appealed the case to the federal Fifth Circuit Court of Appeals. The court of appeals not only affirmed the dismissal, but also wrote a scathing opinion accusing Burzynski of willfully and wantonly violating federal law and the injunction order. The court also went out of its way to declare that patients had no constitutional right to take the treatment. They basically called Burzynski a crook who preyed on desperate patients. This was a major blow to Burzynski and his patients.

The Medical Board Proceedings
By the mid-1980s, Burzynski had survived a civil injunction action with the intent to close him down, a federal grand jury investigation, and a very hostile

---

14   Time and again with Burzynski, we would find a loophole which would then be closed by the government or insurance companies.

federal appellate court.

Next at bat was the Texas Medical Board (then technically called the Texas State Board of Medical Examiners). In 1986, the board initiated an investigation into Burzynski's use of his unapproved treatment. Burzynski hired John Johnson to represent him. John argued that Burzynski was not hurting anyone, and he was helping some people, especially those with incurable cancer. John must have been on a roll, because he convinced the medical board to do some cockamamie, vague agreement.

The board agreed to review the medical records of twenty-two patients. If the medical board's experts concluded that Burzynski's treatment had benefited these patients, then maybe the board would not go after him anymore. The beauty of this agreement was in its vagueness. It didn't guarantee that the board would stop its investigation; it just more or less implied it. So the board wouldn't take any heat for entering into such a ridiculous agreement. I guess they were expecting the results to be negative.

The most important thing the agreement did for Burzynski was to buy time. When you don't have the facts and don't have the law, oftentimes the best you can do is buy time and hope for the best. The last thing Johnson wanted to do was take on the medical board. So buying time was definitely the right thing to do, and when I became involved in the case, it became my main goal as well.

Burzynski and Johnson probably thought they would buy a few months. However, they did not hear from the board for almost two years. Then out of the blue, the board contacted Burzynski and said his records did not show he had benefited any of his patients. They told him he had to stop using his medicine on patients in Texas. Burzynski gave the Texas Medical Board the same answer he gave to the FDA and to Baylor. In response, the Board filed a complaint against Burzynski.

For some reason, Burzynski wanted some new blood or fresh eyes to look at the medical board case. Maybe he blamed Johnson for not disposing of the board investigation, but if he did, it was not justified. Johnson did an excellent job with what he had.

Maybe it was because Johnson did not get along with Burzynski's new public information person, Le Trombetta. Le was riding high at the Burzynski clinic because she got Burzynski on the *Sally Jessy Raphael* show. Before Sally Jessy, Burzynski was in constant financial trouble. After the show, his business doubled virtually overnight. I guess John was a little too Texan and rough around the edges, and Le was a touchy-feely left-wing urban gal from Atlanta. They just didn't hit it off.

Also, John had no expertise in administrative law or medical licensing cases, and Burzynski wanted to find someone who had some specific experience. And that's where the New York law firm of Abady & Jaffe came into the picture. By the time the Burzynski clinic called us in the summer of 1988, we had three associates and had made a name for ourselves in defending Dr. Revici and other maverick doctors throughout the country.

Le Trombetta called Sam about helping Burzynski with his licensing problem. Sam flew down to Houston and impressed them enough to get the case. It looked like an open-and-shut case, in a bad sense. The board's complaint was very short. It just said that Burzynski had been using his medicine in Texas for the past ten years and that it had not been approved by the FDA, which makes it illegal under the *Texas Food, Drug and Cosmetics Act*. It seemed like a pretty good argument.

When in Doubt, Delay
We only got the case about a week before the hearing, and I didn't have time to focus on it. Sam decided to ask for a continuance of the hearing. When in doubt, or when you have nothing, stall. It wasn't elegant, but that's all we had.

Sam asked me to come down for the hearing, mostly for moral support. So we flew down to Austin and met with Dr. Burzynski and many of his supporters the day before the hearing. They were upset. Dr. Burzynski was the only person giving his treatment; many of them felt he was the only person keeping them alive. If the patients had known there was no "plan B," and that their fate and the fate of Burzynski's practice rested on throwing ourselves on the mercy of this hostile board to grant us a continuance, they probably would have been even more afraid. Sometimes people are better off not knowing.

We all showed up at the hearing. Sam made his pitch that we were new counsel and we did not have sufficient time to review everything necessary to prepare an adequate defense. We got a very chilly reception from some of the board members. Quite a few of them appeared to really have it in for Burzynski, and they vehemently opposed even a ten-minute continuance.

But the gods were smiling on us. The board's president asked for advice from its outside counsel, assistant attorney general Dwight Martin. Turns out, Dwight was a fair and reasonable person. He told the board members they were not obligated to give a continuance, but it seemed to him to be the right thing to do under the circumstances. That took the wind out of the sails of the hostile board members, and the board quickly voted to grant us a continuance until the next board meeting, which was in two months. Burzynski had dodged another bullet, and now Sam and I would be dodging them with him.

We flew back to New York and then it became my responsibility to figure out what to do, as Sam moved on to newer challenges. I spent time reading the board's procedural rules and statutes. Back then, the rules were sparse.

I had some questions about that 1986 agreement that John Johnson had worked out, and I had other questions. The board had claimed he had been using his drugs in violation of Texas law since 1977. Hmm…. That meant they thought he was in violation of the old Texas law, before the mini-FDA act had been passed. I had some questions about whether that law really prohibited him from treating patients.

Now, most hearings are held by an administrative law judge. But back then, many of the cases were heard by the entire board. The board had intended to have a complete hearing on this case in less than an hour. We had received a short reprieve, but it was time to really slow things down.

So I asked for a pre-hearing conference to take place before a hearing officer (what is now called an administrative law judge) to narrow the issues and settle disputed points of law. The benefit of a pre-hearing conference is that a hearing officer would rule on disputed legal issues. This would make the hearing before the board run much smoother and quicker, since there would be no need to make legal arguments before the board. And that is how we phrased the request.

There was not much the board counsel could say. Go argue against someone who is trying to save the board time. Our request was quickly granted. The hearing before the board was adjourned again to allow time to hold the prehearing conference.

I spent days, if not weeks, preparing for what the board attorney thought would be a simple prehearing conference wherein the hearing officer would tell both sides that Burzynski was violating the law.

The long and short of it was that the hearing officer eventually agreed that the case was not as simple as everyone first thought. Because of the complex legal issues presented, the only thing we actually accomplished at the first of several prehearing conference was to set up a schedule to submit briefs on the many legal and factual issues I had raised.

Almost as an afterthought, I requested the expert's report on the twenty-two cases per the 1986 agreement. I wasn't expecting to find anything, but Burzynski wanted to see it since he thought the cases he submitted clearly showed that his treatment helped the patients. At this early stage in my working with him, I had not decided whether he was helping people. So like I said, I wasn't expecting much.

And I certainly was not expecting the board attorney to give me a hard time about this report since I just assumed the experts had found no benefit in any of the twenty- two cases. I was more than a little surprised when the board attorney vehemently objected to giving me the report. The harder he argued, the more I thought the guy was hiding something. The hearing officer must have gotten the same impression, and he ordered the report produced to us.

As soon as I received it, I understood. There were three separate oncologists who reviewed the cases. But together, they had only reviewed eleven of the twenty-two cases the board had agreed to review. I couldn't believe how stupid they were. They sat on this case for two years. They hired three experts, but they didn't do the one thing they agreed to do: review twenty-two cases.

I didn't have to be Perry Mason to figure what to do next. I complained to the hearing officer, or in legal parlance, I filed a motion to adjourn the hearing until the board complied with the prior agreement and had all the cases reviewed. The board attorney opposed the motion. The hearing examiner went with us. As a result, the hearing before the Texas Medical Board was put off indefinitely (or *sine die* as lawyers like to say.)

Burzynski, his staff, and the patients were relieved. No one was expecting us to win at this stage. The best anybody could hope for was to buy as much time as possible. And we had just made a very large purchase. Better still, it was a gift that would keep on giving for a long, long time.

That happened in the fall of 1988. We did not have the hearing until 1993. During those five years, the case was litigated and put on the back burner several times by the board.

Working as an attorney for a state agency is a low-prestige, low-paying job. Most board attorneys look at the job as a temporary way station. The original attorney assigned to the case left the board after a year into the case. The next attorney didn't know what to make of the case and did his best to avoid thinking about it. Several additional board attorneys tried to move the case forward, but some procedural issue always seemed to come up. There would be further delays, more hearings before a hearings officer, and more papers. Then that board attorney would leave and a new one would have to be reassigned. The new attorney would have to learn the case and figure out how to get out of the maze.

At some point in the process, Texas changed the law to require medical board cases to be initially heard by an independent administrative law judge (ALJ). That was good news for us since the ALJ would be a professional and probably would not have a bias against an unconventional practitioner like Burzynski.

Maybe I am a conspiracy nut, but I think there was a concerted federal and state effort to put Burzynski out of business. The feds tried and failed in 1983 and 1985. Then in 1986 the medical board surfaces, and in 1988 the board resurfaces and tries to revoke his license.

Enter the Texas Department of Health

By 1992, we had battled the board to a standstill for four years. Then out of the blue, the Texas Department of Health filed an injunction action trying to stop Burzynski from treating his patients in Texas.

I am not paranoid. The assistant attorney general handling the case told me that his office had been monitoring the board case, hoping that the medical board would take care of the Burzynski problem. But after four years, the attorney general's office was tired of waiting, so it took matters into its own hands and filed its own action.

The assistant attorney general was Robert Reyna. He was in charge of the consumer safety section of the attorney general's office. He was competent and highly experienced. We went through some motion practice, and he took Burzynski's deposition; nothing too exciting. But more time elapsed.

A New Sheriff Rides into Town

The medical board, perhaps embarrassed by being unable to conclude a simple licensing case, finally smartened up. Maybe they realized they were being outgunned, or maybe they thought they were just unlucky. Either way, they decided to get their own hired gun, someone who could get to a hearing and rid the state of the likes of Burzynski.

The new sheriff was Dewey Helmcamp III. Consistent with calling himself "the third," Dewey was mighty preppie. About six feet tall, he had longish salt-and-pepper hair, tortoise-shell glasses, and a pleasant but markedly patrician face. He wore conservative Brooks Brothers suits and had just a touch of an effete upper-class Southern accent.

Dewey was chief of the attorney general's litigation section. He had tons of experience litigating cases for the attorney general's office. He was (and still is) a very smart and highly effective litigator. He was not flashy, colorful, or bombastic. In fact, he was rather soft spoken and understated, but those are the guys you have to watch the most. And the worst part of it; he wasn't going anywhere. He was a lawyer who just focused on the job and doggedly pursued his objective.

To my untold relief, Dewey was also a straight shooter. He litigated hard but fairly. Unlike many of my adversaries, Dewey did not bring a big ego to the case. It was all business and competent professionalism.

In the beginning of our four-year adversarial relationship, he had a very low opinion of Burzynski. He didn't think Burzynski helped anyone and thought he was a crook who preyed on desperate people. I made it one of my personal missions in life to change his mind about that, regardless of the outcome of the case. Ultimately, I think I succeeded a little, maybe.

After Dewey took over the case, the licensing case moved methodically toward a hearing. But that was not completely unwelcomed, and maybe I even helped the board's case along. At that point, the Department of Health injunction action was a bigger problem than the licensing case. We had more maneuvering room with an administrative proceeding than a state court injunction action. The licensing case could still be tied up for a couple years after a hearing. But an adverse result in the injunction case would put Burzynski out of business immediately.

So I went back to the Reyna, showed him that the board case was on track, and promised him that the case would go to hearing. Reyna realized that there could be inconsistent decisions if both cases proceeded at the same time. But, if the board ruled against Burzynski and he was stopped from giving antineoplastons to patients, Reyna's case would become moot.

So Reyna agreed to put his Department of Health case on hold. That probably worked out for Reyna as well. He was very busy protecting Texans from all kinds of scams, and he was particularly active against health law violators. But none of those folks were my clients, and I preferred that Reyna focus his considerable skills on someone other than Burzynski.

It was now time to get serious about the medical board proceeding. I tried some last-minute tactics. Several dozen patients attempted to become parties to the licensing case (or "intervene" in legal jargon). We didn't care whether they were called parties or witnesses; we just wanted them to tell their amazing stories of how Burzynski saved their lives with his miraculous medicine. There was a better chance of having them testify if they asked to intervene, even though they might not have a right or legal "standing" to technically join the case. But the judge might allow them to testify as a compromise.

The ALJ, Earl A. Corbitt, was an older guy with a thick shock of white hair. He had a great deal of experience in administrative cases. He rejected the patients' attempt to intervene on standing grounds, but said they could testify at the hearing. We didn't fool either Dewey or Judge Corbitt with this tactic, but we got what we needed.

The Administrative Hearing and the Patients Steal the Show

The hearing lasted several days. The patients were powerful. They just got up and told their stories. All of them had terminal cancer with very short life expectancies. They all found their way to the Burzynski clinic, and they were all disease free, some for many years. A number of them were still on maintenance treatment and, as could be expected, they were very concerned about continued access to Burzynski and the medicine.

Many of the patients were small children with brain tumors. The Kunnaris were one of the families who came to Austin to testify. They lived in upper Minnesota. They were not rich and could not afford to fly down, especially since they would have to take all four of their young children with them. So they all piled into their big station wagon and drove twenty-four hours straight through to Texas, Jack and Marianne switching driving every few hours. They put a bunch of sleeping bags in the back for the kids.

Their son Dustin was just two and a half when he was first diagnosed with medulloblastoma, a virulent form of brain cancer. Surgery was not an option, and he was too young for radiation. The local doctors pressed his parents to have Dustin undergo chemotherapy. However, Jack did some research about conventional treatments for this disease, and he didn't like what he read. The cure rates were abysmal and the side effects were horrifying. He pressed his local oncologists to put him in contact with parents of a few successfully treated children with the same or similar disease. After several days, the oncologist could only come up with one child who was even alive after treatment, and this doctor worked at a large university-related teaching hospital. The Kunnaris decided that conventional treatment was not for Dustin.

Like many others, the Kunnaris found their way to the Burzynski clinic. It wasn't long after undergoing treatment that Dustin's tumor began shrinking. And there were no side effects. Dustin was still undergoing treatment during the medical board's hearing before Judge Corbitt.

So with Jack and the other kids in the hearing room, Marianne came up to testify, with Dustin in her lap. She was understandably emotional as she told Judge Corbitt what they had gone through—that the oncologists told her Dustin would most likely be dead by now and how grateful they were to Dr. Burzynski. It was very moving. No apologies here; you go with what you have, especially in what was literally a matter of life and death for people.

The other highlight of the hearing was the testimony of a physician affiliated with the National Cancer Institute (NCI). At the time, Nick Patronas was the head of pediatric neuroradiology at the NCI-affiliated hospital. He had been one of the NCI doctors who came down to Houston in 1991 to review Burzynski's medical records of a number of brain cancer patients (more about that later). The team concluded that Burzynski's patients had responded to his treatment. He was very impressed by Burzynski's results. At considerable professional risk, Nick flew to Austin to testify for Burzynski.

He told the judge that he had never seen brain tumors "melt away" like they did with Burzynski's patients. He related that the NCI had tested a drug on a few patients which also seemed to make tumors disappear, but that drug was so toxic it killed two of the three test subjects and made a vegetable of the third.

By the end of the hearing, it was very clear that Burzynski's treatment greatly benefited advanced cancer patients and that his patients needed to continue on the treatment.

What Is "Any Drug"?

To have a judge rule in your favor in this type of case, you need to give him the will and the way to do so. We clearly had given Judge Corbitt the will to rule in our favor. I just needed to find the way.

True, the Texas mini-FDA act meant that only FDA-approved drugs could be given to patients in Texas, and regrettably, Burzynski's drugs were not FDA approved. But there was also a law in the medical practice statute that allowed a physician to prescribe *any* drug to minister to the immediate needs of a patient. Given the fact that all of Dr. Burzynski's patients had terminal cancer and would die without it, in some sense, they surely had an immediate need for his drugs, which surely was "any drug" under the statute, to my way of thinking anyway. Maybe my interpretation contradicted the Texas mini-FDA act, but this was a statute right in the *Texas Medical Practice Act,* and it was more specific. This might not have been my most convincing legal argument, but given the equities, we hoped it was enough of the "way" for the judge to come down on our side.

First Round to Burzynski

And it was. Three months later, Judge Corbitt ruled that Burzynski had not violated the *Medical Practice Act* because the statute said he could use *any* drug to minister to the immediate needs of his patients. Corbitt said if the Texas legislature had meant to restrict the "any drug" language to only FDA-approved drugs, they should have specifically said so.[15] It was a wonderful result reflecting the equities of the situation. Corbitt was my kind of judge: equity and people over hyper-legal technicalities.

I talked to Dewey about the decision. Gracious as ever, he congratulated me, but we both knew what had happened, and we knew Burzynski wasn't out of the woods yet—far from it.

Administrative law is an odd duck and has its own set of rules. In Texas, as in most states, an ALJ presiding over a licensing case for a medical or other state board does not make a final decision but rather a "proposal for decision." The ALJ makes findings of fact and conclusions of law, and a recommendation for a sanction, if there is a finding of fault or a violation of the practice act.

But an ALJ's proposal is not binding on a board. With some limitations, the board can change a finding of fact. A board can overrule the ALJ's conclusions of law, and it can completely disregard the recommended sanction.

---

15   Later on, the Texas legislature, at the Medical Board's behest, did just that, probably as a result of Corbitt's opinion.

Why go through the whole ALJ process if it does not make final decisions? The short answer is that you have to. Most licensing boards have too much work to sit through hearings and make a decision on every case. So instead, they farm the cases out to ALJs who make the initial findings. The findings are then submitted to the board for review. Each party has a right to appeal, argue, and make written submissions in favor or against any of the findings, conclusions, and recommendations made by the ALJ. The board members then look at all the material and vote whether to accept, reject, or modify any part of the ALJ's proposal for decision.

So winning before the ALJ was certainly better than losing, but it was not the end of the story. The board had been hostile to Burzynski all these years, and there was no reason to think anything would change just because Judge Corbitt ruled in our favor.

We did what we could in advance. We had politicians write letters to the board in support of Burzynski. We even had one of the most-admired living Texans come to the hearing to show his support.

Burzynski treated a young woman for a rare form of liver cancer. She was not terminal, but it was very serious. She could have taken chemotherapy, and it might possibly have helped her, but there was a complicating factor. She was pregnant, and the chemotherapy would have most likely killed or severely deformed her unborn child. So even though she knew she was putting her life at risk, she refused chemotherapy.

Instead, she went to Burzynski. Burzynski was still treating her when the medical board hearing came up. She and her family were grateful that Burzynski was trying to help her. The woman's name was Lisa Childress and her father was the "Coach," or as he was less commonly known in Texas, Tom Landry (of the Dallas Cowboys).

Round Two Goes to the Noble Healers of the Medical Board

Both Lisa and Tom showed up at the medical board on the day it was deciding the Burzynski case. Most of the board members went up to introduce themselves to him. But he wasn't happy that day. His daughter was sick and wanted to continue Burzynski's treatment. He was just as worried as everyone else.

Judge Corbitt sat between Dewey and me and answered the board's questions. They were hard on him. Indeed, they were brutal. Judge Corbitt not only had white hair but also very fair skin. The more they talked, the more they insulted his decision, and the redder his neck and ears got. He was pretty steamed. He tried to explain to these medical doctors, these "healers," that the patients needed Burzynski's treatment, and that they would suffer and die without it.

But the doctors on the board were card-carrying members of the church of medical orthodoxy, which meant patients be damned in the event of an attack on conventional medicine. They just said Corbitt was wrong and they were reversing him.[16] They would be ordering Burzynski to stop treating patients with his drugs until he received approval from the FDA. (Fat chance of that happening.) They put him on ten years of probation and told him that if he kept treating patients, they would revoke his license. They would be issuing a written decision.

This was a big blow for Burzynski and his patients and supporters. But I assured them that the case wasn't over; we would go to state court, and it was business as usual, until I said so.

Up to State Court where Judge Paul Davis Comes to the Rescue

The board's action was not a surprise, and I came to the hearing with injunction papers already prepared. We didn't need them that day since the board had to finalize a written order. It came soon enough. As soon as we received the order, I drove to Austin to file the injunction papers and seek an immediate temporary restraining order (TRO). We had patients ready to go.

We caught a break, as the case was assigned to Judge Paul Davis, who is a smart, thoughtful, and liberal judge. No doubt he was aware of the case, since by this time it was getting national media attention.

---

16   Corbitt had made one finding against Burzynski, that he was guilty of false advertising. Texas had an odd law that a doctor can't claim a treatment helps a disease, even if it does. Corbitt found that Burzynski was guilty of false advertising, imposed no sanction on him, and said he should stop making claims even if they were truthful.

He agreed to hold an immediate TRO hearing. A number of terminally ill patients who absolutely needed Burzynski's treatment testified on Burzynski's behalf. They had very compelling stories.

Dewey didn't put up much of a fight at the TRO hearing. He had won before the board, but I don't think he wanted to be responsible for pulling the patients off the treatment. By that time, even he was probably convinced that some of the patients needed it. Since Dewey was a very decent fellow, I think he realized there would be no harm if the TRO was issued.

Maybe it would not have mattered how hard he argued, since we had the overwhelming equities on our side. Whatever the factors, Judge Davis immediately granted the TRO and set the case for a preliminary injunction hearing. A few weeks later, we also got preliminary injunction that stayed the enforcement of the board's order pending the briefing of the case, oral argument, and the final decision by Judge Davis on the merits.

That process took several months. Eventually, the day of oral argument came. The case was still in the national media and producers of *48 Hours* were closely following the proceedings. The TV crew had started filming for a big piece on Burzynski and his licensing problems. The crew was at the clinic when I returned from getting the preliminary injunction and filmed me walking into the clinic with my trench coat and my big grey fedora hat, announcing that the judge granted the injunction and that the clinic could stay open. It was a good TV moment (or so I thought).

CBS asked for and received permission from Judge Davis to film the final argument.[17] That seemed a good sign. It would be hard for an elected judge to go on national TV and tell dozens of cancer patients to drop dead, which is what the medical board had done. Maybe we should have brought cameras to the medical board and exposed them to the country.

Dewey and I made our arguments. He still was not at the top of his game, and then we sat down. I was hoping for, but not expecting, an immediate decision. But it was just too good of a television moment.

---

17   Federal courts do not allow cameras in courtrooms, or even in federal courthouses, but many states do, and the review of a Texas state administrative agency decision is in state district court.

The judge announced that he would be giving his decision from the bench. With the cameras rolling and with patients and other news media filling the courtroom, Judge Paul Davis announced that he was overturning the board's decision as an abuse of discretion and reinstating ALJ Corbitt's decision. The entire courtroom broke out in cheers, applause, and screams of joy, all in front of the CBS cameras. That was one of the best days I ever had as a lawyer and those days, few and far between though they may be, are what keeps me going.

As we were leaving the courtroom, Dewey looked over to me with the same pursed-lipped, preppie grin I had seen on him before. He didn't have to say a word. We both knew what had happened and that it still wasn't over for Burzynski; it was just another temporary reprieve.

Still on that day, Judge Paul Davis (maybe with a little help from me) temporarily stayed the death sentences of many of Burzynski's patients and for that, Burzynski, his patients, and I would be forever grateful.

The Court of Appeals Weighs in, but by Then the Horse Could Fly!

Of course, Dewey appealed Judge Davis's opinion. But for some reason, the appeal dragged on. I was busy on other matters, and I had to seek several extensions. Dewey, professional and gracious as always, accommodated me.

It took almost two years for the Austin Court of Appeals to rule on the appeal. Perhaps they also were in no hurry to do what they thought they had to do. Early during the appeal process, Dewey offered us a deal. Stop using the treatment and no probation. That was a far cry from the 1988 board, which wanted to revoke his license. But Burzynski would have none of it. He just wasn't going to stop treating his patients. Not in this lifetime. He didn't get any argument from me. I told him that the court of appeals might overturn Judge Davis's decision. But I wasn't going to advise him to give up and abandon his patients. A different attorney might have done so, but not me. Besides, I was still following Mendel the jester's rule, and we were not yet ready to see if the horse could fly.

By the time the court of appeals issued its decision overturning Judge Davis, in early February 1996, the medical board case was moot. It didn't matter what the board said or did. Burzynski had much bigger problems, which led to a miraculous solution to his problems. Mendel the jester was a smart fellow. The horse would fly!

The Ups and Downs of the Insurance Litigation and the Second Grand Jury

After we had put the medical board case on ice back in 1988 (while I was still practicing in New York), Burzynski started giving Abady & Jaffe more work. We came in as co-counsel in an insurance litigation being handled by John Johnson's firm.

The insurance companies hated Burzynski and hated paying for his treatment. Initially, insurance companies may not have known his treatment was not FDA-approved conventional chemotherapy. The clinic did not exactly broadcast that the treatment was experimental, but it told the insurance companies as soon as they asked.

Early on, his insurance department was run by Cameron Frye. Cameron's mother had been treated by Dr. Burzynski, and the family was grateful for what he did for her, even though she eventually died. Cameron was a real operator, in the good and bad sense of the word. He thought of himself as a modern-day Robin Hood. He took from the rich (the insurance companies) and gave it to the poor (the cancer patients and their doctors).

He devised a short form for describing the treatment on insurance claim forms: "ANPA chemotherapy." For some reason, most insurance companies assumed that this was just one of the many kinds of approved chemotherapy cocktails given to advanced cancer patients. The Burzynski clinic received millions of dollars for ANPA chemotherapy.[18]

But sooner or later, many insurance companies found out that Burzynski's treatment was not FDA approved, so more and more companies started denying

---

18   Frye eventually left Burzynski's clinic and opened up an insurance consulting business. Many of his clients were Mexican and other foreign clinics. For those clinics, he devised another trick. He had them form U. S. foundations or affiliates, mostly in the San Diego area and billed the services out of the U. S. office. It worked, and his clients collected millions of dollars. The insurance companies hated him. Not surprisingly, the feds indicted him on insurance fraud in the late 1990s. But the case languished for years, in part because the federal judge was Lynn Hughes (more about Hughes in Chapter 4). Eventually the case was settled for a civil fine. Frye died of AIDS a few years ago.

the clinic's claims. Eventually there was a financial crisis. The good news was that some of the patients whose insurance companies stopped paying were actually getting much better on the treatment. After John Johnson represented the patients in the 1985 FDA injunction case, some of them hired John to sue their insurance companies for not paying for Burzynski's treatment.

In a few years, John racked up some impressive results. He recovered not only the medical expenses, but also punitive damages for quite a few patients. It helped that some of these insurance companies actually denied payment for patients who had been clearly helped by Burzynski's treatment.

The trick to these lawsuits was that they were all filed in state court. State law generally allows for punitive damages in these kinds of cases. More importantly, under state law, the contract between a health insurance company and an insured person is construed against the insurance company. The patient gets the benefit of the doubt if there is any ambiguity in the policy. It's like the rule that the house wins on ties in blackjack.

This was critical because up until this time, insurance companies had a general exclusion for treatments they did not consider good or standard practice. That language was vague enough to allow most judges and juries to do the right thing and find that a successful cancer treatment was good practice.

The good news was that because of some of these cases, Burzynski was receiving some income from insurance companies even when they knew that his treatment was experimental (though most of the money ended up going to the attorneys and the patients). The bad news was that he was making more and more enemies in the insurance field.

The Killer Aetna Case

Things were starting to slip away from John Johnson in these insurance cases. Johnson had convinced Burzynski to become a party in an Illinois state court lawsuit filed by one of the clinic's patients. The patient died and Johnson continued the case since the suit was about payment of the clinic's treatment for the patient. But something happened this time. Maybe the defense lawyers were better, or Aetna was nastier than the prior companies that John had sued.

Or maybe it was just the wrong case. But whatever the reason, Johnson was getting hammered.

The first thing Aetna did was to have the case removed to federal court. The next thing it did was absolutely devastating. The decedent plaintiff had her health insurance through her husband's employer. That meant that the case was governed by federal employment law, the *Employee Retirement Income Security Act* (*ERISA*), and not state law.

Recovery under health benefit plans governed by *ERISA* is much harder and much less rewarding than suing under a plan governed by state law. Why? Two reasons. First, there are no punitive damages under *ERISA*. If you are lucky, and if you win, you may get attorneys' fees. But the real upside in these health care reimbursement cases was the punitive damages, which did not exist under federal *ERISA*. No lawyer likes to litigate a case and only collect attorneys' fees if they win, unless there is a very big upside like punitive damages, which is usually many times the actual damages and attorneys' fees in the case.

But there is a much bigger problem in *ERISA* cases. There is no jury trial. *ERISA* cases are decided by the judge. But even worse, the judge cannot make an independent determination about whether the treatment is covered under an *ERISA* plan. Rather, the judge is required to defer to the determination of the insurance company, which acts as the trustee disbursing the company's benefits. In an *ERISA* case, the insurance company wins unless the court finds that the denial of coverage was not only wrong, but also "arbitrary and capricious" or "an abuse of discretion," meaning that it has to be completely irrational. That is a very high standard of proof for a patient seeking to overturn an insurance company's denial for payment.

But Johnson had a third strike against him. The insurance contract covering this patient had a specific exclusion barring payment for any therapy that was not approved by the FDA. The irony was that Aetna and other insurance companies made their exclusionary language more specific because of the success of Johnson and other attorneys like him who had convinced judges and juries that the old language was ambiguous.

And if three strikes were not enough, since the patient died of her breast cancer early in the case, Johnson did not have the sympathy factor of a live patient who was being cured by a selfless doctor. In perfect hindsight, this might not have been the best case for Burzynski to have joined.

Aetna Goes on the Attack

And then things just got worse. Aetna looked at its own claims records and determined that it had paid hundreds of thousands of dollars to Burzynski for Aetna-insured patients. In most or all of the plans covering the patients, there was a specific exclusion for experimental therapy. So Aetna at least paid all these other claims by mistake, or so it would argue.

Aetna then upped the ante and employed an aggressive defense tactic: it went on the attack. It filed a multimillion-dollar racketeering counterclaim against Burzynski. So what started as a lawsuit by a Burzynski patient, to collect from Aetna around seventy thousand dollars in medical bills, turned into a multimillion-dollar lawsuit against Burzynski. This may have been another reason that Burzynski was unhappy with Johnson and wanted me to get involved in the case.

As we jumped in, two big things were happening in the case. The Aetna lawyers were starting to depose the Burzynski employees. Just to be extra nasty, they were spending some quality deposition time with Burzynski's family who worked at the clinic.

More troubling, Aetna decided its job was to protect the other poor insurance companies from Burzynski. So as part of their discovery requests, they sought information about all of Burzynski's patients whose treatment was being paid for by any insurance company. The judge was wavering about whether to grant the request. And that's when we came in.

It would have been horrible if Aetna and its hired guns contacted all these insurance companies. We had to stop it and stop it quickly before these jerks could put Burzynski out of business.

What to do? Then as now, I am reluctant to rely solely on my limited powers of persuasion to make a judge see things my way. I needed something bigger, more impressive.

It struck me that what Aetna was asking for was not only bad for Burzynski, but it would also be bad for his patients. If Aetna contacted all these other insurance companies and convinced them to stop paying for the treatment, all of these patients would then be on the hook for this very expensive treatment. If enough of the patients could not pay, the clinic would go under and then no one could get the medicine. That seemed quite dramatic.

Then it hit me. Maybe I couldn't convince the judge, but maybe a patient or two might be more persuasive. And, if the judge might be impressed by a few patients, he might be really impressed by dozens or hundreds of patients. Now I was cooking!

It also seemed to me that Burzynski had an obligation to inform his patients that their insurance reimbursement for the treatment was in danger. So to fulfill that obligation, I sent a letter to every one of Dr. Burzynski's patients letting them know what Aetna was trying to do and suggested that if they had a problem, they should contact the judge. And did they! The judge's office was inundated with letters from desperate and dying cancer patients expressing indignation and outrage at Aetna's plan.

I think these letters helped clarify the judge's thinking. He denied Aetna's request for this information.

I was feeling pretty good about myself for pulling this off, but the feeling was short lived. Within a few weeks, we started receiving reports from a couple patients that their insurance carriers had been contacted by Aetna's lawyers and were told that Burzynski might be defrauding them. A few of the companies were even served with subpoenas for the records of their Burzynski patients. I managed to see one of those subpoenas, and it was odd. Although it carried the same case information as our case, it was signed by another judge in a different division.

I had an idea of what the Aetna attorneys had done, and I was angry about it. But I proceeded methodically. I made a series of motions to try to find out what happened. It turns out the Aetna lawyers went behind our judge's back and had some other federal judge sign subpoenas giving Aetna access to the information that our federal judge said Aetna could not have. Aetna's lawyers argued that it was a "clerical mistake" and that none of the lawyers knew about it. The judge was skeptical, and hit them with over ten thousand dollars in sanctions for that little trick. That was all I could do to them at the time, but I wasn't going to forget it.

John Johnson was still on the case, but things were coming to a head with him. He was insisting that we dismiss the patient's claim against Aetna. He wanted to have the case transferred to a federal court in Houston, and he thought we would have a better shot making a "change in venue motion" if we were not seeking any relief on behalf of an Illinois resident.

There was some logic to the argument, but I felt that we could probably get the case kicked back to Houston even with the claim against Aetna. But more importantly, I thought it would be a mistake to give up the leverage of seeking money and attorneys' fees from Aetna. To follow John's advice would make us just racketeering defendants. If we kept our claim, Burzynski would be the plaintiff in a case where the filthy defendant insurance company filed a frivolous retaliatory counterclaim. It wasn't a close case for me. Burzynski saw it my way. John was disappointed and withdrew as co-counsel.

Aetna Helps Out and Gets Some Help In Return (Probably)
Aetna's attorneys and I went back and forth beating each other up on the case. I got the feeling from the discovery that Aetna was getting help from government entities and that the Aetna lawyers were also doing the investigatory work for these government entities.

My suspicions were confirmed. By mistake, I received a fax from Aetna's attorneys. The fax included a letter from the medical board thanking the Aetna lawyers for their help. There was some indication that the board was also supplying information to Aetna.

One of Burzynski's employees who Aetna wanted to depose was some minor clinic person who may not have had the correct license. It had nothing to do with Aetna's claim. It seemed to me that Aetna was seeking this information just to pass it on to the board, so the board could take action against Burzynski. Aetna's lawyers had made a special trip down to Texas just to depose this person, which seemed odd given how little the person had to do with the case. At the last minute, I canceled the deposition. This time we got hit for sanctions for not producing the employee for the scheduled deposition. But it took a couple months for Aetna to get an order compelling the deposition of that individual. By that time, the person had already left the country. Burzynski was not happy about paying the sanction, but it couldn't be helped.

These Aetna lawyers were really pissing me off. The primary law firm was a many-hundred person Midwest firm. There were three attorneys on the case, two senior attorneys whose arrogance exceeded their intelligence, and a junior attorney, a decent enough person who followed the marching orders of the other two.

As if that was not enough firepower, Aetna hired another big firm in Houston to act as local counsel to assist in whatever had to be done in Houston. But there was a kicker. Aetna apparently hired a junior associate at this big, powerful Houston firm to do the local counsel work. What was so special about her? She had worked in the U. S. attorneys office in Houston, and coincidentally, she had been one of the assistant U. S. attorneys on the Burzynski federal case in the mid-1980s.

That became convenient, since in the middle of the Aetna case, the Houston U. S. attorneys office opened another grand jury investigation about whether Burzynski was violating Judge McDonald's 1983 injunction order barring him from shipping his medicine to his patients.

Then something very interesting happened. For some reason, Aetna's lawyers wanted to depose Burzynski's mailroom clerk, a tall, amiable West African fellow by the name of Bob Mossary. Aetna's lawyers insisted on deposing him. There had been rumors swirling around for years that it was Bob Mossary who was shipping medicine to the patients out of state.

Since Aetna's main attorneys were from the Midwest, and I was still living in New York City, both sides had to come to Texas for depositions of the clinic personnel. As a result, we tended to schedule multiple depositions over the several days. Bob Mossary was scheduled to be deposed per Aetna's group of deposition notices. But for some reason, all the depositions had to be rescheduled. So Aetna's lawyers sent out a new set of deposition notices for the new agreed-upon dates. Bob was again noticed for deposition, along with all of the other people who had previously been noticed. However, due to last-minute scheduling conflicts, I had to adjourn those depositions as well.

Shortly after I had adjourned the second set of depositions, the Houston U. S. attorneys office subpoenaed Bob to testify before the grand jury. He went before the grand jury and denied that he ever sent medicine to any patients out of state.

Here is the interesting part: After Bob gave his testimony to the grand jury, Aetna's attorneys sent out a third set of deposition notices. Everything was the same, except that this time they didn't notice Bob Mossary for deposition. I asked them about it. They just vaguely said they didn't need to talk to him anymore.

Grand jury proceedings are supposed to be secret. Indeed, it is a felony for anyone other than the testifying witness to relate the testimony of a grand jury witness. Yet somehow, Aetna lawyers appeared to know that they no longer needed to depose Bob Mossary. It must have been a lucky guess on Aetna's part. I went after Aetna's lawyers for this. By this time, the case had been transferred to Houston. The Houston federal judge, Kenneth Hoyt, didn't think I had enough evidence to pursue it, so he shut me down. I had to bide my time.

Aetna Switches Horses

The only good news was that Aetna may have been getting tired of its attorneys and it removed both law firms from the case. Since the case was no longer in Illinois, Aetna didn't need a Midwest firm handling the matter, and it didn't rush to have the junior Texas attorney take over the case. Whatever the reason, it was the right call for Aetna, since arrogance and a lack of smarts are a bad combination in a lawyer, and Aetna's lawyers had too much of both.

Aetna hired a smaller insurance defense firm. They were just as nasty, but much smarter. But then, I guess I hadn't been warm and fuzzy to Aetna either, and if I had my way, it was going to get much worse for them. I was not going to forget what Aetna and its lawyers had pulled in Illinois or in Houston.

The Second Grand Jury Comes and Goes; Better Lucky than Good

By 1990, my last year practicing in New York, between the Aetna case and other Burzynski matters, I was spending most of my time on Burzynski's business. Some of it was what I would call "light corporate"—short agreements for various business deals, interacting with his Securities and Exchange Commission (SEC) counsel and accountants, and dealing with employee issues.[19] I was acting as his general counsel. In addition to the Aetna case, there were other insurance litigations that I, with the help of Cathy Helwig and Matt Dineen, was handling for Burzynski.

But things became even busier. We knew the government had another grand jury going because it was calling some of the clinic's employees, like Bob Mossary, to testify. But we had not expected it would go anywhere, since we knew that Mossary said he was not shipping any medicine across state lines.

Two things changed our minds. By mistake (I assume) I had received from Aetna a copy of the government's prosecution memo outlining the criminal charges to be filed against Burzynski.[20] It was a long, detailed, and frightening. And Burzynski started hearing credible rumors that he would be indicted the following month.

Burzynski was mighty worried. He was looking to me to stop the indictment. That was a tall order, even for a fairly smart New York Jewish lawyer. It is very difficult to stop an indictment. There is an old saying that a prosecutor can indict a ham sandwich if he wants to. The prosecutor on the case was highly experienced and had handled the 1985 grand jury investigation. This time around, I knew, or suspected the government was receiving and possibly sharing information with Aetna.

I spent several days thinking about all of this. Since I had started working for Burzynski, I had felt like I was playing whack-a-rat. You whack one rat back into a hole, and then another one pops up from a different hole. This was getting

---

19   In the 1980's Burzynski's research corporation became a public company and changed its name to the Burzynski Research Institute, Inc.

20   After receiving the U. S. attorney's prosecution memo, I began to wonder whether I was getting these documents showing Aetna's counsel's interaction with the government by accident. Maybe someone didn't like what Aetna was doing. I never found out whether it was an accident or someone was quietly helping us.

ridiculous. Aetna was helping and possibly being helped by the Texas Medical Board, the United States government, probably other insurance companies, and a whole cadre of quack-busters, who are professional consultants intent on putting alternative practitioners out of business. This was really pissing me off.

But I was most aggravated by the fact that the U. S. attorneys office appeared to be working with Aetna and sharing what should be secret information with a private party in a civil litigation. That just wasn't right, and I decided to do something about it.

I needed something that would make a splash. Since Aetna was suing Burzynski for racketeering, I decided to return the favor but with a twist. I sued Aetna, its attorneys, and the quack-buster consultants who were helping Aetna.

The twist was that I also sued a number of unnamed government employees who violated grand jury secrecy laws and conspired with Aetna and its attorneys to commit various illegal acts against Burzynski. Although I didn't name any names, I presented in the complaint some of the information I had uncovered about the communications between Aetna's lawyers and the unnamed government attorneys. I picked a nice round number for the damage claim: $200 million. I was told the complaint read like a novel. We filed the complaint and the same day put it out on the business wire. It had the desired effect.

It took a few weeks for things to percolate, but then we started to hear some amazing coincidences. After we filed the action, the U. S. attorney for the Southern District of Texas announced that he was resigning and going back into private practice. That was a welcomed happenstance.

We then heard that the assistant U. S. attorney handling the Burzynski grand jury investigation also decided to go into private practice and move out of Texas. Yet another welcomed coincidence. Maybe I was just a lucky guy. If so, it's better to be lucky than good. And that was the last we heard from the second grand jury investigating Burzynski.

Aetna II Gets Thrown Out, Over and Over

After the second grand jury investigation ended, I had trouble with my racketeering lawsuit against Aetna. The case was assigned to Houston federal district judge Sim Lake. At the time, he had only been on the bench a few years. Lake had been a young and up-and-coming litigation partner at the Texas powerhouse law firm of Fulbright & Jaworski. He was very smart, maybe the smartest guy in the Houston federal court building, but very conservative, which was not surprising given his background. The other thing I heard about him was that he was almost never reversed on appeal.

For this lawsuit, Aetna hired perhaps the most aggressive and well-connected firm in Texas, Susman & Godfrey. They assigned two sharp lawyers to the case. They called me to ask for an adjournment to answer or otherwise move. I knew what was coming: a dismissal motion. They made it and it was a good one. We filed answering papers. The judge set the case for argument on the motion, but it turned out it was just an opportunity for the judge to read his lengthy dismissal of the case.

I thought Lake was wrong on the law and took him up on appeal. We had an excellent panel. One of the judges was a circuit court judge from California who was sitting in on a Texas case. He asked many questions at the oral argument and seemed favorably disposed to us, which was surprising given how harsh the Fifth Circuit had been to Burzynski and his supporters in its 1987 decision.

The court of appeals reversed Judge Lake's dismissal of the lawsuit and sent the case back to proceed through discovery.

As soon as Judge Lake got the case back, he scheduled another conference. Although he accepted the court of appeals' ruling, he announced that he was dismissing the case again on different grounds, without any discovery or any further proceedings.

I asked him if he was going to write a new opinion or just use the transcript of this conference call as his dismissal decision. He told me he had said everything he had to say. As politely as I could, I asked for a copy of the transcript, as I would need it to return to the court of appeals to seek a mandamus. Judges do not like to hear the word "mandamus." A mandamus is when you seek an order personally against a judge for doing something wrong or exceeding his boundaries or jurisdiction.

I didn't know what that guy was thinking. The court of appeals had ordered him to allow the case to proceed, yet the first thing he did when he got the case back was to dismiss it on slightly different grounds. And the funny thing was, Aetna's lawyers had not even made a new motion to dismiss. Presumably even they understood that the case was supposed to proceed.

So once again, I went back to the court of appeals, this time on some abstruse issues partially relating to racketeering law. The court of appeals once again reversed (and clarified this point of racketeering law, which became a legal precedent in the Fifth Circuit). The court also conditionally granted the mandamus motion. They said they would issue an order against Lake unless he reinstated the case and let it proceed.

Judge Lake would later joke in the Burzynski criminal case that I was the only lawyer who had ever reversed him twice in a single case. I was sorry he remembered that unfortunate episode and feared that he would hold it against Burzynski. To his credit, and with my abounding gratitude, Lake was scrupulously fair with Burzynski when we really needed it.

After two expensive trips to the court of appeals, Burzynski was tired of paying me for working on this case, which he viewed as not essential to his business. He found two lawyers who were willing to take the case on a contingency fee, something I was not willing to do since I viewed this case as defensive, even though we were nominally the plaintiffs. So I was off the case. I was not unhappy, since I got what I needed from the case early on. Anything else was gravy or a distraction, depending on your point of view.

Burzynski's new lawyers did some discovery. Several years later, Susman & Godfrey succeeded in having the case dismissed on summary judgment. This time the dismissal stuck. And so ended the second Aetna case.

During the time I was repeatedly being thrown out of Sim Lake's court on the second Aetna case, I was still litigating with Aetna on the first case, the one involving the Illinois patient's claim and Aetna's racketeering case against Burzynski. It was a nasty, killer litigation—the worst experience I ever had in civil litigation.

Of course, it didn't help that in the second Aetna case, I had sued the attorneys representing Aetna in the first Aetna case while I was still litigating against them. Maybe they took it personally.

Aetna I Is Finally Over

I had moved to Houston in 1991, and by that time, Houston federal judge Ken Hoyt was overseeing the first Aetna case. It was easier for me in that I was living in the same state, but I was now practicing alone and no longer had Matt or Cathy to help me.

Thankfully, discovery finally ended. Both sides moved for summary judgment, dismissing each other's claims and seeking judgment on the respective affirmative claims. The papers flew back and forth between me and Aetna's lawyers. My basic point was that Aetna was a big company, and they had a great deal of information about Burzynski in their files. And whenever any Aetna claims person asked the clinic for information about the clinic, they would always be given accurate and complete information. I argued that these facts refuted Aetna's claim of fraud, since Aetna did not "rely to its detriment" or in legal jargon, there was no detrimental reliance.

During a conference, Judge Hoyt suggested that we should settle the case. I was more than happy to withdraw the patient's seventy thousand-dollar claim, but Aetna and/or its attorneys were out for blood—Burzynski's blood. Even though they had only paid Burzynski six hundred thousand dollars for all its insureds, Aetna demanded over two million dollars from Burzynski to settle the case. I thought this offer was outrageous and inconsistent with what Hoyt wanted us to do with the case. It was like saying "Screw you" to the judge, and they were telling me they were going to bury Burzynski. Okay, if that's the way they wanted it.

So I sent Hoyt a brief note indicating that the parties had not been able to reach a settlement per his recommendation. I attached to the note my letter offering that both sides walk away and Aetna's attorneys' letter demanding two million dollars on its six hundred thousand-dollar claim.

Maybe settlement letters are supposed to be confidential and not disclosed to the judge. Aetna's lawyer thought so, and as soon as he saw my note to Hoyt, he called me and started screaming and cursing at me. After a few minutes, he stopped to take a breath. I told him it was his letter and his demand, and he should take some pride of authorship in his work. And if he was so concerned about the judge knowing Aetna's demand, then maybe he should have made a reasonable offer. For some reason, that only made him angrier. Again, he started screaming and cursing at me. I just laughed and hung up. Screw you too.

Maybe my note gave Hoyt a clearer picture of the situation. Ken Hoyt was plenty smart, and he had a well-developed sense of justice. He figured out what was going on and what should be done. In due course, he issued his decision. In the finest Solomonic tradition, Hoyt granted each party's motion dismissing the other's claim, which was exactly what I had offered to Aetna.

The first Aetna case was over. We had fought to a draw, and that was plenty good enough to me. In fact, it was better than good because Hoyt's dismissal of this Aetna case happened when I was still bouncing back and forth between Lake and the Fifth Circuit on my racketeering case against Aetna. So while Aetna was finished with Burzynski, I wasn't finished with Aetna.

We're Not So Lucky in the Other Insurance Cases

Although I did good work for Burzynski in the Aetna cases, we were still having trouble with the other insurance companies, and regrettably, I was not as successful in some of those other cases.

The federal government filed an action to recoup a small amount of money that it had paid Burzynski with the apparent misunderstanding that his treatment was FDA approved. After looking the case over and discussing it with Burzynski, we decided to refund the money.

A couple of the Blue Cross entities also filed lawsuits. We ended up paying some money back to them as well, but they had to work hard for it.

The biggest setback in the insurance fraud cases came from a small pension plan from the great Northwest. It filed suit in Oregon. I had the case transferred to Texas. Once there, the fund hired some local attorney I had never heard of who was part of a small firm with a former prosecutor by the name of Rusty Hardin.

I don't know what happened in that case, but somehow, the plaintiff's lawyer, Brad Beers, managed to convince then Chief Judge Norman Black to grant summary judgment against Burzynski on the fraud case. I couldn't believe it. It is usually very difficult to win on summary judgment, especially on something fact specific like fraud. But in this case, a federal judge had granted judgment without a trial on a fraud claim.

I was confident I would have the decision reversed on appeal—too confident. At the oral argument, there was a judge who must have been around ninety-five, and he kept on insisting that I had not filed the appeal within the ten-day time deadline and hence my appeal could not be heard. The judge was dead wrong. But the judge kept on insisting the appeal was untimely. Based on what happened, I wish I had conceded the point and let them simply throw out the appeal.

I didn't have the paperwork proving he was wrong with me at the oral argument, but they had a copy in the clerk's office. The other two judges seemed to know I was right, and they just told me to come back and bring the paperwork showing that the appeal was timely filed.

I then did one of the dumbest things I had ever done practicing law. It was all ego. I went to the clerk's office, got a copy of the piece of paper showing that the appeal was timely filed, and returned to the courtroom. By that time, there was another case being heard. I went up to the clerk's desk, maybe a little too dramatically, and with too much of a flourish, I handed the clerk the paper, looked at that old judge, and then walked out of the courtroom. I guess I had showed him.

I was feeling good on the way back to the airport. (The oral argument was in New Orleans, which is the main office of the United States Court of Appeals for the Fifth Circuit.) I shared a cab with Brad Beers. Brad is an excellent lawyer. You couldn't ask for a better adversary, except maybe for him not to be so good. I was feeling magnanimous after the oral argument, since I had proven that the old judge was wrong. So I treated Brad to the cab ride. I told him that anybody who could win a fraud case on summary judgment deserves a free cab ride. What a smoo I was.

Several months later, the old judge responded. He wrote the opinion affirming the District Court's finding of fraud, but in the process he went out of his way to rip Burzynski to shreds. He cited the 1987 court decision against him and said that despite being told he could not ship medicine out of state, Burzynski continued to do it.

It was a nasty opinion, as bad as or worse than the Fifth Circuit's opinion seven years before in the FDA case. I became nauseous after reading it and had to lie down. This guy had just painted a bull's-eye on Burzynski's back. I knew then that Burzynski would eventually be indicted. I didn't have all that long to wait. All the defense work I had done up until then had just gone up in smoke.

The Third Grand Jury Investigation Bites the Dust

But even before I got hammered by the Fifth Circuit, there had been renewed activity in the grand jury. For a couple years after the second grand jury in 1990, all was quiet on the grand jury front. We had heard that a room full of Burzynski grand jury files had been moved from one assistant U. S. attorney (AUSA) to another. But it finally landed on someone's desk who decided to do something. This AUSA was a career trial prosecutor who had tried a number of complicated white-collar cases in the past, and he was not afraid to sink his teeth into Burzynski.

He again subpoenaed several Burzynski employees to testify before the grand jury. I accompanied many of the employees down to the grand jury. The AUSA was unhappy about that since I was the company's attorney and not the personal attorney of the witnesses.

This time, the prosecutor also tried to obtain information from Burzynski's most visible, high-profile supporter, Harris County Attorney Mike Driscoll. Burzynski had treated Mike's first wife for breast cancer. She eventually died, but he and Burzynski became good friends. Burzynski put Mike on the board of directors of the Burzynski Research Institute, and Mike was very supportive of Burzynski's efforts to help cancer patients.

As county attorney, Mike was the chief attorney for the county, which included the city of Houston. Having the support of someone as high profile as Mike was very helpful to Burzynski. It gave Burzynski some much-needed credibility. The prosecutor was apparently unhappy with Mike's behind-the-scenes efforts to help Burzynski and decided to go after Mike.

In a seemingly unrelated investigation, the spokesman for the U. S. attorneys office announced that it had served a subpoena on the Harris County Clerk's Office to obtain campaign donation records from Mike Driscoll's most recent campaign for reelection as Harris County attorney. The statement implied there was an ongoing grand jury investigation about improprieties in Mike's campaign finances. The story was splashed across the front page of the Houston newspapers and did not make Mike look good.

I don't believe in coincidences. It struck me as odd that at the precise time the government was working on its third grand jury investigation of Burzynski, the feds just happened to be investigating a Harris County official who happened to be on Burzynski's board of directors and was Burzynski's most visible supporter. I didn't buy it.

The really odd thing about the subpoena was that all of the information the subpoena requested was a matter of public record and was available to the U. S. attorneys office or to any member of the public just by walking over to the Harris County Clerk's Office and asking for it. I just didn't understand why the government had to serve a subpoena in order to get the information. Maybe they didn't want to pay the copying charges.

I asked Mike to fax over a copy of the subpoena. The subpoena contained other odd coincidences. The same case agent who signed the Burzynski subpoenas signed the subpoena for Mike's campaign contribution records. Not only that, the records were returnable to what appeared to be the same grand jury that was hearing the Burzynski case. The same assistant U. S. attorney was handling both investigations. For a guy who doesn't believe in coincidences, this all looked highly noncoincidental.

Some problems take much thought and planning. This wasn't one of them. Mike was being trashed by the media with an innuendo that the feds were conducting an investigation into illegal campaign finances. I believed there was no such investigation and that the publicized subpoena was just a smear tactic by a vindictive prosecutor to hurt a high-profile Burzynski supporter.

I made a few calls to media people I knew and laid it all out for them. Within a day, the story had taken a new twist. Was there really an investigation of Mike Driscoll? Was the government retaliating against Driscoll for being a Burzynski supporter? Why did the feds issue a subpoena for records available to anyone in the public?

Suddenly, the feds were taking heat. At first, the U. S. attorneys office had no comment, citing the secrecy of grand jury proceedings. (I got a laugh out of that one.) But the new spin on the story would not die.

Eventually, the government admitted there had been no separate investigation of Mike's campaign finances. Shortly thereafter, a new spokesman for the U. S. attorneys office issued a statement saying it had conducted an investigation and found no improprieties. The statement also announced a reorganization at the office. The assistant U. S. attorney who was handling the Burzynski investigation was being reassigned to the civil appeals section (not a big promotion for a high-profile trial attorney). The assistant who issued the first press release against Mike was being replaced by a new spokesman. That was the extent of the reorganization. And so ended the third Burzynski grand jury investigation.

The National Cancer Institute (NCI) Is Impressed but Every Silver Lining Has a Cloud Inside of It

It was not all bad during these times. One of the first things the National Institutes of Health's office of alternative medicine did after it received funding[21] was to arrange for researchers from the NCI to visit Burzynski's clinic and review a "best case" series of cases to see if the treatment merited further investigation.

Investigators, including Nick Patronas, spent almost two days at the clinic reviewing the records of seven patients, all of whom had advanced and incurable brain cancer. This was not some hatchet job orchestrated by the Texas Medical Board. These scientists really wanted to know whether Burzynski was helping his patients.

---

21   The creation of the office of alternative medicine is discussed in more detail in the beginning of Chapter 5.

After the site visit, the group wrote a report and found that in every single case, Burzynski's treatment had caused either a partial or complete response. They concluded that tumors were shrinking or disappearing because of Burzynski's medicine. This was the first time any government agency concluded that Burzynski's treatment had benefited patients.

As a result of the site visit report, the NCI set up a clinical trial to have the medicine tested. The two sites chosen were Memorial Sloan-Kettering in New York and the Mayo Clinic in Minnesota. The Mayo Clinic and its lead cancer investigator Charles Moetrel were infamous in the alternative medicine community because they tested or mistested Linus Pauling's claim that vitamin C helped cancer patients. There were accusations of bias surrounding these tests.

Memorial Sloan-Kettering was not any better; it had been involved in the testing of laetrile. According to cancer activist and author Ralph Moss, who at the time had worked in Memorial's PR department, some of the testing showed that laetrile had anti-cancer effects. According to Moss, Memorial suppressed these results and knowingly published false negative results about laetrile.[22] I was very wary of all this good news.

The clinic spent many months wrangling over the details of the protocol for the clinical trial. From the beginning there was trouble. My impression was that the Memorial and Mayo investigators wanted only the sickest brain cancer patients; those who were literally on death's doorstep. Of course, the more advanced the patient, the less likely it was that any treatment would work. Burzynski wanted to limit the trial to brain cancer patients who had a reasonable chance of responding. Ultimately, the protocol and the entry requirements were worked out to both parties' apparent satisfaction.

Burzynski wanted to use a new, more potent form of antineoplastons he had recently developed. This was not only a clinical trial. Presumably, the investigators would also be trying to save the lives of the participants, and his new medicine, which was ten times more powerful than his prior formula, seemed like a no-brainer, so to speak.

---

22   See Moss, Ralph, *The Cancer Industry* (New York: Paragon, 1989) Chapter 9.

Unfortunately, the investigators didn't see it that way and insisted that the old, weaker formula be used. As illogical and uncaring as that seemed, such was their position. Reluctantly, Burzynski had to give in. This did not bode well for Burzynski or the patients.

As news from the study started trickling in, Burzynski started to get worried. Despite the specific written entry criteria, the investigators were admitting patients into the protocol who were in far worse shape than what had been agreed to. Burzynski fired off a series of letters complaining about it. In addition, for some reason, the investigators were not giving full doses of medicine. This was starting to look like a fiasco.

After watching what was going on, we reached the unhappy conclusion that the investigators were not interested in fairly testing the drug. It also looked like the investigators were willing to let the test subjects die rather than follow the protocol for a drug that possibly could have helped them. It was time to pull the plug. I wasn't going to let what happened to laetrile, vitamin C, and Revici happen to Burzynski.

So I sent a letter to the investigators at both institutions. I made it clear that if they continued misusing the drug and mistreating the patients, there would be litigation consequences, not only from Burzynski, but most likely from the patients once they found out how the investigators sacrificed them just to sabotage the clinical trial. That letter got their attention right quick. After a series of exchanges and communications with the NCI, it was decided that in the best interests of all concerned, the trial would be terminated.

The investigators eventually wrote tentative findings on the aborted clinical trial. They found no responses to the treatment. But because the trial had been stopped and included only a few patients, the negative effect of the publication was minimal. This was not what we wanted, but no test was better than a biased negative test. And so ended the attempt to have these two august cancer institutions test Burzynski's drugs.

This experience left a deep impression on me. I had studied the history and philosophy of science in undergraduate and graduate school at the Hebrew University of Jerusalem in the 1970s. At the time, the prevailing theory was paradigm shifts by Thomas Kuhn. Although the model accounted for new ideas and clashes between new and old theories, science was still viewed as a relatively clean, theoretical, and gentlemanly endeavor.

I had left graduate school because I was tired of just seeing ideas bounce off other ideas. I wanted action. In many of my cases, but especially the Burzynski case, I was doing what I would call applied philosophy of science.

But these battles were not esoteric and gentlemanly. They were brutal and fought in the trenches of life. Real patients were involved and their lives were at stake. These Burzynski NCI trials showed me up close how dirty, unscientific, and immoral medical science could be. It was a far cry from what I learned in my philosophy of science classes two decades earlier. Most people probably don't realize how unscientific and all-too-human so-called objective medical science can be. Regrettably, there is very little written about the subject.[23]

The Fourth Grand Jury and Off We Go to Congress

We didn't get much of a reprieve from the government on the criminal front. In early 1995, we became aware that the government was starting its fourth grand jury investigation.

This time, the government had three attorneys assigned to the case. Michael Clark, the chief of the criminal division, would be supervising the case. He had two highly seasoned federal prosecutors working with him, George Tallichet and Amy Lequoc. In addition, there was a postal inspector as well as an FDA inspector, both of whom appeared to be working full time on the case.

One day they came in unannounced, maybe a dozen people with a search warrant. Here we go again. They took the medical records of dozens of patients. After they carted off the records, in order to see the medical records of his own patients, Burzynski was required to install a copier in a prosecutor's office at his own expense and send someone down to make copies.

The prosecutors were initially very hostile to me. Maybe they were wary. Three of their colleagues who had come in contact with me on the prior Burzynski grand jury investigations, plus the former U. S. attorney, had either

---

23   For a listing of some of the books which discuss the bias involved in the testing of alternative remedies see the "For Further Reading" section at the end of this book.

left government service or been demoted (all by coincidence of course). Two law firms that had represented Aetna had also been replaced. The new prosecutors were also in touch with the Texas Medical Board and they knew that the board's case, which had been filed in 1988, was still tied up in the court system.

They were surely aware of my racketeering lawsuit against Aetna and its lawyers as well as the unnamed government employees who had allegedly conspired with them. They also knew that Judge Lake's two dismissals of my racketeering case had been reversed.

As mentioned before, I had settled a small insurance case with the U. S. attorneys office on Burzynski's behalf. Burzynski had paid back the government insurance company for some treatment he had given to a patient. I ran into Sam Longoria, the assistant U. S. attorney who had handled the case at my health club around the time of the fourth grand jury. I liked Sam. He was a good guy and a straight shooter. Sam came up to me and thanked me for making him look so good at his office. I didn't know what he was talking about. He explained to me that he was the only government attorney who ever got something from me and kept his job after dealing with me. He said that gave him status in his office. I'm sure he was only kidding, but it gave me a good laugh.

So I can't say that the new prosecutors' hostility toward me was completely unexpected. What followed were more grand jury subpoenas and more Burzynski employees before the grand jury. The government lawyers were annoyed that I was in the grand jury waiting room and met with all of the Burzynski employees before and after they testified. They made noises about indicting me for obstruction of justice or moving to disqualify me since I was Burzynski's attorney.

There is nothing wrong with a grand jury witness telling anyone what happened at the grand jury. Despite this, the government lawyers threatened the witnesses that if they talked about their testimony, things would be bad for them.

From what I heard, the prosecutors were hard and nasty toward some of the witnesses and needlessly so. This finally came to a head.

They were particularly harsh with the clinic's receptionist. She was a middle-aged woman from Eastern Europe. They must have thought she was involved in some great conspiracy to ship medicine to dying patients. Unbeknownst to the prosecutors, she had a mild heart condition and was upset after she finished testifying. That evening, she had a heart attack. She lived, but was out of work for several months. Don't think I didn't complain about that.

These prosecutors were disrupting Burzynski's business, harassing his employees and patients, and this time, they might get an indictment. These people were smarter and much more careful than their predecessors. And by then, they had the Fifth Circuit's recent decision in the insurance case (which I had lost) in their back pocket, and that decision all but invited the government to indict Burzynski.

I didn't have much to work with, except that this was already the fourth grand jury proceeding over a ten-year period dealing with the same issues. That's what I had, so that's what I went with.

I made some calls to people in the field, complaining about the government's tactics in this and the previous grand jury investigations. Eventually I talked to someone at the Washington Legal Foundation, a prestigious and highly successful advocacy organization that protects the rights of individuals and goes after government abuse and misconduct.

One of their former staff attorneys, Alan Slobodan, was working as counsel to the House Committee on Energy and Commerce's Subcommittee on Oversight and Investigations, which was chaired by Republican Representative Joe Barton out of Ennis, Texas. I gave Alan a call, and he was very sympathetic. They had heard about the Burzynski case but did not have many details. I spent a great deal of time filling him in.

After consulting with Barton, he got back to me. They would be interested in having testimony about the Burzynski case before the subcommittee in one of their upcoming hearings on government abuse and foot-dragging by the FDA.

As I was familiar with the case, he asked me to prepare the hearing, in terms of finding and prepping the witnesses who would testify before the committee. I gladly and instantaneously agreed.

During the fourth grand jury investigation, I was busy preparing for this hearing. We had a number of terrific patients and parents of child patients come and testify before the committee. Mary Jo Siegel, Marianne Kunnari, Mary Michaels, and others testified before the committee. It was wonderful. They told story after story about how Burzynski had saved their lives or the lives of their children.

My job at the hearing was to hammer the FDA and the government for their actions over the past ten years. "Four grand juries; dirty tricks; collusion between government attorneys and private insurance carriers; foot dragging by the FDA on a treatment that NCI investigators confirmed had tumor response in incurable cancers; calls for overhaul of the FDA and replacement of enforcement personnel." I got a lot off my chest that had been building up for years. Some of the Democrats gave me a hard time, but mostly they stayed away from the hearing. Barton and then Congressman Richard Barr were especially sympathetic to the plight of the patients.

Chairman Barton assured us the committee would look into why the government kept on harassing Dr. Burzynski. The FDA never showed up to the hearing. Some news shows photographed the FDA's empty reserved seats. The FDA sent a written statement saying there was nothing they could say because of the ongoing criminal investigation.

I also filed a complaint with the ethics department of the attorney general's office complaining about the government's tactics in this and the other investigations. I was not hopeful that the complaint would go anywhere, but I wanted the government boys (and girl) to have something to think about, besides indicting Burzynski.

I used one other small tactical maneuver. The government made countless requests for documents to be produced to the grand jury. Some person with knowledge had to come to the grand jury to authenticate the documents before the grand jurors. On one of these occasions, I had Burzynski himself bring down the documents.

It is a given amongst criminal defense lawyers not to let targets of a federal criminal investigation go before the grand jury. There are too many dangers, like the danger of being indicted for perjury, if the government does not like the target's testimony. I decided to take the risk here, in large part because the government would not be expecting Burzynski to show up just to authenticate documents. So I didn't think they would be prepared to interrogate him. The upside was that it would give Burzynski a chance to meet the people who would decide his fate. I thought it might make it harder to return an indictment if the grand jurors actually saw who they would be accusing of a crime. We were not dealing with a bank robbery but a cancer treatment. So on balance I thought the risk was worth the upside. It might have been worth the risk, but it did not stop the indictment.

Burzynski Is Finally Indicted, and the Cavalry Arrives (Sort of)

On November 20, 1995, Stanislaw R. Burzynski, MD, PhD, was indicted on a seventy-six-count indictment; thirty-four counts on insurance fraud, forty-one for violations of the FDA act, and one charge for violating the 1983 injunction order.

I remember the exact day because it was the first day in my new office. All of the attorneys I shared offices with had moved over the weekend and Monday, November 20, was our first day in the new suite. I remember thinking to myself that it was slow for me, and I wondered when things would pick up.

After I returned from lunch, I received a hysterical call from one of the Burzynski people saying that it was on the radio and TV that Burzynski had been indicted. And so began what I feared would be the final chapter of the Burzynski wars.

The first thing that happens after an indictment is that the defendant has to appear in court, usually before a federal magistrate. The initial proceeding is an arraignment and bail proceeding. My biggest concern with bail was whether the government would be playing hardball and ask that as a condition of bail, Burzynski not be allowed to treat patients with antineoplastons. I had seen this trick in a few other cases. The government argues that as a general condition of bail, the defendant cannot commit any crimes. Since Burzynski was indicted for treating patients with unapproved new drugs and was also accused of committing insurance fraud, how could he be allowed to continue these so-called criminal acts while he was on bail? I was prepared for the argument, but fortunately, the government didn't make it, at least at the bail hearing.

The bail and arraignment went smoothly. Burzynski was processed through the system and released. He had to surrender his passport and was required to seek permission to travel to medical conferences throughout the country. But all in all, it was not too bad.

It was clear from the indictment that the government had pulled out all the stops. The trial would take at least a month. The government had three trial attorneys and two full-time investigators on the case, and who knows how many paralegals and support staff. Up until that time, I had handled all of the Burzynski litigation and other Burzynski matters myself in addition to handling several other big cases around the country for other clients. There was no way I could handle a case this big on my own. It was time to get help. Burzynski told me to put together the best team I could.

In Houston, the two most prominent attorneys were Dick DeGuerin and Mike Ramsey. DeGuerin was probably more famous since he had recently been one of the attorneys in the Branch Davidian/Waco criminal trial (David Koresh's group). I heard he did a lot of drug work. Ramsey was slightly less well known, but he also had an excellent reputation. He had just come off of a big trial that resulted in an acquittal of one of the most prominent real estate developers in Houston.

I called DeGuerin first, but he was out of town. He had not called me back by the middle of the afternoon, so I called Mike Ramsey. Mike wanted to see me immediately. We spent over an hour discussing the case. He was the real deal.

Mike was fifty-seven, six feet tall, with a full head of white hair and steel-rimmed glasses. He sounded like a good ol' Texas boy. He had a deep Texas twang and a soft whistle every time he said a word that began with "s." He wasn't bombastic or showy. If anything, he was understated. Despite the Texas good ol' boy routine, you couldn't miss his penetrating intellect or droll sense of humor.

He was upfront with me that he had an extremely full trial schedule and couldn't try the case or even focus on it for over a year. I smiled to myself and thought about Mendel the court jester and told him that was okay by me.

Mike was the right man for the job. So I called Burzynski and told him that I had found the guy I was looking for. After a brief meeting between the three of us, Burzynski agreed.

Ramsey and I appeared together at the first court appearance before Judge Lake, the purpose of which was to set a trial date. Ramsey appeared on behalf of Burzynski personally, and I appeared for the Burzynski Research Institute, which had also been indicted. Ramsey explained to Sim Lake that he was tied up for the next year on federal criminal cases before other judges in the district. Most of the top criminal practitioners are booked up at least a year in advance, so it was no surprise to Lake. Besides, federal judges also are booked up far in advance with the cases lawyers like Ramsey work on, so Lake went along with the delay. Although Ramsey was a terrific lawyer and I was excited to have him on board, I was also very interested in finding someone who could not try the case until some distant time in the future. The case was set for January 1997. That would give us over a year to prepare and see what trouble we could stir up in the meantime. So far, hiring Ramsey was paying off.

Ramsey was a solo practitioner, but on big cases he brought in another prominent Houston criminal defense attorney, Dan Cogdell. Ramsey wanted me to check him out because he wanted Dan on the team. So I went down to watch Dan on a case he was trying before Judge Rosenthal, another federal district court judge in Houston.

I was only moderately impressed. Dan was a tall, handsome guy who looked the part of a defense attorney. He also had the good ol' boy Texas twang, but initially, anyway, I thought he was too brash and aggressive.

But Cogdell had a string of previous successes, and I knew that Ramsey and Cogdell worked well as a team. Neither of these guys knew anything about cancer, healthcare law, or insurance law, but I figured that would be my job. I also thought we needed at least three attorneys to try the case, and I didn't have anyone better in mind, so I agreed that Cogdell should come on board. That turned out to be a good decision, as Cogdell was an excellent attorney, and he was extremely effective at the trial.

By the time of the trial, we had a fourth attorney working on the case, John Ackerman. Ackerman was in his late fifties, with balding white hair, a big gut, and tons of experience trying cases. He had also been a state district court judge. John is a very smart and thoughtful individual. But he only started seriously working on the case a month or two before the trial.

Burzynski Goes Out of Business (Almost)

After that initial appearance, Ramsey basically disappeared to try all the other cases he had lined up before the Burzynski trial. The other two attorneys came on board later on, and neither knew any of the issues in the case nor anything about health or insurance law. So it was still just me on the day-to-day work and trial preparation.

I was hoping things would be quiet for a few months, as I had plenty of other non-Burzynski work to keep me busy. My New Jersey chiropractor case was in the final phases of discovery, and the case was heating up.[24] *Dateline* was working on what I thought would be a big exposé on the illegal activities of the New Jersey state government. So I had other things to think about. But it was not to be.

Within a few weeks of the arraignment, the government did what I feared it would do and moved to modify the conditions of release to bar Burzynski from treating any cancer patients with antineoplastons, since it was not an FDA-approved drug.

It was a complicated issue. By the end of 1995, the Austin appellate court had still not ruled on Judge Davis's reversal of the medical board's decision that Burzynski was violating state law. So we were still okay on the state law issue.

The prosecutors took a strict view of federal law and the interstate commerce issue. They argued that because Burzynski treated people who came from other states, and because the clinic and manufacturing facility obtained supplies from out of state, that was enough interstate commerce for Burzynski to be in violation of federal law.

---

24   That case is the subject of Chapter 6.

It was getting close to Christmas, and I figured that Judge Lake probably didn't want to spend a lot of time on this, especially since the trial was over a year away. I decided on a volume approach, more specifically, weight and inches. My written response to the motion with exhibits was at least four inches thick. It was mostly exhibits, but I discussed all of them in the motion.

Clarity would not be the main objective of the response. Like I said, it was Christmastime, and I knew that Lake was an efficiency freak. I was sure he was going to give his decision before the end of the year and probably before Christmas. The more complicated and unclear the issue seemed, the better.

It worked. He wrote an opinion stating that on the record he had before him, he could not say it would be illegal for Burzynski to continue treating patients. Another bullet had been dodged, but more were coming.

February 1996 would be a very busy time for me. I was scheduled to try the New Jersey chiropractic case, but on the day of trial, the case settled on favorable terms. (See Chapter 6.) Since I had worked like a dog for weeks preparing that case for trial, I was hoping to take it easy for a while. Didn't happen.

In early February 1996, the Austin court of appeals finally came out with its decision. It reversed Judge Davis's decision reversing the medical board, which had reversed Administrative Law Judge Earl Corbitt. We had now gone full circle, twice. The decision showed no sympathy for the patients and blamed Burzynski for everything that did or would happen to them. So it was now illegal for Burzynski to use his medicine on patients in the state of Texas.

The federal prosecutors were in touch with Dewey, the medical board's attorney both before and after the Austin appellate court's decision. They were hovering around like vultures over dying prey, and we were the prey.

Shortly after the court came down with its opinion, the prosecutors filed a new motion to modify Burzynski's conditions of release to bar him from treating his patients, as it was now illegal under state as well as federal law.

I suspected it was Mike Clark, the lead prosecutor, who was behind the motion. I could see it in his eyes. He was a heartless bastard. He looked at the case like any other of the criminal cases he worked on. He had no empathy for the patients. There was no use working on him. The patients could all drop dead as far as he was concerned, or so it looked to me.

I didn't get that feeling from the other two prosecutors. I ran into Tallichet a couple of times, and he seemed genuinely concerned about the patients, though he didn't have a high opinion of Burzynski. Despite his prosecutor's façade, I could tell that Tallichet was a decent fellow. He had the same kind of mentality and outlook as Dewey. Neither would go out of their way to cause imminent harm to the patients. This was Clark's show.

Even though I had done some pretty nifty work in the past keeping Burzynski in business, this time I knew we were in big trouble. My prior tactic of inches and weight was not going to work with Judge Lake this time.

Of course, I would file a petition for review with the Texas Supreme Court to overturn the Austin court's reinstatement of the medical board's decision, but until the Supreme Court ruled, the law of the case was that Burzynski's treatment of his patients was illegal under state law.

Besides, I knew that the "any drug to minister to the immediate needs of the patient" argument was over. It had served us faithfully and well, and we had bought years with it, but it was over. The Texas Supreme Court was not going to adopt it.

Also, since we made that argument, the medical board had convinced the Texas legislature to change the law. The new law was now clear that the "any drug" language could not be used by Burzynski or any doctor to supply non-FDA-approved drugs to patients, or indefinitely supply any drugs to patients. Another loophole had been closed.

We were at the end of this particular road. I put in opposition papers. I made it clear to Judge Lake how important it was that the patients continue on treatment, regardless of anything else. But I knew that we would not be able to reach the criminal trial—which was still eleven months away—with the patients on treatment unless we had a new and bigger plan. But I needed just a little more time. And that's where the patients came in (once again).

The Patients Come to the Rescue

For years, Burzynski had a loyal and devoted group of patients. They helped us dearly in the medical board case. They had appeared at the hearing before Administrative Law Judge Corbitt, at the medical board, and throughout the proceedings before District Judge Davis. Of course, they were also at the oral argument before the Austin court of appeals. (I had a bad feeling at that one when the clerk of the appellate court insisted that the patients remove their green armbands, which they wore as a sign of support for Burzynski.)

The patients were closely following the criminal trial. They had created a formal patients' group that was headed by Mary Jo and Steve Siegel and Rita Starr.

Mary Jo Siegel had been diagnosed with advanced non-Hodgkin's lymphoma. She was unsuccessfully treated by conventional medicine before she found her way to Dr. Burzynski. Burzynski put her into complete remission, and she has stayed cancer free since then. But she was still on maintenance therapy at the time of the criminal trial.

Her husband Steve was a manufacturer's rep of some kind. He was devoted to her, and they both were devoted to Dr. Burzynski. Mary Jo had been the star of the *48 Hours* segment on Burzynski. In her midforties, Mary Jo was cute, perky, and the perfect poster person for Burzynski's successful treatment.

Rita Starr's mother was successfully treated by Burzynski. Rita's family ran a big bakery in South Florida and she was very grateful to Burzynski. She was dogged and good at convincing people.

All the patients had an obvious interest that Burzynski be allowed to continue to treat patients until the criminal trial. Because of his other criminal trials, Ramsey was mostly available for brief telephone consultations, and I would frequently ask his advice. We were both interested that he get up to speed in the case and talking to him about these issues was a good way for this to happen.

In our discussions and conversations with the patients, we came up with the idea that the patients should have their own attorney to protect their interests as the criminal case proceeded. As an old-time Houston criminal attorney, Mike knew most everyone in town. He introduced the patients to one of his lawyer acquaintances, Cynthia McMurray.

Although in her early forties, Cynthia had only been practicing law a few years. I think she had been an actress or a model prior to going to law school.

She was drop-dead gorgeous in a Hollywood way; long, straight, most assuredly bleached-blonde hair, high cheekbones, chiseled features, perfectly tanned, tall, and appropriately thin. She looked like you would think a movie star should look life in real life, only better. And she had a movie-star life, as it was known that she was seeing Frank Sinatra, Jr. (whom she would later marry, then divorce).

I was not crazy about her. She didn't have much experience. She didn't know anything about the field. I didn't see what she brought to the table. Frankly, and much to my discredit, I held her looks against her. Maybe I was just balancing things out since Mike, and probably most other lawyers, had probably helped her out because of her looks.

Despite my tepid non-endorsement, Cynthia was hired to represent the patients. This allowed us to in effect "double down" at the second bail proceeding. It was very nice that Mike and I as Burzynski's criminal attorneys argued that the patients had rights and that they should have a say in what happens pending the trial, but we felt it would be much stronger if the point was made by a separate advocate for the patients.

But despite all of our efforts, Judge Lake was not moved. This time he granted the prosecutors' request. He modified Burzynski's conditions of release and barred Burzynski from treating patients until he had the FDA's approval.

We did get one absolutely critical concession from Judge Lake, much to Mike Clark's annoyance. He granted our request to stay his decision pending the appeal of his decision, which we told him we would do. I had already reversed Lake twice in the second Aetna case and maybe that weighed on him. But I think he stayed his decision because he is a decent human being. He might be obligated to apply the law, but I don't think he wanted to pull the plug on all these dying patients.

So Judge Lake gave us a break. Everyone knew the appeal would take several months. Lake was basically saying to us that we needed to find another solution. So over Mike Clark's strenuous objection, the patients would stay on the treatment and live a little longer. For that concession, the Honorable Sim Lake will always be a hero in my book, especially since with the time he gave us, we did find another solution.

But even before Clark had renewed his motion to shut Burzynski down, I had a sense that the end was near. I had been hoping for the best from the Austin appellate court in the medical board case, but I did not have a good feeling about those judges, or the ability of our "any drug" argument to keep working.

Clark was a very determined character, and I assumed he would come back to Lake sooner or later. He was the typical overaggressive prosecutor. I think he also had some ego issues. He was going to do what none of the previous prosecutors had been able to do—shut Burzynski down, and outsmart Burzynski's attorney. So when Clark came back to Lake again to close the clinic, it was not a surprise. And I had been quietly preparing the move to higher ground, the political arena.

Mostly what I did was keep in very good contact with Alan Slobodan, Joe Barton's House subcommittee's counsel, and staffers of other congressmen. I let them know privately of my fears and expressed my hope that if the worst happened, the committee would jump into action and help the patients. By this time, Slobodan, Barton, and many congressmen and their staffs were invested in the Burzynski case and especially his patients. They all knew that it was a matter of life and death for them.

So the first thing I did after Judge Lake modified Burzynski's conditions of release was to call Alan Slobodan and some staff of other congressmen who were following the case to let them know that we desperately needed their help.

In very short order, Barton, Dan Burton, and other congressmen were calling the FDA, outraged by what the government attorneys had done to Burzynski's patients. It was no longer about Burzynski; it was about the patients who needed to stay on the treatment. Burzynski had not been convicted of anything, and yet he could not treat any of his patients. There was a loud uproar against the FDA. The congressmen threatened the FDA with all kinds of congressional actions and investigations.

Barton and Burton's staff coordinated with us to arrange to have some of Burzynski's patients go to Washington and do anything they could with the FDA to get it to back down. The patients held a rally on Capital Hill that was covered by the media. They walked the halls of Congress looking for support. They met with FDA officials. Congressman Dan Burton even held another hearing. All this put considerable pressure on the FDA.

This was the patients' show. The leaders of the patient group, Mary Jo and Steve Siegel and Rita Starr, did a spectacular job running the event. They, along with other patients, advocated, cajoled, and pleaded with congressmen, FDA officials, reporters, and anyone else who would listen. They developed a close relationship with Congressman Burton and his key health legislative aide, Beth Clay.

Steve Siegel is a tremendously effective individual. He was dogged to the point of bullying people. Rita Starr just got things done. It didn't matter what it was. Ask her to do something, and it got done somehow. Mary Jo was the embodiment of all the emotion, hope, and frustration involved in the case. People had a hard time saying no to her. There were, of course, many other patients and their families involved, like the Kunnaris and the Michaels, but these three took on the responsibility to lead the charge. They were intensely determined and extremely focused. I have encountered many patients' groups over the past twenty-plus years, but the Burzynski patient group was by far the most effective group I have ever encountered. And that was in large measure due to the efforts of Mary Jo and Steve Siegel and Rita Starr.

The Horse Learns to Fly!

Sometimes miracles do happen, and we badly needed one now. Word came from Barton and Burton's people that over the vehement objections of the prosecutors (read Mike Clark), the FDA was going to back down. The patients had won, and by doing so, they had saved their own lives.

The FDA would allow Burzynski to file emergency INDs to treat all of his patients and even future patients. Normally it would take months or years to gather the data necessary to file INDs for just one form of cancer. But the FDA was going to waive all of those requirements and approve INDs covering all of Burzynski's patients regardless of what type of cancer they had.

That was terrific news. I went over to talk to Burzynski about what had to be done. The FDA was giving us a very small opening. I didn't think the window would stay open long or that we would be able to go back repeatedly each time Burzynski wanted to treat a different kind of cancer.

So we decided to hit the FDA with everything at the same time. All of his current patients would be covered in a single clinical trial which Burzynski called "CAN-1." As far as clinical trials go, it was a joke. Clinical trials are supposed to be designed to test the safety or efficacy of a drug for a disease. It is almost always the case that clinical trials treat one disease.

The CAN-1 protocol had almost two hundred patients in it and there were at least a dozen different types of cancers being treated. And since all the patients were already on treatment, there could not be any possibility of meaningful data coming out of the so-called clinical trial. It was all an artifice, a vehicle we and the FDA created to legally give the patients Burzynski's treatment. The FDA wanted all of Burzynski's patients to be on an IND, so that's what we did.

CAN-1 allowed Burzynski to treat all his existing patients. That solved the patients' problem, but not the clinic's. A cancer clinic cannot survive on existing patients. It needs a constant flow of new patients. So in addition to getting the CAN-1 trial approved, we had to make sure Burzynski could treat new patients. Mindful that he would likely only get one chance to get them approved, Burzynski personally put together seventy-two protocols to treat every type of cancer the clinic had treated and everything Burzynski wanted to treat in the future. I believe it was the largest number of protocol and clinical trial applications ever submitted at one time by any institution. We heard that the FDA had to put together a fifty-person task force to review all of the protocols Burzynski submitted.

By regulation, a clinical trial can start thirty days after submission to the FDA of the IND, unless the FDA puts it on clinical hold. This time the FDA let all of the clinical trials go through. Miracle of miracles, all of Burzynski's patients were now on FDA-approved clinical trials, and he would also be able to treat almost any patient he would want to treat!

The modification of Burzynski's bail conditions of release was now moot. And it was a good thing because, as we expected, the Fifth Circuit affirmed Judge Lake's order modifying the conditions. But who cared. The medical board's decision was also moot. With one metaphorical stroke of the pen, the FDA had made it legal for Burzynski to treat all his patients, and that satisfied the medical board's condition of probation. We then settled the Texas Department of Health case for a relatively small payment for the state's legal and investigative costs. The horse had learned to fly!

Mike Clark was unhappy. He was given the mandate by his client, the FDA, to shut down Burzynski's clinic. And through his skillful lawyering, he had arranged for that to happen months before the criminal trial even started. He had succeeded in doing what all of the previous federal prosecutors, state attorney generals, and insurance attorneys had failed to do. And right when he was about to nail Burzynski's (and his patients') coffin shut, his client blinks. He was disgusted with the FDA and told me so. Burzynski had dodged another bullet, but not completely. A piece of the bullet had grazed him.

The Burzynski Clinic Is Wounded but Manages to Survive

Burzynski's indictment was a big story in the alternative health community and beyond. News traveled fast, but it didn't always travel accurately. After the first and second times the prosecutors sought to modify the conditions of release, rumors started circulating that the clinic had been shut down, which was untrue, or that it was about to be closed, which was closer to the truth. In addition, many prospective patients simply did not want to deal with the uncertainty of whether the clinic would remain open.

As a result, the clinic was not attracting the numbers of new patients necessary to sustain it. It was very expensive to keep the doors open, and the patients were just not coming through the doors fast enough.

There are many things that saved the clinic during this period. One of biggest was Burzynski's business manager, Barbara Tomaszewski. She was a very savvy businessperson. As the patient numbers started to decline, she came up with dozens of ways to cut costs and increase income. Some of the services that had been farmed out, like pharmacy supplies, were brought inside the clinic, and buildings were refinanced. She did whatever she had to do to squeeze or save every dollar she could. Another important task was to keep in touch with Julian Whitaker and his staff, and Julian was an important external reason the clinic stayed open.

Julian was a complementary medical doctor. He had a clinic in Orange County, California. More importantly, he had a newsletter called *Health and Healing,* which had a circulation of upwards of two hundred fifty thousand. He was (and still is) a very powerful voice in the alternative medical community.

Julian was from Georgia and spoke with a deep Southern country drawl. After medical school, he worked at the Pritiken Institute for a few years and then opened his own complementary clinic in California. Julian had a big mouth and was always outspoken, but through the 1980s, he was just one of many alternative doctors who had a small following.

Two things happened in the 1990s which raised his profile. First, Jonathan Wright, one of country's most highly regarded complementary physicians, was raided by the FDA. Julian Whitaker became one of Wright's most visible and aggressive supporters and fundraisers.

This was also the time when Congress was considering limiting access to nutritional supplements. In response, Julian helped organize the American Preventive Medical Association, which was a lobbying organization representing the rights of supplement companies, alternative practitioners, and people who wanted to take supplements. The organization gave Julian a vehicle to advocate things close to his heart. In subsequent years, Julian put his money where his mouth and heart were and funded many important lawsuits against the FDA.

What really catapulted Julian into the national spotlight was a large media conglomerate, Phillips Publications. Phillips approached him about doing a newsletter on alternative health. Whitaker agreed, and within a few years, his newsletter became an important force in the alternative health community.

Whitaker didn't know Burzynski personally, but after the indictment, Whitaker flew down to Houston to check things out. He looked at patient records and talked to patients. He was very impressed by the results. He also hit it off with Burzynski personally. They had a lot in common, even though they had grown up in different parts of the world.

Burzynski was cultured and sophisticated. He was gracious and highly mannered in an old-school sense. He had a good palate for food and loved fine wines. When out in a group, he would always pick up the check. Burzynski was also extremely well-read on a wide variety of subjects. He was sort of a Renaissance man, but he was also a very shrewd businessman and entrepreneur.

Although much louder than Burzynski, Whitaker sounded like a courtly Southern gentleman. And Whitaker also had an appreciation of the good life. Since hooking up with Phillips Publications, life was extremely good to Julian. Whittaker had his hand in many things related to health. In addition to his clinic and newsletter, he wrote a series of best-selling books. Like Burzynski, Julian was also a very shrewd businessman.

So after visiting Burzynski, and being impressed by Burzynski's results with patients, Whitaker promised that he would help in any way he could. Whitaker was always up for a good fight, and this was shaping up to be the biggest fight against the FDA in history. I am sure Whitaker wanted to be a part of it.

So when things got bad and new patients stopped coming, Whitaker started writing stories about Burzynski and the amazing results he was achieving on different kinds of cancer. Every time he wrote a story or editorial on Burzynski, new patients appeared. Julian's articles and editorials helped keep the clinic open.

With the existing patients now being treated under FDA-approved clinical trials, and new patients coming in, the clinic began to operate normally. I still had a number of insurance litigations pending. But the medical board case and the Department of Health case were behind us, and we still had a few months before the criminal trial would start.

Ackerman Picks Up the Slack

By this time, we had our full complement of lawyers. Ramsey was still tied up trying all his cases, as was Cogdell. However, Ackerman started picking up some of the slack. He was a very methodical, detail-oriented attorney. He seemed to have a knack for jury instructions, and I was able to shift all of those issues in the criminal case to him. He did multicolored jury charges, which Judge Lake really appreciated.

Ackerman was also extremely knowledgeable about evidentiary issues, and he took over all of those issues as well. Ackerman was a very decent and kind person. He was a terrific attorney and worked well in a team environment. His skill set was complementary and in many ways superior to mine. I was beginning to like this multi-lawyer approach to the case. It was nice to spread around the burden and the headaches, and I learned quite a bit about lawyering from Ackerman in the process.

Legwork

I spent several months focusing on a couple of big projects. The biggest one was the exhibits. Burzynski wanted to prove his treatment worked. By then, there were hundreds of articles published about antineoplastons, and for a variety of reasons, we decided to submit every one of them as potential exhibits. At the very least it would keep prosecutors and their consultants busy, and that would be a good thing.

Federal jury trials are highly scripted and planned in advance. Well before the trial, it is necessary for each side to prepare its lists of exhibits and provide the court and the other side with a copy of every exhibit the party intends to offer into evidence. Since I had been Burzynski's attorney for eight years, I was the obvious man for the job.

We ended up listing something like 550 separate exhibits. Some exhibits were only a page, while other exhibits were 150 pages long. We had maybe twelve four-inch black trial notebooks that contained our exhibits. My secretary and I put them all together. We did not know how much it would help, but it looked impressive. And the hope was that it would keep the prosecutors busy reading it all and make them prepare against this paper onslaught. (It turned out we didn't use a single article at the trial. It might have helped the judge get a clearer picture of the case, but who knows.)

My other major task was to prepare expert witnesses as part of our effort to prove that the treatment worked. Unfortunately, Nick Patronas got into trouble for testifying in the medical board case, so he could not testify at the criminal trial. But we found several other doctors who agreed to help out.

Somehow, we found our way to Dr. Dieter Schellinger who was the assistant head of pediatric neuroradiology at Georgetown. We arranged to have him fly down to Houston to review the scans of a couple dozen of Burzynski's brain cancer patients.

I spent almost two days with him in a tiny room with a light box. One case after another, looking at the before, during, and after scans. Schellinger was from Germany and spoke with the German accent. When he spoke, it reminded me of Artie Johnson's German soldier character on *Laugh In*. "Very interresssting" both of them would say. This was very detailed work, but it wasn't rocket science. He would take something that looked like a measuring compass and measure the tumors on the images. After most of these patients he would say, "Ah, this is fairly remarkable. I don't think I've ever seen anything like this before" in his German-accented English. By the end of his stay at the clinic, Schellinger was convinced Burzynski was on to something. As a result, he agreed to testify if we needed him. We lined up a few other doctors who were equally impressed.

Of course, the government was not going to make it easy for us. In fact, they were taking the position that the efficacy or effectiveness of the treatment was irrelevant to the case. We would go back and forth on this both before and during the trial. The problem was that the government was also arguing that Burzynski committed mail fraud and that part of this scheme was over-selling the benefits of the treatment. Based on this claim, we felt we had the right to talk about the benefits of the treatment and that Burzynski did not oversell it. Unfortunately, the judge didn't agree.

Whereupon a Lawyer Ascends Mount Sinai and Receives the Word
As the trial approached, I tried a variety of tactics or angles. Most of them did not work out. Obviously a big issue was Judge McDonald's 1983 civil injunction order. What exactly did it mean? Judge Lake told us he thought it meant that Burzynski should not be treating patients. What to do?

One day it hit me: we should go right to the source. So I tracked down Judge McDonald. She had been working at The Hague as a judge in the Serbian war crimes trials, but she happened to be in Houston on a visit home when I came up with the idea to call her.

I was very nervous. Maybe it was not appropriate for me to call her, and for all I knew she would contact Judge Lake to complain or file a complaint against me. But it was close to the trial, and like a gunfighter in the old West,

I was looking for an edge. I explained to her that I wanted to know what she meant in her 1983 order that Burzynski could not introduce the medicine into interstate commerce, but that he could give it to patients if it was "wholly intrastate."

Judge McDonald is a very smart lady. She would not come right out and say what she meant. Maybe she was afraid I would subpoena her to the trial. (Not likely that I was brazen enough to subpoena a former federal judge to explain a decision. The law is clear that decisions have to stand on their own, and outside [*parol*] evidence even from the horse's mouth is not admissible.) But inquiring minds wanted to know, and I needed to know.

She did not answer any of my questions. Instead, she led me down a Socratic path with just a few questions.

"Was there any evidence in the record of the1983 hearing that Burzynski was giving medicine to patients who were then taking the medicine out of state?" she asked.

"There surely was such evidence in the record, Your Honor," I answered.

"Since it was in the record and I assume I knew of it, did I expressly prohibit him from treating these patients?" she asked.

"You did not," I replied.

"Well, then, you have your answer, don't you?" she said.

And I guess I did. I thanked her profusely.

In her carefully crafted, terse questions, I had received the Word from the Source. I intended to be her prophet and carry her Word to the chosen, that being the jury. Thank you, Judge Gabrielle McDonald. Your wise and compassionate words were much needed and greatly appreciated.

Final Preparations and It Starts Coming Together

For weeks before the trial, the four defense attorneys were preparing for the trial in earnest. It was nice to finally have the other lawyers focus on the case consistently and for an extended period. All four of us had egos. All of us had been around the block, but there were few disagreements. Ramsey and Ackerman would represent Burzynski personally. Both of them had white hair and were in their late fifties.

The youngsters, Cogdell in his early forties and me at forty-five, would represent the Burzynski Research Institute. The prosecutors had made a significant tactical mistake by indicting and keeping the Institute in the case. This allowed us to have two bites at the apple. For jury selection, for every witness, and for every evidentiary point to be argued to the judge, we had two attorneys who had identical interests arguing against the prosecutors.

This turned out to be critically important since the four defense attorneys had overlapping strengths. None of the other three had substantive knowledge about the FDA, health insurance law, or cancer treatment. Ackerman seemed to be the best versed on procedure and evidence, and Ramsey and Cogdell had tons of experience before juries and were consummate showmen.[25] Being able to "double down" or hit the government twice every time it made a point was simply invaluable.

Picking a Jury

We were all concerned about the jury and the jury pool. There had been much publicity about the case, and we felt people would have strong feelings, both for and against Burzynski. Having tried many high-profile, well-financed cases, Ramsey often worked with jury consultants and wanted to use Robert Hirshhorn, his favorite jury consultant. I did not have any objection. Any help would be appreciated, but I did not see a need for a jury consultant in this case.

By that time, I had been in the field a dozen years, and I had a good sense of what kind of people would be sympathetic to the issues raised in the case and the converse. I was much more concerned that we would not be able to identify our friends and enemies in the relatively short time allotted to *voir dire*, or jury selection.

My solution to that problem was a jury questionnaire. Basically a questionnaire is prepared asking the prospective jurors for information about themselves. In a case like this, there would be some questions about cancer.

---

25   During the trial, after Ramsey and Cogdell together just tore apart one of the government witnesses, I remember thinking, "I can't believe I'm getting paid to watch these guys work."

The answers would tell us what we needed to know. The other attorneys had used questionnaires in the past, and they all thought it was a good idea.

So I prepared a multiple-page jury questionnaire. The primary focus was family history with cancer, experience with insurance companies, and work experience. There were also some questions about alternative health and unconventional medicine. It seemed obvious that people who used alternative remedies would have an open mind and be sympathetic toward Burzynski. I think the jury questionnaire is the single most important pretrial preparation for any case in this field. I ask for it in every case. After we were all satisfied with it, we sent it to the prosecutors, and we made a motion to have it included.

The prosecutors more or less agreed, but Judge Lake thought it was a good idea. He was sensitive to the fact that the case could cause emotional difficulties for people who recently lost a loved one to cancer, so he also wanted a jury questionnaire. He took our version and the government's and cobbled his own version. It did what we needed it to do. The jury questionnaire was sent out to the jury pool with the jury summonses.

We received a copy of the completed questionnaires of all of the people in the jury pool and were given a few hours to study it.

The responses were extremely helpful and eye opening. The most amazing thing was that even to a bunch of lawyers, it was clear that cancer is sometimes genetic. Many of the potential jurors had no family members who had cancer. But cancer had ravaged the families of some potential jurors. A few had all their immediate female relatives die of breast cancer. Others had multiple family members with various kinds of soft-tissue cancers. It was just startling to see. It was almost like watching the Angel of Death passing over the houses of the Israelites, while striking the firstborn of the Egyptians.

The questionnaires also revealed that some people used many alternative health modalities while others had no experience with anything unconventional. The jury pool mirrored the population in that the more-educated jurors with higher-level jobs were more likely to have had some past experience with alternative remedies. From what we could tell, we had possible supporters and people who would be skeptical or have a bias against us.

I was inclined to strike anyone who worked for the government, especially if they had held the job for a long time. But I was most anxious to strike anyone who had anything to do with an insurance company. By that time, I hated insurance companies. I had already worked on too many insurance cases for Burzynski, including the killer first Aetna litigation. I had just finished my case against the New Jersey department of insurance (see Chapter 6), and I had tangled with insurance companies in other cases. I thought anyone employed by an insurance company was the scum of the earth, and I wanted to get them as far away from the Burzynski jury as possible.

My hostility to insurance folk led to one of the few conflicts I had with my co-counsel. It turned out to be one of the biggest mistakes I made during the trial.

Ramsey and Cogdell did the *voir dire* (questioning of the jury) for our side, while Ackerman, Hirshhorn (the jury consultant), and I observed, made notes, and conferred. In jury selection, you don't usually end up with the most sympathetic jurors to your case, because these are the folks who are struck by the other side and visa versa. If you are lucky, you get a few who appear to be moderately good, and hopefully you can remove those who are the most hostile or fit some worst-case profile.

After using most of our peremptory strikes (strikes not for cause) we were left with a couple of less-than-ideal choices. One of those was a white fifty-ish guy. He seemed smart, sophisticated, and very smug, but all I needed to know was that he was the president of a nationwide property casualty insurance company. I really wanted him off. The last thing we needed was a smart guy who is used to being in charge and who spent his life taking excessive insurance premiums from hardworking people and then coming up with disingenuous reasons why the company won't pay claims. (Hey, I said I didn't like those guys.)

But Cogdell had some idea that Mr. Insurance Executive gave him a wink or that he knew some friend of a friend but did not acknowledge it. Cogdell thought this juror would be good for us because he had a rapport with him.

The other two lawyers and Hirshhorn wanted to defer to Cogdell's gut feeling. I didn't know anything about Cogdell's gut, friends, winks, or secret handshakes. I had spent much of the seven years fighting with insurance companies, and did I say that I despised these people? But with all four of the other professionals against me, I backed down and we struck someone else. Although we didn't know it at the time, Burzynski almost went to jail because I caved in.

The Media Weighs In

We had our jury, and we were ready to begin. The trial had generated a great deal of public interest. The *Houston Chronicle* was at the trial most of the time, as were the wire services. CBS had a crew covering the case. Its previous *48 Hours* shows on Burzynski had received high ratings. Also, the producer and some of the reporters were closet supporters of Burzynski.

Like in all these cases, the media was a mixed bag. Some of the wire services were quite hostile toward Burzynski. *The New York Times* was a little better. Its general reporters were fair and balanced, but I could not get through to the medical reporter, Gina Kolata. She was skeptical and hostile to Burzynski. On the plus side, Gabe Pressman was still very interested in alternative health and he did a number of TV programs which included Burzynski's struggles with the FDA.

But for the criminal trial, the national media did not matter. What did matter was the local press. In Houston, there is only one newspaper, the *Houston Chronicle*, and we received balanced and sometimes favorable press from it.

The primary *Houston Chronicle* reporter covering the Burzynski case was Deborah Tedford, the federal court reporter. Despite spending many dozens of hours talking to her over the phone and in person, I never learned much about her. Deborah was extremely interested in the Burzynski saga, and unlike some of the other media folks I dealt with, she actually took the time to talk to the patients at length. And she got it. There were just too many terminal patients who had been cured for this to be a hoax or a fraud.

It was clear to her that I was a passionate advocate for Burzynski, having by then worked for him for nine years. I was knowledgeable about all facets of the case and the clinic. It also helps that I try to be a straight shooter.

So with Deborah and the rest of the media, I played it straight, admitted the problems, and tried to maintain focus on the good points. Much of the time I would be the one to bring up the negative points or the other side of things.

Deborah was terrific and I guess it was "one hand washing the other." The Burzynski story was big news, and her stories on the Burzynski case got her on the front page often, which is a good thing for a reporter. She wrote countless stories about Burzynski, his clinic, the patients, and the federal government's efforts to shut it all down.

Deborah's stories were always balanced. They always told the government's point of view, usually by way of a short and heartless quote from Mike Clark. But when you have story after story about technical legal positions versus a treatment many patients believed was saving their lives, that is just about all a guy like me could hope for. In the end, I think Deborah's numerous stories were very helpful for the public to understand what was really involved in the case.

In addition to Deborah's stories in the *Houston Chronicle*, all of the local TV stations covered the case and parts of the trial. We mostly received fair to positive coverage. With all the cancer patients involved and the government attempting to put their doctor in jail, it was a good TV story.

Standing Room Only

Because of Deborah's articles and the TV coverage, the courtroom, which was quite large, was too small to fit in all the people who wanted to attend. So if you can believe it, Judge Lake had to disburse tickets to attend the trial. We received an allocation, as did the government and the press. The media had to do some pooling because of lack of room. It was like the premiere of a blockbuster movie. There were purple velvet ropes with the metal rope stands. The federal marshals acted as the ticket takers. When we would come and go into the courtroom, people outside would ask us if we could get them in. It was the closest I have ever felt to a rock star (or a bouncer).

So we started. The judge gave both sides plenty of time for the opening.

The government gave a very solid presentation of what they thought the evidence would show. Much to my dismay, they quoted liberally from some prior Burzynski opinions and my abortion of an opinion from that old judge. The government's view was that in 1983, Burzynski had been ordered to stop treating patients in interstate commence and was ordered to obtain FDA approval to test his drug. He did neither, and he was knowingly treating patients illegally since that time.

He also hid from insurance companies that his treatment was illegal and experimental, which caused them all to pay based on the mistaken assumption that the treatment was legal and standard chemotherapy.

The insurance companies were further duped because the medical code he used (CPT or current procedure terminology) tricked them into thinking he was administering his treatment in his office when in reality the patients were home and self-administering the treatment with a pump. The government attorneys were good. After their opening, even I thought Burzynski was a crook, and I worked for the guy!

But then our turn came. Ackerman started things off and gave Burzynski's personal story. He was terrific. He barely spoke over a whisper. He spoke modestly and almost as if he was in pain or discomfort. But whatever it was, it seemed very effective. The other three of us also spoke. Cogdell was louder, more confident, and aggressive. He and Ramsey were righteous indignation.

I tried to focus on the errors and technical problems with the government's case, and we all talked about the big-picture issues like freedom of choice. This would be an important concept in the trial because it would be hard to argue that there were not perhaps some technical violations of the FDA law.

Actually, our main strategy was jury nullification. Judges and prosecutors hate this, but sometimes the best argument the defense can make is that the jury should not follow the law, because there is a higher law. You can't exactly tell that to a jury, because the prosecutor would object and the judge would go nuts. When they take their oath, jurors swear to apply the law to the facts regardless of their personal feelings. But people are just people, and sometimes it's hard to follow the law, or so we were hoping. Our job was to show the jury that Burzynski was saving the lives of his terminal patients, and a bunch of government bureaucrats should not be allowed to kill all these people just because of some ridiculous FDA hyper-technicality, which in fact had been resolved by one stroke of the FDA's pen. (Clark was right in thinking we would use the FDA's backing down against them. We did, and it proved effective.)

In a criminal prosecution, the government presents its case first, and Clark and his colleagues took several weeks. There were a half a dozen insurance companies named in the indictment, and a representative from each testified. They all said the same thing. Their insurance policies exclude experimental treatment, and they paid Burzynski's clinic thinking that the treatment was conventional. They all also testified that they would not have paid for "chemotherapy administration" if they had known that the patient was administering the treatment himself by way of a pump in their homes.

Because of my prior experience on these insurance issues, I took the lead on the cross-examination of these witnesses. I made them admit that they would not pay for an experimental treatment, even if it cured their insured patient. Greedy insurance companies. This might have been somewhat helpful, but since the government chose insurance companies whose insureds had died, it surely was not a home run.

Supposedly the insurance companies didn't know the treatment was self-administered at the patient's homes. But all the insurance companies paid for the surgery to have the IV line installed in the patient's body, and they also paid for the self-administered pump. So I argued, they had to know that the treatment was self-administered since they paid for the self-administered delivery system? The insurance people talked about computers and how no one really knows what is going on. Maybe that also helped, and maybe we were chipping away at the government's case.

Based on of all the prior Burzynski insurance litigation, the main thrust of our cross was that all the insurance companies knew or had access to information about the clinic's treatment, and the clinic knew the insurance companies had such knowledge. These facts tended to negate key elements of fraud, namely reliance and intent to defraud.

In addition, the witnesses all admitted on cross that their companies eventually asked the clinic to provide information about the treatment. They were forced to admit that when asked, the clinic always provided truthful and complete information.

"Aspirin Is a Very Dangerous Drug"

A major part of the government's case was the interstate shipment of medicine. The government brought in a senior FDA employee. His job was to explain the FDA drug approval process, its necessity, and how the FDA regulates interstate commerce.

I caught a break with him on cross-examination. I made some reference to the fact that not every drug is as benign as aspirin. It was just an offhand comment. But the FDA witness corrected me and said that aspirin was a very dangerous drug. I looked at him in astonishment. And I wasn't the only one who was surprised. Before he could stop himself, Judge Lake turned to the witness and said, "You mean taking a child's dose of aspirin every day is dangerous?" Everyone in the courtroom knew that Lake was taking aspirin, just like many of us were.

The FDA witness turned to the judge, looked him dead in the eye, and said, "Yes, it is." And then he said something even more remarkable. He said that if aspirin was up for drug approval now, the FDA would never approve it. He said aspirin was just too dangerous and there are too many other, better things out there to treat headache pain and aches. Lake was speechless.

Sensing a moment here, I raised my arms in an overly dramatic gesture and said half seriously, "Your Honor, I rest my case." Everyone in the courtroom laughed, and I think the point was made.

There were a number of humorous moments during the prosecutor's direct case. However, these guys were deadly serious about putting Burzynski in jail, and they were presenting a competent and persuasive case.

Bob Mossary Becomes the Man of the Hour

Bob Mossary's situation was more complicated than we first thought. During the grand jury process, the postal inspectors were closely observing the clinic.

One day Bob appeared at the local post office when the postal investigators happened to be there, and he shipped the medicine to a few patients out of state. They followed him back to the clinic.

The government called Mossary as a witness. He could not deny he had shipped the medicine out of state, but to everyone's relief, he said that he did this on his own and that nobody else at the clinic knew about it. George Tallichet, the prosecutor who was examining him, kept on questioning about his actions. George insisted that other people at the clinic must have known what he was doing or helped, because it was such a big and complicated project. Bob kept on insisting that he acted on his own.

Tallichet then changed tacks and asked Bob if it wasn't hard for him to keep it all straight in his head. Bob looked at George said, "No it's not that hard, Mr. Tallichet. Even you could do it." The entire courtroom burst into laughter.

I guess that annoyed George, because then he started asking Bob about some of the technicalities of the FDA law and interstate shipping. Bob looked like he was completely lost and turned to George and said, "What you're doing is like trying to explain music to the deaf or color to the blind." Another burst of laughter from the courtroom.

Everyone seemed to like Bob, and they liked that he was sticking it to the prosecutors. If the government intended for Mossary to be one of their star witnesses, they were sorely disappointed.

"A Little Bit of Chemo" Opens the Door

Not all of Burzynski's patients were happy with him. All of them had advanced and terminal cancer. Some only had weeks to live before they came to the clinic. So naturally, many of his patients died.

The government called a few disgruntled family members of deceased patients. A couple of them went out of their way to hurt Burzynski. One particularly vicious woman made some crazy comment that she had heard that Burzynski adds "a little bit of chemo" to his medicines and that the chemo was responsible for whatever small results he had.

The defense team had agreed that Cogdell would take the first crack at all of the hostile patients. Cross-examining them did not require much technical knowledge, and Cogdell was a terrific cross-examiner. He lowered his jaw and scrunched up his face and mimicked her "a little bit of chemo" comment and then he went after her, hard. She did not have a specific recollection about who told her, when she was told about the "little bit of chemo," what type of chemo, or anything. By the time he was finished with her, everyone in the courtroom knew she was lying. It was one of the most effective pieces of cross-examination in the entire case.

I think the government planted that information to try to dirty Burzynski up. But the tactic backfired. Because this person had talked about what other patients told her, this allowed us to call many patients to rebut her testimony. Up until that time, the government was taking the position that we could not call any patients because they did not have any relevant information to the charges in the indictment. But this opened the door for us, and Sim Lake let us drive a Mack truck through it. I think he also understood that the witness made the whole thing up, and the government knew it.

On and on the government went. It took them over almost three weeks to finish. They had covered all their bases and did a very credible job. I think we took the sting out of much of their evidence on cross, but who knew what the jury thought.

From body language, it looked to us that at least several jurors thought Burzynski was a crook. But several jurors seemed put off by the prosecutors and their witnesses. How much of this was reality versus wishful thinking was hard to say.

Now It's Our Turn

I had received a lot of face time before the jury on the government's case, as most of the witnesses had technical information, and I had the most substantive knowledge. But of course either Mike Ramsey or John Ackerman also cross-examined every witness. We had many sidebar conferences with the judge on evidentiary issues as well and numerous conferences, arguing various points out of the jury's presence.

It was obvious to all of us that Judge Lake was giving me the hardest time. I just could not make any headway with him. I would make a legal argument, and he would reject it. Then the argument would be recast by Ackerman or Ramsey, and Lake would accept it. He also seemed much stricter with me on rules of cross-examination. He would let the other three get away with much more. And he had me on the carpet much more than the other defense lawyers. Maybe I have that effect on judges, or maybe the other three had more technical skills than me, or maybe they knew better how to stay out of trouble. Who knows?

Perhaps in part to make up for that, the jury gave a bag of candy as a Valentine's Day gift to both sides. Judge Lake gave me the gift for our side, either as a peace offering or to show the jury that he did not have anything against me personally. But I did what I had to do, and I thought I had made some headway tearing apart the government's case on cross-examination.

Because of all this, the team decided I would take a lower profile in presenting the defense case. I still would examine a few of the technical witnesses. But for anything nontechnical and controversial, like the patients who hopefully would make our case, Cogdell would handle it for the Research Institute.

One of the tactics I came up with was to have the entire staff of the clinic and Research Institute appear in the back of the courtroom. All of them had on their white coats or scrubs, different colors for different departments, depending on their function. I think this made a big impression with the jury for many reasons. I don't think the jury initially understood how big an operation Burzynski had. It's one thing to accuse a doctor of being a crook. It's another to think that over a hundred people, many of whom are nurses and PhDs, are all involved in some grand conspiracy and fraud scheme.

To reinforce the point, we had some of the department heads of the Research Institute testify about what they and their departments did. We were trying to show that there was a great deal of time, money, and effort put into cancer research for what the government claimed to be just a fraud scheme to dupe insurance companies.

This was just one example of how the prosecutors made the mistake of over-prosecuting and taking their arguments to a ridiculous end point. By showing all the research, all the quality control, and all the people who were involved with producing the medicine, we went a long way to dispelling the idea that this was a fraudulent scheme.

To rebut the insurance fraud allegations, we called both of the clinic's senior insurance coordinators. They gave terrific testimony. In fact, one of them, Gabrielle Howard, had actually written to the people who put together the procedure codes. She had asked them whether there was a more appropriate code for billing the services that Burzynski called "chemotherapy administration." She got a vague letter back from them saying there was no more appropriate code and suggested the clinic apply for a new code. That seemed to be very persuasive evidence that there was no fraudulent intent to dupe insurance companies.

Also, the two insurance coordinators appeared to be decent, hardworking, and honest people. Again, it is one thing to say in the abstract that Burzynski is a crook, but we were presenting the actual people who worked in the insurance department, and they seem like reasonable people.

They also testified that any time an insurance company would ask about the treatment, the clinic's insurance department would send volumes of information about Burzynski, the clinic, the treatment, and scientific publications written by the Institute's researchers. They were very proud of the clinic and would readily share this information with the insurance companies. Ramsey and Cogdell did the direct examination of the two insurance coordinators and their questioning was skillful, and their skills were certainly needed as insurance fraud was the nastiest part of the case.

Slowly but surely, we were neutralizing the government's insurance fraud case, or so we hoped. The FDA aspects of the case were harder, at least in terms of the facts. All of Burzynski's employees knew that most of his patients came from out of state. They all obviously knew that somehow the medicine got to the patients in their home states. Most of the employees said they thought the patients made arrangements for people to pick up the medicine at the clinic and have it shipped privately to them at their homes. It was a combination of the ostrich defense and jury nullification. As some of these witnesses were testifying, I could not help thinking about Sergeant Shultz on *Hogan's Heroes*. "I seee nothinggg, nothinggg." You do the best you can with what you have.

As Usual, the Patients Are the Stars of the Show

By far, the most effective part of our case was the patients, and in particular the mothers of some of the younger patients. Two of the most spectacular results Burzynski achieved were with Paul Michaels and Dustin Kunnari. By the time of the criminal trial, Dustin was in complete remission.

Paul Michaels was diagnosed with inoperable brain cancer when he was just seven. His prognosis was poor, and his doctors thought he would be dead within a year. His parents, Ken and Mary, found their way to Burzynski. Burzynski ended up treating Paul for many years and eventually his tumor completely disappeared. Even his conventional doctors were amazed.

The family lived in upper Michigan, but they were devoted to Burzynski. Each time we needed them for a court appearance, like the Kunnaris, they packed their car and drove to Texas. They also testified at all of the congressional hearings for Burzynski. And of course, they testified for us at the criminal trial. By that time, Paul was in his mid-teens. He was strong and all but cancer free. He was still on a small maintenance regime. His mother Mary testified, and she was just stupendous. She really brought home what this case was about for her and to people like her.

Of course, Mary Jo Siegel testified, and she was her usual combination of effervescence, humility, emotion, and gratitude. We had many other patients testify.

The rub was that based on Mike Clark's argument that the efficacy of the treatment was not an issue in the case and would unfairly prejudice the jury in Burzynski's favor, the judge wouldn't let any of patients say they had been cured by Burzynski.

But we were four fairly clever lawyers, and we didn't let that minor setback stop us. So we came up with a template for the questioning of the patients. We (or since I was voted off this aspect of the case, the other attorneys) would ask the patients about their disease. The patients would then give a narrative about their illness and the prognosis. All the patients had been diagnosed at least several years previously and were given only six months to a year or two to live. They had all gone to Burzynski after they received their terminal diagnoses. They were testifying in court, and they were all healthy. As lawyers say in a different context, *res ipsa loquitur*; the facts speak for themselves. And in this case, the facts were speaking volumes.

The patient testimonies were going so well, that just for grins, the boys allowed me to do the direct on one of patients. Sure enough, Judge Lake shut me down pretty quickly. We all laughed about it, and that was the last time I got up to handle the direct of any of the patients.

The Only Witness We Didn't Call

We had the insurance people testify. We had the scientific staff testify. We had the clinic's administrator, Barbara Tomaszewski testify. We had many witnesses testify. The one person we did not call to the witness stand was Burzynski himself.

In some cases, it is a tough decision whether to call the defendant as a witness, but not in this case. We all thought that we were doing pretty well. Burzynski's employees and patients were making all the points that needed to be made. There would be much downside to calling Burzynski. First, a couple of these court of appeals cases had taken a very harsh view of him. Calling him to the stand would allow the prosecutors to hammer him over and over with the opinions of all of the judges who criticized him.

Also the issue about whether Burzynski knew the patients were taking the medicine out of state might cause us some trouble. This guy was an MD, had a PhD, and ran a multimillion-dollar cancer clinic. It would be hard for him to say that he did not know. What his knowledge meant might be another thing. In these kinds of high-stakes cases, the fundamental question is do you absolutely, positively have to call the defendant as a witness to defeat the government's case? The team felt we did not. That was our feeling at the beginning, the middle, and at the end of the trial. So the one witness who did not testify was Burzynski himself.

I had one funny but disquieting episode. I got on an elevator at the ground floor. The only other passenger was a tall attractive woman. She had a "juror" tag, but I didn't recognize her as being on my jury, so I smiled at her and asked what case she was hearing. She looked hurt and said, "You don't recognize me? I'm on your case." I froze and had a recollection of the *Schneider v. Revici* trial and specifically Sam, the moron juror, and Judge Motley, but this time I was the moron and Lake was already giving me a hard time. The door opened on a floor below our courtroom. My mind was mush. I gasped or gurgled something like, "I gooo nowww," and in one hop lurched out of the elevator. I later found out that the juror, Darlene, related the event to the other jurors and they all got a big laugh, at my expense.

Eventually we came to the end of our case. The government did not put much on in rebuttal. We had a jury charging conference, and Lake came up with a set of charges taken from both sides which everyone thought was fair.

The government did its closing first, and they also had time after our closing for a rebuttal closing. They were very good; technically proficient, arguing the technicalities of the case. Not much soul, in my opinion, but they were prosecutors and they were doing their job.

All four defense lawyers spoke at the closing. I tried to stick to the themes I had worked on the opening, which were some of the technical problems with the government's case as well as the big-picture items. My big phrase to the jury was that they had to draw a line in the sand to protect people's rights. There was no doubt that Burzynski was helping people and saving their lives, and because of that, the government had no right to come in the way they did and try to stop him.

The other three lawyers were very articulate. Ackerman spoke last. He was particularly moving, pleading with the jury. At one point he told them he was scared to sit down, in case he forgot something important; very humble and very moving. He was great.

The judge gave the charge, and the case was submitted to the jury. And then we waited, and waited.

The jury had a few questions. Each time the jury would send a note with a question, the lawyers would be summoned to discuss the response. Then the jury would be called in and the judge would give the response.

This went on day after day after day. The defense started thinking in terms of a deadlock, which would result in a mistrial. After five or six days, the jury announced that it was deadlocked.

When this happens in a jury case, most judges will give what is called an "Allen" or dynamite charge. The judge tells the jurors to search their conscience and open their hearts to the other jurors. The Allen charge strongly encourages the jurors to reach some decision, any decision, because if they did not, the case would have to be tried before a new jury, which would be facing the same issues. Defense lawyers hate the Allen charge. In most criminal cases, there are usually one or two people holding up a guilty verdict. So the Allen charge is thought to be directed to the jurors holding up a conviction.

Judge Lake gave the Allen charge and the jury went back to deliberate. But it didn't help. At that point, the judge had no choice. He declared a mistrial, and the first criminal trial was over, almost.

Judge Lake Comes through, Big Time

As a matter of form, at the end of the case and before the jury went to deliberate, the defense moved to dismiss all the charges on all counts as a matter of law. These motions are never granted but are always made. Judge Lake had reserved decision, which meant he was going to let the jury deliberate and do its work and then he would address the motion.

After Lake declared the jury deadlocked, he did something that flabbergasted everyone. He granted our request to dismiss all of the insurance fraud counts. In simple but cogent reasoning, he found that whether the insurance companies knew at the beginning that Burzynski's treatment was experimental, not FDA approved, and self-administered by the patients, the Burzynski staff always told the insurance companies the truth whenever they were asked. He said that was inconsistent with insurance fraud, and this fact was acknowledged by every insurance witness called by the government (at least under cross-examination). So Judge Lake dismissed all thirty-four of the insurance fraud counts. The lead story in the *Houston Chronicle* was "Burzynski Acquitted of Fraud." And so ended the first Burzynski criminal trial.

After the end of jury trial and after Lake dismissed the insurance counts, he brought all the attorneys to the jury room so we could talk to the jurors.

When you try a case before a group of people, you really don't know what they are thinking. You may think you do, and you might be right sometimes and with some jurors, but you never really know.

Turns out the jury split six to six. Most distressing, the leader of the six who wanted to convict was the president of that property insurance company—the guy I wanted to strike but got outvoted. He was adamant that Burzynski was guilty of everything, and he used all his management and persuasive skills to convince the six holdouts. He even told them that nothing would happen to Burzynski—that he would just get a slap on the wrist and the clinic would stay open. These arguments were patently false. Fortunately, the holdouts would not budge.

One of the leaders of the holdouts was Darlene, the woman I encountered in the elevator. Darlene also shared something that made me feel pretty good. Although deadlocked on the charges, they did agree that I was the most sincere and believable attorney.

That night we had a big celebration at a local restaurant for the Burzynski staff and supporters. The media was also there in force. We also invited all the jurors. The six holdouts came. None of those who voted to convict attended. Maybe Clark took those folks out to dinner to commiserate with him.

Between Trials: To Try or Not to Try, That Is the Question

I was feeling good after the trial. True, we had a hung jury, and the case might have to be retried, but the insurance fraud counts were gone, and that was very good news. The government was given some time to decide whether to seek a new trial on all of the FDA counts. Since the jury was six to six deadlocked, we all hoped that the feds would do the right thing and drop the case. But this was the FDA and the federal government, so maybe we were hoping for too much.

A few weeks before the scheduled retrial, the government wanted to meet with us to discuss resolving the case without a new trial. Ackerman had already left for Bosnia to represent war criminals in The Hague (Cynthia McMurray was also over there). So he was out of the picture.

Ramsey, Cogdell, and I went to the U. S. attorneys office to see what they had in mind.

Initially, they wanted Burzynski to plead to a misdemeanor. Ramsey and Cogdell seemed willing to do that. From their wealth of experience defending hard-core criminal cases, any day you get a serious felony charge reduced to a misdemeanor was a very good day. But I would not agree. By that time, Burzynski was the sponsor and principal investigator for seventy-two clinical trial protocols under several INDs. I didn't trust these government lawyers as far as I could throw them. I was afraid that if Burzynski signed off on the deal, those bastards at the FDA would close the trials because he had pled guilty to a criminal offense.

Having held firm, the government lawyers agreed to drop the requirement that he plead guilty to any crime. Instead, they proposed that Burzynski pay a hundred thousand-dollar fine.

That sounded more like it. Ramsey and Cogdell were really excited. Only legal magicians could transform a felony into a civil fine. There was one sticking point. The government wanted the payment to be called a fine, and Burzynski had to acknowledge that it was a fine, presumably for violating the FDA act. I was okay with him paying money, but I didn't want it to be called a fine, again because of my fears that the FDA would use it as a reason to remove Burzynski as the clinical investigator for all these trials or shut down the trials completely.

Ramsey and Cogdell leaned on me to acquiesce. My counter position to them and the government was that the payment would be uncharacterized. We would agree that the FDA could call it whatever they wanted, and we could characterize it however we wanted (except maybe a gift or charitable contribution). Apparently, Mike Clark did not have the power to make that deal, so they called in the U. S. attorney, Gaynelle Griffin Jones, to take part in the negotiations. It was her call. Her prosecutors were inclined to accept it, but she rejected it.

Ramsey and Cogdell thought we should take the deal as a fine. Mike said, "It's our case to lose." He said we could do a whole lot worse than paying a fine and a civil settlement. In any other case, I would have jumped on the deal in a heartbeat. But this case was different. Burzynski, his patients, and others needed him to keep testing his drugs. And since he agreed that he would only give his treatment to people under FDA-approved protocols, if the FDA shut down the trials, there would be no more treatment for any patients. I thought it would be a tragedy if as a result of this case, the FDA managed to stop the trials.

I had one other reason for taking a hard line. Perhaps because of financial and time constraints, a few weeks before our meeting, the government had dismissed all of the FDA substantive counts. The only charge they could take to trial was the contempt of court charge for the alleged violation of the 1983 injunction order.

I was very familiar with the injunction order, as it came up in many of the civil insurance cases I had handled for Burzynski. I had also been involved in three of the four grand jury investigations. I felt that if there was one charge in the whole case we could actually win, the contempt charge was it. Of course, having spoken to Gabrielle McDonald also gave me considerable fortitude.

Neither Ramsey nor Cogdell really understood the contempt charge, so I thought I was in a better position to make an assessment about the likelihood of winning a second trial.

Since we were close to the second trial, the prosecutors insisted on an answer during the meeting. In a separate room we called Burzynski. Mike made his case, and then I made mine. By this time, I had a pretty good understanding of Burzynski, and I strongly suspected that he was too proud and stubborn admit that he was paying a "fine," the implication being that he had violated the FDA act. He didn't even think about it. He just said, "Okay, we go to trial." And we did.

The Second Trial and the Two-Word Verdict

The second criminal trial was much easier and there was less pressure, for the lawyers anyway. Seventy-five of the seventy-six criminal counts had been dismissed. The remaining count, although serious and with the possibility of some prison time, was not as bad as the potential penalties of the first trial where Burzynski was facing more than a decade of jail time.

Because it was a smaller case, the legal teams got smaller as well. Ackerman was gone and the government reassigned Amy Lequoc to other matters. And of course, the postal investigator was no longer involved since her part of the case had been dismissed. So it was just Mike Clark and George Tallichet for the government and Ramsey, Cogdell, and me for the defense.

The government presented pretty much the same FDA case it presented at the first trial, and so did we. While the government's substantive case did not change, the tone dramatically changed.

For reasons we did not know, Clark and Tallichet did not get along at the second trial. They would snipe at each other. Mostly it was Clark belittling and undercutting Tallichet. Tallichet would try to do something or agree to something, and Clark would overrule him, oftentimes in front of the jury. At times it was unpleasant and embarrassing to watch. Tallichet looked like a guy who just didn't want to be sitting in that courtroom next to Clark. But Tallichet was a consummate professional, so he sat there and took it. Clark was acting like a jerk before the jury. But that was fine with us.

At this trial, the only real issue was the meaning of the 1983 injunction and whether Burzynski had violated it by treating patients and letting them leave Texas with his unapproved drug.

Of course I had spoken to McDonald, and I knew what she meant. I kept hammering away at the FDA, the government, and to the jury that Judge McDonald knew that Burzynski was treating out-of-state patients and could have specifically prohibited him from doing so, but she didn't. That was my mantra during the whole trial, and Ramsey and Cogdell were also chanting it. We had Gabrielle McDonald herself to thank for the mantra. And it worked.

We wrapped up the second trial in about a week. The jury went out and we waited, but this time it took less than a day. As the jury was being escorted into the courtroom to announce its verdict, an intense wave of panic enveloped me. It was the four of us at the table: Burzynski, Ramsey, Cogdell, and me. I played back in my mind the meeting at the U.S. attorneys office where Ramsey and Cogdell argued and pleaded with me that Burzynski should pay the hundred grand "fine." What if they were right? What if Burzynski was convicted and went to jail because I told him not to pay a fine? I had some very tense moments as the jury ambled back to their seats.

Fortunately, it was a two-word verdict. The last of the seventy-six criminal counts had been dismissed.

We had another party after the second trial. Some of the jurors came to the party. One of the jurors took me aside and told me that they all felt I was the most effective attorney at the trial. After nine years fighting the Burzynski wars, that was nice to hear.

Postscript

It has been over ten years since the Burzynski criminal trials. The clinic is still open and still saving the lives of many of its patients. Some of the clinical trial protocols have been closed, either due to lack of patient enrollment or in some cases, after Burzynski saw that his treatment was not affecting some forms of cancer, like lung and breast cancer. A few of the trials have been completed, and the results of some of them are excellent, especially in different forms of brain cancer and certain kinds of lymphoma.

A few years back, Burzynski even got orphan drug status for antineoplastons as a treatment for brain cancer. But he continues to be stuck in the morass of the FDA approval process. My fear is that the FDA will never approve any drug with his name on it. And from my perspective, that is a tragedy and an embarrassment for American medicine.

In all the years I have worked in the field, Burzynski's treatment is most clearly and consistently saving the lives of advanced cancer patients. Recently, the clinic celebrated its thirtieth anniversary with a big party. Most gratifying to see were the many young adults who Burzynski treated when they were children. They were alive, well, and at the party because the Burzynski clinic kept its doors open during those dark days. To the extent I helped, well, that's as good as it gets.

CHAPTER THREE

What about Kids?

Can children use unconventional therapies? The short answer is yes, so long as they don't have a life-threatening disease for which there is a proven conventional treatment. If they do, then all bets are off.

There Are No Christian Scientist Children with Serious Illnesses

Let's start with the basics. Adults can refuse treatment, conventional or alternative. Christian Scientists and others do not believe in modern medicine. Instead, they trust in God to provide them health care. (That is surely one way to reduce healthcare costs.)

While these folks can reject medical care for themselves, they cannot reject care for their children. State law holds that the refusal by a parent to provide necessary medical care constitutes child neglect, which can result in the state taking legal and possibly physical custody of a child. In short, parents can be Christian Scientists, but their young kids cannot, at least not if the child has a serious or life-threatening medical condition.[26]

What about a child with cancer? Can parents forgo conventional care and seek out an alternative cancer remedy? This issue has come up often in the last thirty years. One of the first cases involved a child by the name of Chad Green who was diagnosed with cancer. His family refused chemotherapy, evaded U.S. authorities, and eventually fled to Mexico to receive laetrile. The treatment was unsuccessful and unfortunately, the child died.

We had our first case like this over twenty years ago. The young child was diagnosed with acute lymphocytic leukemia (ALL), which used to be a death sentence for children. However, by the mid-1980s, it was clear that chemotherapy was highly effective at curing the disease.

Of course, the treatment is very rough, and children experience all the symptoms of chemotherapy, like hair loss, nausea, vomiting, and their immune systems are severely compromised. The standard course of chemotherapy is given for up to a year. After the disease goes into remission, chemotherapy is continued under what is called "maintenance therapy." Chemotherapists do maintenance therapy in order to maximize the chances the disease will not return. Recurrent ALL is much harder to treat and is usually fatal. So the chemotherapists are absolutely adamant that ALL patients take maintenance therapy.

The child of our New York clients had the initial chemotherapy and the cancer went into remission. However, the parents resisted the oncologist's plan to give their child maintenance chemotherapy.

The doctor called the New York State Child Protective Services (CPS). CPS unsuccessfully tried to convince the parents to allow the child to take the maintenance therapy.

CPS then filed criminal charges against the parents and also moved for custody. That's when Abady & Jaffe came into the picture (circa 1988, when

---

26   The older the child, the more likely a judge will allow the child to decide whether to take conventional treatment. There was a case a few years back involving a sixteen- or seventeen-year-old, and his wishes were respected. Recently a judge allowed a fourteen-year-old Jehovah's Witness the right to refuse a transfusion. But in a Texas case, a similarly-aged girl was forced to take chemotherapy. However, a Utah judge would not force a twelve-year-old boy to take chemotherapy because he and his family were adamantly against it.

we were deeply involved in the Revici malpractice litigations). Unfortunately, the parents did not have a specific and reasonable alternative to the maintenance chemotherapy. They had talked to one unconventional practitioner and made an appointment to see some other alternative doctor in the Midwest. They wanted to explore dietary options like macrobiotics. But there are no proven alternative treatments for ALL, obviously, and most alternative doctors have little or no experience with the disease.

My partner Sam eventually had the criminal case dismissed, but legal custody was transferred to CPS. The child was forced to take maintenance chemotherapy. Twenty years later, the child (now an adult) is still cancer free.

Since that time, I participated in a number of these cases throughout the country. Most of them involved kids with inoperable brain tumors. The state wanted the child to take chemotherapy and radiation, and the parents wanted to take their child to the Burzynski clinic. Chemotherapy is largely ineffective for most brain tumors, but chemotherapists continue to provide it, if for no other reason than because patients want some treatment and conventional doctors prefer patients to take ineffective conventional treatment rather than unconventional treatment.[27]

Prior to treating patients only on FDA-approved clinic trials in 1996, Burzynski treated a number of these children in his private medical practice. Some of these families were successful in having the courts allow them to use Burzynski's treatment because he had a track record with some types of brain tumors even though the treatment was not FDA-approved. I assisted in some of these cases by preparing some of the legal paperwork in support of the parents' efforts to bring these kids to Burzynski's cancer clinic.

But since 1996, Burzynski has only treated patients under FDA-approved clinical trials. That mostly eliminated his ability to treat children with untreated brain cancer, unless the patient was terminal and could not benefit from (ineffective) chemotherapy or debilitating radiation. The effect of these conventional treatments can be devastating and fatal.

---

27 Chemotherapists admit this, calling it keeping the patient "properly oriented."

The Navarros Fight to Get on Burzynski's Treatment

These situations are hard on the family. Thomas Navarro and his parents Jim and Donna fought one of the hardest battles I have ever seen.

Jim was a take-charge kind of guy, to a fault. He was only around five feet ten, but he was big and completely bald. Jim had been in the military—the military police to be exact. He was in the retail law enforcement supply business. His wife Donna had a background in the health care field, having been a combat nurse and also a physician's assistant. They lived in Tucson, Arizona.

Jim and Donna had five children ranging in age from the early twenties down to three years old. In 1999, when he was four years old, their fourth child, Thomas, was diagnosed with medulablastoma, a deadly form of brain cancer. Thomas initially had surgery that removed most of the tumor. He had some visual and motor problems as a result of the surgery, but he eventually made a full recovery. Unfortunately, surgery is usually not a cure for most forms of brain tumors. Even if the surgeons think they got it all, the tumors usually grow back.

The standard postsurgical treatment for brain cancer is chemotherapy and radiation. The cure rate is not good, but that's all conventional medicine has to offer. The side effects of these treatments on kids are horrendous. The Navarros did some research as to the effectiveness and side effects of conventional therapies, and they were horrified to learn that basically all children who took chemo and radiation suffered severe and permanent mental retardation, if they survived, and almost half of those receiving treatment did not.[28]

Many parents would have accepted their fate, gone with conventional treatment, and hoped for the best. But not Jim and Donna. They did some more research and found out that Burzynski's clinic had successfully treated

---

28   One of the most comprehensive studies they found was from the St. Jude's Cancer Clinic in Memphis, published in the December 1999 issue of *Journal of Clinical Oncology*. The study reported that a third of the patients had died within two years despite treatment, and half of those who died may have died from complications from the therapy. Only about half of the patients were alive after five years. But all of those who were alive became severely mentally retarded as a result of the treatment, and they experienced other debilitating side effects and deformities, all from a treatment that works, at best, half of the time.

many kids with brain tumors without the horrible side effects of chemotherapy and radiation.

They heard about Dustin Kunnari who had the same type of cancer, medulablastoma. Dustin was even younger than Thomas and was in full remission with none of the side effects of chemo and radiation. They decided that Burzynski's treatment was for them.

So they packed up Thomas and traveled to Burzynski's clinic in Houston. They thought it would take a few weeks to get the FDA's permission to have the clinic treat Thomas. But unfortunately, they were just at the beginning of their long ordeal.

Thomas did not meet the entry criteria for any of Burzynski's clinical trials since he had not received chemotherapy or radiation (the irony was that no form of chemotherapy had been specifically approved for medulloblastoma in children), so the clinic applied to the FDA for a special or compassionate use exception to give Thomas the treatment.

The FDA is the high temple of the church of medical orthodoxy, so it was no surprise when it refused to let the clinic treat Thomas. The high priests of the church did not have to watch Thomas or the other kids suffer the side effects of the conventional treatments.

As much as I didn't like what the FDA was doing, I didn't think the Navarros had a chance in hell of getting Burzynski's treatment for Thomas, at least not before he had chemotherapy. And I repeatedly said so to Jim and Donna, much to Donna's dismay and Jim's anger.

Like I said, Jim was a gung-ho guy. But he had no background in alternative health. He came to the clinic several years after the Burzynski wars had ended and knew nothing about clinical trials or FDA policies. But he was going to do what many others had failed to do: persuade the FDA to allow his son to take a drug under clinical investigation before conventional therapy.

I thought Jim had more confidence and certitude than his background justified. Every chance I got, I would tell him he needed another plan for Thomas, as the FDA would not allow him on Burzynski's treatment before conventional treatment. And every time Jim would tell me that I didn't appreciate what a powerful force he was and that his training in the military was going to make it happen. I always wished him luck.

For months, the Navarros tried to get Burzynski's treatment for their son. They contacted politicians, the media, celebrities, anyone they could think of, all to no avail. The state of Arizona made noises about bringing an action against them for child abuse for not providing conventional care to Thomas. When the Arizona authorities heard the Navarros were in Texas, they called the Texas authorities. The Navarros had to go underground, since Child Protective Services from both states were now looking for them.

Because they were not making any headway in obtaining Burzynski's treatment and with the government authorities on their heels, they fled to Mexico to try some other unconventional treatment. The treatment was not successful, so they came back to Texas to keep trying to get on Burzynski's treatment.

Jim, still the persistent and naïve guy that he was, kept working all angles he could think of. They were introduced to Congressman Dan Burton's staff. Burton eventually submitted the *Thomas Navarro Access to Treatment Act*, which would allow Thomas and patients like him to receive non-FDA-approved treatment.

That really fired Jim up. But Burton's access to treatment bill garnered as little support as the prior access to treatment bills.[29] Burton's bill went nowhere. But Jim didn't know or appreciate the history of all this, so he felt that Thomas's treatment was just around the corner.

Jim was especially adept at getting media attention focused on Thomas's plight. The story was widely covered in the TV and print media. Thomas's picture made the front page of the *New York Post*. The story appeared in *People* magazine. But perhaps his greatest coup was that he managed to get two Republican presidential candidates running in the 2000 election to focus on Thomas's problem with the FDA. During one of the debates, Alan Keyes mentioned Thomas's situation and criticized the FDA and the federal government for interfering in the parent's right to choose the best treatment for their child. Jim and Thomas and the rest of the family were backstage and met with several other presidential candidates, who expressed their support.

---

29   See Chapters 5 and 9 for a discussion of the other access to medical treatment bills.

But all this media didn't change the FDA's policy against experimental treatment as first-line therapy when there were approved remedies that were "effective."

I wasn't representing Jim, as he was marching to his own beat. In fact, I thought he was doing a disservice to Thomas, and I told him so. One time we almost came to blows. (Actually I didn't know we had almost come to blows until he told me many months later that he almost coldcocked me, as he put it, for telling him what I thought about all his efforts.)

He also didn't like that I told him he was enjoying himself too much with all of the media attention he was getting from Thomas's cancer situation. He would tell me about his latest media coup, all the while thinking that if there was just one more story, the FDA would back down. I thought he was living in la-la land (and I guess I told him that too). All the while, Thomas was continuing to go untreated. Maybe it wouldn't have mattered, since he was only giving up conventional treatment, which is mostly ineffective and harmful in pediatric brain cancer cases.[30]

Who knows, maybe all his ranting to the press did move the FDA, a little bit anyway. Eventually a deal was worked out. Thomas would take three rounds of chemotherapy and if it didn't work, he could go on Burzynski's treatment. The FDA also agreed that in light of his age, Thomas would not need to undergo radiation. I am sure in Jim's mind, he had reduced the FDA to its knees, but to me this was what the FDA would have agreed to from the beginning.

So the Navarros traveled up to New York for three rounds of chemotherapy, to be administered at Beth Israel Hospital in New York City. One of the hospital's top medical oncologists had agreed to supervise the therapy. The first course proceeded normally, and the side effects were tolerable. Donna did some research and gave Thomas a bunch of supplements and other things

---

30   I had one other problem with Jim's decision-making. Thomas's battle became the family's entire life. They uprooted themselves from their home in Tucson. Whatever business Jim had was gone. They had no money and lived off of public calls for financial help. This battle became Jim's profession and livelihood and it made me, as well as the Burzynski clinic and some in the Burzynski patient group, uncomfortable.

that mostly eliminated the immunosuppressive effects of the chemotherapy.

However, the second course did not go as well. Unfortunately, the primary oncologist was on vacation and some lesser-skilled doctor supervised the chemotherapy administration. Apparently, Thomas was overdosed and had a horrible reaction. Thomas's white blood count was almost at a fatal level. The doctors told Jim and Donna that Thomas might not survive because of his reduced white blood count level.

Donna went back to the Internet and got in touch with parents of other children who had similar problems. She was told a vitamin A compound could dramatically reverse Thomas's immune problem. So without the doctors' knowledge, she gave Thomas a high dose of vitamin A. Within a day or two, Thomas was no longer in a life-threatening situation, but he was still very sick and severely immunocompromised.

Because of this last experience with chemotherapy, Jim and Donna were finished with conventional chemotherapy. It had almost killed their son.

They went back and forth with the FDA. At this point, and despite the chemotherapy, Thomas's tumors were increasing at a very rapid rate, a sure indication that the chemotherapy had failed—big surprise. As a result of the failure of the two treatments, the FDA waived the requirement to undergo the third round of chemo and allowed Thomas to be treated by Burzynski.

So the Navarros flew back to Houston to start Burzynski's treatment. There were no side effects from the treatment, but Thomas was continuing to suffer effects from his immunocompromised condition due to the chemotherapy.

Thomas went in and out of Texas Children's Hospital for infections and pneumonia. He would develop a high fever, have trouble breathing, and be taken to the hospital by ambulance, to be revived by a bevy of skilled pediatric and emergency room doctors.

But amazingly, despite his immune problems and his several visits to Texas Children's Hospital, the scan after the first few weeks on Burzynski's treatment showed that some of the tumors were shrinking dramatically, and other tumors were no longer growing. Burzynski's treatment was working, just like Jim and Donna had hoped it would.

I have seen this many times with Burzynski's patients, kids and adults alike. Their tumors start to shrink, but because of a severely impaired immune system resulting from prior chemo and radiation, their general condition deteriorates, slowly at first, but then more quickly.[31]

Thomas was starting to win his cancer battle, but his body was losing the war. Each time he would get an infection or pneumonia, he would become progressively weaker. This took an emotional toll on him and the rest of his family.

I went to see Thomas and his family at the hospital and at the Navarros' home. My problems with Jim were in the past. They had plenty of support from the Houston community, but every little bit helps. Thomas was fighting for his life, and I was just as emotionally involved with Thomas and his battle to live as many others were.

After the third or fourth time he was admitted to Texas Children's Hospital for pneumonia, he was just tired. Up until that time, Thomas would tell his parents that he wanted to keep fighting the disease and all of the infections and pneumonia caused by his weakened immune system. But this last time, Donna asked Thomas whether he still wanted to fight, and Thomas said, "No, Mommy, I've had enough. I want it to end. I just want to sleep." Thomas died shortly thereafter.

Could Burzynski have saved Thomas if he had treated him before his immune system had been ravaged? Obviously there is no way to know. But

---

31   Although I cannot prove it, based on my years in the field, I believe that the actual cause of death of many cancer patients is cancer treatment, and specifically immune system and other complications resulting from aggressive multiagent chemotherapy coupled with radiation. Most death certificates have separate entries for an immediate and underlying cause of death, but nothing about what caused the immediate cause of death. Many cancer patients die of infection, pneumonia or respiratory problems, and they don't have cancer in their lungs. In many such cases, the cause of these problems is that the cancer treatments weaken the immune system making the patients more susceptible to these conditions.

I also believe that better nutritional support could alleviate some of these problems, but that is not likely to happen so long as the registered dietitians continue to have a stranglehold on the nutrition needs of cancer patients in hospitals and other medical facilities. See Chapter 8, "Food Fights: Who Should Control the Nutrition Field?," for a further discussion about the problem with the dietitians.

given the fact that the standard treatments for this kind of disease are so risky and that the known side effects for kids are so horrendous, it is worth asking whether the FDA really should be in the business of stopping families from seeking a milder form of treatment. Remember, while Burzynski's treatment may not be FDA-approved for commercial marketing, it was in clinical trials, and there was documentation from the NCI itself that the treatment caused partial and complete responses in certain forms of brain cancer. I hold the FDA responsible for ruining any chance Thomas could have had to live, and it angers me to this day.[32]

---

32   I had lost touch with the Navarro family. I recently learned from Jim that he is starting CancerBusters Foundation to help families deal with children undergoing treatment (www. cancerbusters.us).

CHAPTER FOUR

Sue Spenceley against the World

I returned from lunch one day and received a message from a Sue Spenceley who said she had been referred by Gerry Spence and that she and other patients needed my help. I returned her call. She was a patient at M. D. Anderson and, along with other patients, had been receiving an experimental therapy. But the treatment had been interrupted, and since that time, she and others had been desperately trying to get back on it. They even went to Congress, which had been instrumental in forcing the FDA to allow Burzynski's patients to continue treatment. They consulted with some of the top FDA attorneys in the country, but nothing had worked. Now six months had passed since their treatment had been stopped, and some of them were close to death.

These Folks Need a Miracle

Because of the urgency, I told them to come right over. I met Sue, Jimmy Hagen, and their doctor, Huibert Vriesendorf. After listening to their story, it was clear that they needed help, but probably nothing short of divine intervention would get them back on the treatment because they faced obstacles from the federal government in the form of the FDA and the Texas state government because M. D. Anderson is a state institution.

Sue Spenceley was a tall, attractive woman in her midforties with short brown hair. She was the dynamo in the group and did most of the talking. On a jury, she would be considered the ramrod; the one who takes charge. She worked in a hospital in San Clemente, California, as the medical records coordinator. Health wise, she had a normal life until a few years previously when she was diagnosed with Hodgkin's disease, a cancer-like malignancy of the lymphatic system. She went the normal route of chemo and external beam radiation, but unfortunately, like at least 25 percent of all Hodgkin's patients, the multiple treatment regimes were unsuccessful, and her disease continued to ravage her body.

Jimmy Hagen was a twenty-something kid and he came to my office with a white tee shirt with the message "Give Us Our Treatment." He was a semi-professional mountain climber, which didn't sound like much of a living to me. He was quiet, serious, and determined, a characteristic not uncommon among advanced cancer patients. Like Sue, he had numerous previous treatment regimes, and he also was refractory to other forms of treatment, meaning it was this treatment or nothing, and nothing meant death. Sue told me that the handful of other patients who had been undergoing the treatment were all in the same boat.

Hub's Patient-friendly Treatment

They had all found their way to Houston's M. D. Anderson Cancer Center to be treated by Dr. Huibert Vriesendorf, or "Hub," as he is known to friends and patients. Hub was a conventional doctor all the way, but it would turn out that he had the same radical independent and anti-authoritarian streak that characterized most of my physician clients.

Hub had both a medical degree and a PhD. He trained and worked initially in Holland but came to the United States in the mid-1980s, working at Johns Hopkins before moving to M. D. Anderson. His specialty and life's work is the use of radio-labeled antibodies in Hodgkin's patients. After a few years, he had treated approximately eighty patients. His results were pretty good considering the patient population.

RIT (radio-labeled immunoglobin therapy) is a form of radiation. While other institutions had been using RIT, Hub at M. D. Anderson was the only physician using this type of treatment on Hodgkin's patients.

RIT differed from conventional radiation as far as the delivery system; RIT attached a radioactive particle to a monoclonal or polyclonal antibody. It was like a heat-seeking missile. The process was as follows: First, find an antibody that seeks out either a cancer cell, or in this case, the fluid surrounding a Hodgkin's cell. Second, irradiate the antibody. Third, deliver the irradiated antibody to the patient. The theory is that RIT is a more selective cancer treatment with a higher therapeutic ratio (i.e., more efficient in killing cancer cells versus normal cells) than chemo or standard radiation. Not only is it more efficient, but it also has much fewer side effects than traditional chemo or radiation.[33]

The actual treatment was given over a week or two. First, the patient received an injection of radioactive iridium as kind of a test or dry run. In theory, the iridium would travel through the body and seek out the tumor site. After the injection, the patient would be given a gallium scan to see if the iridium was taken up by the tumor. If it was, then the treatment with the actual antibody, antiferritin, would probably be successful. If not, then the patient would not likely respond to the treatment, and hence it would not be given.

This was an experimental therapy which had to be approved by the FDA. Hodgkin's disease is considered curable. As indicated in the previous chapter, if a patient has a cancer that is considered curable by some approved medicine, then the patient has to get conventional treatment first before taking an experimental drug in a clinical trial. Only after the patient has failed one

---

33   Almost all types of chemotherapy work by interfering with a cell's ability to divide and hence reproduce. The problem with cytotoxic chemotherapy is that it kills all cells, normal cells as well as cancer cells. The theory is that cancer cells divide more quickly or more often than most normal cells, so when you give chemo over a course of a few weeks, more cancer cells than normal cells should be killed, theoretically at least. But some of the body's normal cells divide rapidly as well, like hair cells, and the cells that line the stomach. Chemo kills these normal cells as effectively as it kills cancer cells, which is why the expected side effects of chemo include hair loss and nausea. Chemo is, of course, no magic bullet; it's more like a scorched-earth approach to treatment. Sometimes it works, but much of the time it doesn't.

or more conventional treatments can a medical institution that is testing an experimental agent offer it to the patient. Thus, the patients whom Hub treated had all failed conventional treatment and were considered incurable and terminal.

The RIT treatment, according to Sue and Jim, was very patient-friendly. It has none of the horrible side effects normally associated with chemo or radiation. On the other hand, the treatment is not a cure. It just reduces the size or eliminates tumors on a temporary basis, and thereby could extend a patient's life. But for a terminal Hodgkin's patient, the idea of a treatment that is not life-threatening, does not have horrible side effects, and can give the patient more quality time is a mighty attractive option.

The Patients Play Ping Pong, but They Are the Ball

According to Sue and Jimmy, all was going well until late October 1995, when out of the blue, the FDA wrote to M. D. Anderson and put the clinical trial "on hold," thereby disallowing any patients from obtaining the treatment. While the FDA has the power to oversee clinical trials, under federal regulations, it is not supposed to suspend a clinical trial unless there is some very serious risk of patient harm. The "clinical hold" letter they showed me did not come close to establishing such imminent harm. Indeed, the letter didn't even say there was imminent harm. It was just the bureaucrats at the FDA throwing their weight around, God bless them.

What they described next sounded like a malevolent game of ping pong, with the patients as the ball. Within a six-week period, the FDA withdrew and reinstated the clinical hold several times. By early December 1995, the FDA agreed to allow past patients to be treated and new patients to be treated under so called "compassionate use" exceptions.

In the first few days of December, one new patient received the initial pre-treatment iridium injection. On the morning of December 6, Vriesendorf sought and received permission to treat the patient with the actual treatment. So the patient was prepped and his IV was started with saline solution. But just before the injection with the treatment, Vriesendorf received an emergency call from the FDA and was told to stop. Once again, the treatment was put on hold. Then M. D. Anderson closed the study, later reopening it, but refusing to accept any of the patients for treatment.

That all happened about six months before they came to see me. In the interim, they made the rounds through Congress, including Joe Barton's subcommittee on oversight and investigations. Joe Barton had almost single-handedly forced the FDA to put Dr. Burzynski's patients on clinical trials so they could be treated—all two hundred plus of them. But in this case, he couldn't do anything.

Sue and the others consulted with the country's top FDA attorneys, and I mean several former FDA general counsels—lawyers way above my pay grade. They went to the news media. Finally, they asked Gerry Spence to take the case. He wouldn't or couldn't and apparently suggested they contact me, I assume because of my work with Burzynski. The kicker was that they didn't have any money to pay a lawyer.

These Folks Really Need a Miracle, Now

After I heard them out, I gave them my legal analysis, and I was none too hopeful. They had two separate but related problems, each of which was almost insurmountable. First, they had to take on the federal Food and Drug Administration. It would have to be argued that placing the clinical trial on hold was arbitrary and capricious and otherwise convince a federal judge that the FDA's medical decision was so wrong that a federal court needed to step in.

Most federal judges feel very comfortable about deciding legal issues but are extremely uncomfortable in deciding technical medical issues involving public health and safety. That is the reason we have agencies like the FDA in the first place. So it had to be very clear for a federal judge to step in and overrule the judgment of the FDA.

Fortunately, in this case the FDA's actions seemed heavy-handed since the clinical hold letter did not even attempt to identify the supposed serious harm. That was fairly typical for the FDA, in my experience.

But the FDA would likely argue that it had ultimately let the study continue, and it was M. D. Anderson that had closed the program. And the

FDA would be right to make that argument. It was M. D. Anderson that had closed Vriesendorf's clinical trial. But it was widely rumored that it did so because the FDA threatened to close every single FDA-approved study at Anderson unless Anderson closed this study. Then Anderson filed another IND to treat the previously treated patients. But six months had gone by and Anderson put one road block after another in the way of the patients. Clearly Anderson did not really want to treat these patients with RIT.

So in addition to challenging the FDA's actions in initially closing the studies, they would have to take on M. D. Anderson, which is a Texas state facility. Both of these problems were difficult as the federal and state governments are enshrouded by a variety of legal doctrines that makes them hard to sue. Going after both levels of government in the same lawsuit would make a "Hail Mary" pass look like a sure thing.

These were just the general problems. These folks also had specific substantive difficulties. Although the problems that precipitated the closure of the study were not life-threatening to patients, the FDA had identified several dozen protocol violations committed by Vriesendorf and his co-investigators. With one patient, antiferritin was taken from a pig rather than from a rabbit, as called for in the study. A few patients were admitted into the study even though their white blood cell counts did not come close to meeting protocol eligibility requirements. There were numerous other violations in documentation, reporting to the institutional review board, and other technical protocol violations. We could expect the FDA to argue that these protocol violations were endangering the lives of the patients.

But life was short—literally for these patients—and I quickly agreed to take the case. As to money, well, we (the royal we that is) would just have to worry about that later. I dropped everything else I was doing and spent the next several days preparing papers: federal complaint and motion for preliminary injunction. If I do say so myself, I ended up with a pretty good set of papers. Ah, who am I kidding—there was absolutely no legal precedent for what I was asking, and there was the small fact that the FDA and M. D. Anderson uncovered all of the protocol violations. I desperately wanted to help these people, but I am just a lawyer, and I knew that most federal judges looking at these papers would have just shaken their heads, expressed sympathy, and told me that the FDA and M. D. Anderson knew best about when a study should be closed.

Coming Right Up, One Miracle

I went down to the courthouse to file the papers. These people needed my help, and I needed a miracle.

His name was Lynn Hughes. In federal court, new cases are assigned to judges at random. In some places, they used to have a drum with every judge's name written on a card. Your judge is who the clerk picks for you, but more recently, the clerk's computer randomly assigns cases to the judges. It's basically a lottery. And after filing the case, I hit the lottery!

I don't know anything about Lynn Hughes's background. I had only appeared before him once before; he didn't grant my request to quash a subpoena served on a prominent government attorney who was trying to keep an embarrassing sexual condition out of a grand jury room. But I knew enough about him to know that Lynn Hughes was the only judge who would even consider ordering the FDA and Anderson to treat these patients.

Hughes was well known as a tough, no-nonsense guy who had a deep mistrust of the government and maybe even government personnel. The first time I met him in chambers (when he did not grant my motion to quash), he showed me and the three federal prosecutors arguing against me a cartoon of government agents with a caption calling them "thugs in blue suits." I guess it made the two federal prosecutors who wore blue suits uncomfortable, but no doubt that was Hughes' intent.

For government lawyer types, appearing before Lynn Hughes was probably as disheartening as being a bathing suit salesman in a nudist colony. But then again, both situations have their good and bad points. Lynn Hughes was still a federal judge, not a doctor or a scientist. The FDA's job is to oversee new drug trials in this country. M. D. Anderson is one of the top cancer treatment centers in the world. So convincing Judge Hughes that both institutions were wrong and that he should overturn their joint decision to close the clinical trial would be a challenge.

In short order, I received answering papers. The U.S. attorneys office in Houston and Main Justice out of Washington, D.C., answered and appeared on behalf of the FDA. M. D. Anderson hired Terry Tottenham from Fulbright & Jaworski. Terry was the top health care defense attorney in Texas and beyond. He literally wrote a manual on Texas medical jurisprudence, which I used as a resource in preparing my motion papers. (Thanks, Terry.) The individual Anderson administrators I sued had a separate set of counsel. Anderson also had a couple of assistant attorney generals on the case.

All told, there were between six and eight lawyers filing papers against us, all trying to prove that the government and Anderson were right in stopping these people from taking this potentially life-extending treatment, basically because the investigators didn't do the paperwork to the FDA's satisfaction! You've got to love these bureaucrats.

The law was against us, but we had a few extremely compelling, irrefutable facts, namely that all of these patient were going to die for certain if they didn't receive this treatment. Anderson and the government were so busy pointing their fingers at each other that they were missing this point. But institutions like the FDA think in macro or generic terms, "public safety," "public health." They were uncomfortable with or completely forgot about individuals like Sue Spenceley and Jimmy Hagen. My job would be to make sure Judge Hughes understood that this case was not about public safety with a capital "P" but about these individual patients who needed the treatment right now.

Within ten days of filing the case, Judge Hughes had all the attorneys in his chambers. (The main justice lawyers participated via telephone.) We had quite a crowd. I made my pitch to the judge. He seemed reluctant to second-guess the FDA, but I kept at him. Frankly, I didn't think I had made my case with him, and I was plenty worried.

He then let all of the other attorneys speak. Fortunately, the attorneys for Anderson and the FDA didn't help their case as much as they could have. They blamed each other and Vriesendorf, and neither side felt any responsibility toward the patients, except they all professed their heartfelt interest in protecting the "Public." It was a good thing I came to the conference on an empty stomach. Fortunately, there was one other person in the room who apparently shared my opinion about the defense counsels' arguments, and that was Judge Hughes.

After hearing all counsel, he ordered me to send the medical records of the patients to the attorney general's office and they were given a few brief days to tell him whether there were any patients for whom the treatment was medically too dangerous, considering the fact that they were terminal. We were on our way to getting these people treated!

We didn't get everything we wanted. There were a number of patients who had not received the treatment previously. These patients had been enrolled in the program, but the protocol was shut down prior to them receiving the treatment. The judge would not go that far. He would only force Anderson to treat patients who had previously received the RIT and needed re-treatment. It was my unpleasant duty to tell the families of these as yet untreated patients the bad news. Since these patients had already failed other conventional therapies, I was delivering a death sentence. It was one of the worst things I ever had to do as an attorney.

But I had over a dozen patients we were going to push through to get treatment. Within a day, we had all the information the judge ordered. Without too much trouble, Sue, Jimmy, and most of the others were scheduled to take the treatment. We lost one of the patients to the disease during the time between the filing of my lawsuit and processing the people per the judge's order.

The judge issued a short written opinion.[34] When I read it in chambers, I didn't think it made much sense, and in a moment of perfect stupidity, I jokingly told the judge so. Given the gift he had given me, I guess he was a little miffed by my comment. (Note to self: keep my mouth shut unless I have something important and substantive to say, which should cut down considerably on what I say to judges.)

Upon reflection, Hughes was probably concerned that I or someone like me would use his decision to wreak havoc with the FDA's oversight of clinical trials. So he wrote a short opinion, which looked like he denied all relief and

---

34 *Spenceley v. M. D. Anderson*, 938 F. Supp 398 (S.D. Tex., 1996).

"poured us out" of court (as they say in Texas) but for the small fact that he ordered the FDA and M. D. Anderson to treat the previously treated patients. This was an absolutely staggering result. But the case had no precedential value to adversely affect the FDA. It was a very shrewd and extremely humanitarian decision. Exactly what you would expect a judge to do, but quite uncommon in the real world, at least in my experience.

And Sue, Jimmy, and the Others Get Their Treatment
This would be the perfect end to the story, but life is sometimes messy. I convinced Hughes to allow the patients to be re-treated, but Anderson and the FDA convinced him that Vriesendorf should not be involved in the treatment because supposedly his multitude of protocol violations evidenced a lack of competence to act as a clinical investigator.

Hub and the patients were obviously not happy about that. He had developed a strong bond with his patients. He was also the most knowledgeable and experienced person concerning the treatment. But my job was to get patients re-treated. Frankly, Hub was a liability to the case. He had not followed the FDA's rules, and the FDA was punishing the patients as a result of Hub's infractions. I felt that some distance between my clients and Hub wouldn't be a bad thing. Turns out I was at least partially wrong, but it wasn't up to me anyway.

Apart from ego, Hub was concerned that the other doctors at Anderson were not clinically competent to administer the treatment. But ultimately Hughes could not completely disregard the FDA's and Anderson's concerns, so he ruled that Anderson could decide who administered the treatment. And there was no way Anderson would let Hub near the patients given all the protocol violations that had caused the FDA to close the clinical trial protocol in the first place.

Regrettably, it turned out that Hub's concerns were justified. Anderson used a diagnostic radiologist, rather than a therapeutic radiologist, to supervise the treatment. He had no experience whatsoever with RIT or therapeutic radiology in general. Hub, who was still at Anderson, worked behind the scenes and did what he could to make sure the patients were properly treated.

But unfortunately, the Anderson staff did not take proper sterile precautions. Within a few days of receiving the treatment, one patient died of infection from the treatment. (No one had previously died from infection as a complication of the treatment.) The good news was that all of the other patients survived the pretreatment and treatment and seemed to benefit greatly from it. Sue, Jimmy Hagen, and the others would live awhile longer.

Round Two: Getting the RIT from M. D. Anderson's Sticky Fingers

Hub, however, continued to have problems at Anderson, in part because Anderson found out he had still been involved with his RIT patients. Like most physicians at Anderson, Hub worked under a one-year contract. At the end of the year, not surprisingly, Anderson did not renew his contract. Hub found another job in a private cancer facility in Arlington, Texas. He intended to move his RIT program with him, but Anderson had other plans.

Making the radio-labeled antibodies is a long, complicated, and expensive process. Before Hub moved to Anderson, he had made enough to treat over a hundred patients. There was still much of the material left when he was planning to leave Anderson.

I recommended that he just take all of the material from the freezer and transport it to his new lab. Possession is nine-tenths of the law. And since Hub had brought the material with him from Johns Hopkins and Anderson did not pay for it, what claim could Anderson possibly assert to hold the medicine? There might have been some FDA issues, as the material was the subject of a clinical trial, albeit one that was no longer active. But I thought it would be easier to address those issues with the material in Hub's hands rather than trying to pry the materials out of Anderson's fingers.

Hub chose not to follow my advice and notified Anderson that he intended to take his materials with him. They said no. They moved the materials and put them under lock and key. That was the end of the matter as far as Anderson was concerned.

The irony was that Anderson had no intention of restarting the program; they just didn't want Hub to have the materials. Very nice, but not a big surprise.

Hub went back and forth with Anderson for a long time but got nowhere. I wasn't involved and didn't even know about the problem. Finally he asked for my help. In for a dime, in for a dollar. (Not precisely applicable here since I never received that first dime for my work for Sue and her group.)

But Sue, Jimmy, and the others needed another round of treatment, and from my past experience, I was certain that the noble healers at M. D. Anderson would never voluntarily relinquish the material, nor would they ever re-treat the patients.

Back to Judge Hughes, but He's Not Happy to See Me
Well, here we go again. I drafted injunction papers and called the local press. But this case was different. Now I was representing Hub Vriesendorf, who was seeking the return of materials he brought to Anderson and which he intended to use on cancer patients, FDA permitting. This was arguably or technically a completely new case, especially as it had been almost two years since the patients' case had concluded. I probably should have filed a completely new lawsuit and accepted the lottery pick of the judge. But I wanted Judge Hughes since he was familiar with the situation, and he did right by us before. The only way I could guarantee getting Hughes was to file the new injunction papers under the case name and number of the first case. It might not work, but it was worth a try.

Reluctantly, the deputy clerk accepted the papers under the old case number even though the case was marked "closed." I also hand-delivered a courtesy copy of the papers to Judge Hughes's chambers to expedite his review of the motion. Within a day or two, I received a call from his office to appear for a conference. The advantage of having filed the papers under the old case number was that names and addresses of Anderson's attorneys were already in the court's record, so we didn't have to wait for the usual legal niceties like allowing them to carefully study the papers or submit a written response. Judge Hughes's office just called them up and told them to get right on down to the courthouse. That was my kind of justice!

I appeared at the conference and Anderson's lawyers were not happy. Judge Hughes had some words for me. He was pretty clear about the fact that the old case was closed and these papers should have been filed as a new lawsuit. Point taken.

But as I hoped, Hughes wasn't going to let a small technical defect get in the way of administering justice. And the Anderson lawyers were in a difficult position. Vriesendorf had brought these materials with him from Johns Hopkins. Anderson was not giving the medicine to patients. Their only interest in the drugs was possessory. They had the material, and they were not releasing it to Vriesendorf, probably as payback to him and his patients for causing Anderson so much grief with the FDA and for making the cancer institution look bad in the media. As could be expected, Anderson's nonargument did not impress Judge Hughes.

After politely listening, Judge Hughes looked Anderson's attorney dead in the eye, pointed his finger at him, and said that Anderson had twenty-four hours to turn it all over to Vriesendorf. As we were walking out of chambers, he also made it clear to me that I was not to file any more motions under this closed case.

By this time, I was a little smarter, so all I said to him was, "Yes, Sir," and, "Thank you very much, Your Honor," and I removed myself as quickly as possible from his chambers. Sue, Jimmy, and the rest would get their treatment again.

The next day I went to Anderson's in-house counsel's office and picked up all the materials. Somehow, Channel 11, the Houston CBS local affiliate, found out about the time and place of the transfer and appeared at Anderson's counsel's office and filmed the scene. The station was doing a story about Anderson's attempt to hold up the treatment yet again. They decided to run the story on TV sweeps week, and teasers of the story were aired dozens, if not hundreds, of times during the following weeks. It probably didn't do much for Anderson's reputation or fundraising efforts, but as far as I was concerned, they got what they deserved.

Vriesendorf picked up the material from me, and once the FDA pa[...] was filed, he began re-treating the patients. I didn't get paid for th[...] Nonetheless, it was one of the most rewarding experiences [...] attorney.

Postscript

From the beginning, everyone knew that antiferritin RIT was not a cure. It only temporarily blocked the progression of the disease. Despite Vriesendorf's efforts, the patients who fought their disease and then fought the government to obtain treatment eventually died. Jimmy Hagen died within six months after Vriesendorf moved to the Arlington Cancer Center. One by one, they all passed. Sue Spenceley was the last to pass. She was brave, determined, and a wonderful human being. I learned much from her.

Vriesendorf unfortunately continued to have professional problems interacting with colleagues and superiors. He left the Arlington Cancer Center after a year and had another job or two after that. While his dealings with patients were exceptional, he continued to have difficulties with the administrative staff.

Hub now practices *in locum tenens* on short stints around the country filling in for other radiologists. Recently, he has been flying back and forth to Beirut, Lebanon, to help out one of his former residents. That's classic Vriesendorf; whatever it takes and wherever it takes him to help patients.

Vriesendorf is a brilliant scientist, and a most compassionate healer, but he shares personality traits with many of the maverick doctors I have encountered: an intense anti-authoritarian streak coupled with an unwavering certainty of purpose and a sense of righteous indignation against all who oppose him. Maybe these are character flaws, but with these flaws—and perhaps only because of them—Hub Vriesendorf gave Sue, Jimmy, and others an invaluable gift: time. And I was glad to help him deliver that gift.

CHAPTER FIVE

Even World-Class Scientists Have Troubles

Lyme Disease, Allergies, and Why the Feds Decided to Study Alternative Remedies

Up until the late 1980s, the federal government largely ignored unconventional health remedies. Despite the billions of dollars the feds spent on health research at the National Institutes of Health (NIH) and all the money it doled out to researchers at institutions throughout the county, nothing was allocated to complementary and alternative health modalities. That changed primarily because of one case of Lyme disease and a guy who had allergies.

The Lyme disease patient was Berkley Bedell. Before going into politics, Berk founded a company that made a very popular line of fishing tackle, aptly named "Berkley Tackle." After he sold his company, Berk served in the U. S. Congress for several terms. However, he was forced to resign because he contracted what was first a mysterious disease, which was later diagnosed as Lyme disease.

Berk received many forms of conventional medical treatment. Since he was a U.S. Congressman, he had access to the country's best medical care. But nothing helped. Finally, probably more in desperation than in actual hope of relief, he started taking bovine colostrum produced by a Minnesota farmer.

Colostrum is a lactating female's first milk. It is extremely high in many immune-stimulating components and has been given to people with a wide variety of illnesses. Although you can't find it administered at any hospital or conventional medical center, it has a large following in the alternative health community. It's available in bulk powder or in capsules. For therapeutic doses, you have to go right to the cow's first milk. The product Berk received was produced specifically for Lyme disease by injecting the cow with killed Lyme disease germs prior to the birth of the calf.

Miracle of miracles, the colostrum worked, first alleviating his symptoms and then completely curing him. This little-understood product, which conventional doctors do not recognize as having any therapeutic benefit (other than for young calves), did what the best medical doctors treating a prince of the U.S. government could not do.

This event refocused Berk's life. He became a tireless advocate of the benefits of alternative health. When in Congress, he had served with fellow Iowa Congressman (later Senator) Tom Harkin. Harkin knew of Berk's illness and forced retirement, and he was amazed by the results. In part as a result of witnessing Berk's recovery, Tom Harkin became the main advocate in the Senate for alternative health.

Harkin was not some naive true believer (which is how his detractors like to portray him). He had his own experience with unconventional remedies. Harkin suffered from severe allergies. Despite the finest products of modern medicine, his only real relief came from bee pollen. So Harkin was a natural and willing ally for Berk.

The other main early ally for Berk was Senator Tom Daschle. Berk from the outside and primarily Harkin and Daschle on the inside became the core effort to get the U.S. government involved in unconventional medicine.

The first thing they did was request that the congressional Office of Technology Assessment (OTA) undertake a comprehensive study of alternative medicine and its actual and potential benefits. The OTA investigated and researched most of the popular alternative health remedies and several cancer doctors who were my clients.

After over a year of investigating, the OTA published a draft report. It invited public comments and decided to hold hearings inviting the subjects of the reports and others to testify before the authors of the report. I appeared on behalf of Burzynski (and was not in town to take my wife home after the birth of our daughter as a result of that appearance).

I don't think any of the presenters altered the OTA's position on anything. I also worked with the OTA in revising the report's chapter on insurance reimbursement issues. (I was then deep in the process of getting my PhD in insurance litigation at Aetna's school of hard knocks.)

The study concluded that most forms of unconventional or unapproved treatments do not have sufficient scientific evidence to conclude they are effective and that further research was needed to evaluate the claims made by the proponents of these treatments.

What a shocker! By definition, unconventional or unproven treatments are unproven. But sometimes the strategy and logic of government is different from ordinary logic.

Armed with the OTA's recommendations, the Toms (Harkin and Daschle) and their colleagues organized Congress to pass legislation creating the office of alternative medicine, which was put into the National Institutes of Health. The purpose of the office was to study alternative health remedies, which is what the OTA had in effect recommended.

Congress then began to fund this office, first in small amounts but by the end of the millennium, it was receiving upwards of thirty million dollars annually. (In recent years, the funding has increased dramatically and it is now called the National Center for Complementary and Alternative Medicine.)

The office is not without critics from both sides of the issue. In the early days, most of the money went to the major conventional medical institutions. These institutions didn't usually study the main unconventional cancer treatments but focused on adjuvant therapies like prayer for helping patients cope with conventional therapy. Many in the conventional medical establishment thought the entire office was a giant waste of taxpayer money.

In any event, but for Berk Bedell's Lyme disease and Tom Harkin's allergies, the office of alternative medicine would likely never have been created, and there would be no government support whatsoever for alternative medicine.

In addition to his work on the OTA and the Office of Alternative Medicine, Berk was also a good friend to maverick doctors and their patients. He testified in a few cases in which alternative doctors had been attacked by the government. And he drafted and shepherded into Congress legislation that would have allowed people the freedom to take a treatment even if it had not been approved by the FDA. It was called the *Access to Medical Treatment Act.* It was a good bill, though it had some flaws. Tom Harkin and Tom Daschle were big supporters of the bill in the Senate. Unfortunately, the bill never garnered widespread support in Congress.

Still, Berk Bedell is probably the most influential legislative advocate of unconventional medicine outside of government. I had only occasional telephone contact with him and then only in terms of passing information between him and Dr. Burzynski, so I was surprised and more than a little honored when he called me to ask for my help.

Even Former University Medical Professors Have Problems

Hugh Fudenberg, a friend of Berk's and a world-class immunologist, had gotten himself into trouble. It seems that he had written a few prescriptions for mild sleeping pills for someone else and then used the pills himself. Berk didn't think Fudenberg was being adequately represented because, with his lawyer's blessing, Fudenberg agreed to an indefinite suspension of his medical license. That seemed a severe penalty for a minor self-prescribing problem. I thought that either there was more to the story or Fudenberg had received poor legal advice. (It turned out that both were true.) Berk asked me to give Fudenberg a call and see what I could do for him.

I did some research on Fudenberg before I called. Berk was right. Fudenberg was a world-class immunologist. He was formerly a full professor at the University of California and later at the Medical College of South Carolina. He was highly regarded in the international scientific medical community. He had edited one of the classic textbooks in immunology, which had been used by a generation of medical students. This was a welcome change, as many of the folks I represented were considered pariahs or worse by the medical community. It sounded like an easy case.

Later that day, I talked to Dr. Fudenberg. After his second sentence, I changed my mind. Maybe it was my vast and varied experience, or perhaps it was my highly developed sense of intuition. But actually it was neither: Fudenberg's speech was horribly slurred. He spoke very fast, too fast for someone with a severe speech slur. He also kept flitting around from topic to topic. He was like a verbal strobe light. If it had not been the middle of the day and he was not a world-class immunologist, I would have thought that he was drunk.

The month before, a former nurse at his office claimed he was a Demerol addict and filed a criminal complaint against him. South Carolina was one of only a few states in which a private person could swear out a complaint and have someone arrested. Fudenberg had been arrested and signed an incriminating statement because he was told that if he didn't, he would be locked up in a detox center.

The South Carolina Board of Medical Examiners, which had been pursuing him on unrelated charges, heard about this criminal incident and threatened to immediately suspend his license. Fudenberg had two attorneys and with their "help" worked out a deal. Fudenberg had to surrender his license indefinitely until such time as the board decided that he could have it back.

This was the worst deal I had ever heard. There was no hearing, no findings, no due process, no mandatory review of the order, and worst of all, no time limit on the license surrender.

Fudenberg explained that the whole case arose because he wrote a few prescriptions for mild sleeping pills, and some legend drug, and used the drugs himself.[35] He did it because he was out of town when he ran out of his own medications and couldn't renew his prescriptions, which had been written

---

35   A legend drug is a drug that requires a prescription but is not a scheduled drug. Examples of legend drugs are Premarin, birth control pills, prescription antacids, and the like.

by his physician. When he got back to his hometown, he had his physician refill the prescriptions.

His story seemed straightforward. It was surely in violation of some South Carolina criminal statute and a board rule, but that story didn't justify the indefinite surrender of his license. From my conversation with him and his office manager, it looked like he could use my help.

He had several interrelated problems. He had criminal felony warrants outstanding on the fraudulent prescription case. This was the issue that caused his indefinite license suspension. There was no formal board complaint against him based on these criminal charges, but that would be coming.

He also had another licensing case pending about his treatment of patients over the previous ten years with an experimental drug. In that case, there had already been a day of hearings before three medical board members.

And lurking in the background was an equally potentially difficult problem: once they heard him speak, the board might challenge his competency to practice medicine on physical or mental grounds.

I reported back to Berk and told him that with his lawyers' help, Fudenberg was in a big mess. I wasn't sure there was anything I could do because the licensing case dealing with his use of experimental medicine had already started, and he had already agreed to surrender his license temporarily and indefinitely.

But Berk asked me to get involved, and I wasn't about to say no to him. Besides, I was a pilot, and by that time I had my own little single-engine airplane. I didn't need much of an excuse to take a nice 750-mile excursion from Houston to South Carolina. So I flew to Fudenberg's office in Spartanburg, South Carolina, and met with him.

Chronic Fatigue Syndrome

Fudenberg, it turns out, had a severe case of chronic fatigue syndrome, and that's what caused his slurred speech. However, when he concentrated and spoke slowly, his speech improved.

I had worked on a few cases involving chronic fatigue syndrome (CFS) or fibromyalgia, as it is sometimes called. CFS is a tough diagnosis. Many conventional doctors do not recognize it as a disease. When patients with this condition come to conventional doctors and their testing does not show an organic problem, the doctors often refer these patients to psychiatrists. Many patients find this insulting.

CFS presents itself over a short period of time. Normal, highly functioning people suddenly become very ill with strange symptoms. They have horrible muscle pain. They have a hard time sleeping but can't stay awake. They have cognitive issues, which are sometimes described as "brain fog." It is such a debilitating disease that many CFS sufferers cannot function normally; they cannot go out and are bedridden.

There is no conventional cure for CFS because conventional medicine doesn't offer a cure for something it doesn't recognize as a disease. As a result, the study and treatment of CFS has been relegated to unconventional medical practitioners. Interestingly, most of the researchers in the CFS field have the condition. Who else would spend their life in the study of a disease not recognized by conventional medicine, where the cause is unknown and a cure is unheard of? Being a researcher in this field is a dead end, career-wise, and treating the disease is frustrating since there is no cure. It's all about management of symptoms.[36]

So Fudenberg's need for mild sleeping pills was understandable. He also could not work more than four or five hours at a time. He had difficulty walking and used a cane. He also looked older than his sixty-seven years. But aside from that, he was normal—or normal for an absent-minded, disheveled, brilliant professor.

We talked at length about his life's project, finding immunological subsets of diseases most scientists did not recognize as immunologically related until Fudenberg came along.

---

36 Recently, the drug LYRICA has been approved for fibromyalgia, but there is still a debate in the medical community about whether the disease even exists. Some experts assert that two to four percent of Americans suffer from the disease.

Fudenberg and "Transfer Factor"

Up until 1991, Dr. Fudenberg was a professor at the Medical University of South Carolina (MUSC) and head of the department of immunology. He did extensive investigation with his medications, which he called "transfer factor." Transfer factor is a product that is usually distilled from the blood of a patient's relative. Fudenberg and other researchers believed the blood contained immunological factors beyond the standard lymphocytes, T cells, and macrophages. They believed there were many of these immunological factors, and sometimes a disease expressed itself because of the absence of the immune factor relating to that disease.

Fudenberg treated patients by first determining whether the disease was caused by a lack of an immunological factor, and if so, making a serum of the factor from a relative and then transferring it to the patient. He called the process and serum "transfer factor." He used it to treat a variety of illnesses including autism, Alzheimer's disease, retinitis pigmatosis, and chronic fatigue syndrome. The results he achieved were sometimes staggering.

The important point was that by virtue of the fact that these patients responded to an immunological-based treatment, it proved that certain subsets of these diseases were immunologically based. Fudenberg and other researchers wrote numerous articles about their findings and published them in some of the world's leading immunology journals. Fudenberg was at the forefront of this work. But to this day, some scientists are still skeptical of his claims. However, the data he established and published in peer-reviewed journals seems largely unassailable.

Among Fudenberg's many talents, keeping meticulous paperwork is not one of them. And since he was treating patients under FDA-approved clinical trials, good paperwork was what the FDA wanted and expected but did not get out of Fudenberg. There were lapses in meetings at his institutional review board, and he did not do all his annual reports on time. He acted like an absent-minded professor who only cared about treating his patients, which is a dangerous course of action in American medical science, especially when involved in FDA-approved clinical trials.

Probably because of all the paperwork violations, the FDA raised concerns about the safety of the treatment, even though there were no patient complaints. Ultimately, the FDA allowed him to keep treating patients.

Along the way, Fudenberg made some important enemies at MUSC because of his habit of curing patients and not doing all of his paperwork. Because of these problems, he was forced out of the university in 1991. He then opened a private practice in Spartanburg, South Carolina, treating a wide variety of patients but mostly patients with chronic fatigue syndrome.

At some point, the South Carolina medical board commenced an investigation regarding his practices at MUSC based on complaints from MUSC administrative staff who were unhappy with his work. The board eventually filed a complaint charging him with a variety of violations having to do with his treatment of patients at MUSC.

I briefly reviewed some of his publications, the books he wrote and edited, and the international scientific publications in which he was the principal editor. This guy might have chronic fatigue, but he was very prolific and had accomplished a great deal in his life.

I also met with Fudenberg's attorneys. They were decent guys and seemed like reasonably adept lawyers. They were advising Fudenberg to agree to a voluntary permanent surrender of his license. Their thinking was that the board could revoke his license on either the FDA counts or the drug charges, and it would be better for him to permanently surrender his license voluntarily and hope that it would not have any repercussions in the other states in which he was licensed.

I thought their advice was bad and their rationale wrong. They might be smart guys, but they didn't know anything about medical licensing law. If they had, they would have known that a voluntary surrender in the middle of a board case would be reported to the National Practitioner Data Bank, which keeps a record of things like that. New York, where Fudenberg also maintained a license, would undoubtedly find out about the license surrender (and Fudenberg would be under a legal obligation to tell the New York board), and New York would probably request the same result as in South Carolina.

Fudenberg's situation was difficult. He had multiple interrelated problems, but after spending many hours that day with him, it was clear that he was a brilliant scientist and an incredibly dedicated physician. He had spent his life trying to help incurable patients. His treatment approach was unique; he was helping people, curing illness that no one in this country could cure. It would be a tragedy if America lost this man because of these relatively minor problems. If I felt this way, I was sure I could make the board see this also and allow him to continue to practice medicine.

The substance of his transgression didn't bother me. Doctors, like the rest of us, make mistakes. Fudenberg had no criminal record, no history of drug abuse, and he was a world-class scientist. As far as the prescription-writing violation went, I felt it could be worked out as long as the prosecutor was reasonable. And they had every reason to be, given how much good Fudenberg had done in his life.

As to the FDA clinical trials, I'd figure something out when the time came. After I went back to Houston and read the transcript of the first day of the hearing and reviewed the charges, I felt I could defeat or at least greatly mitigate the impact of the charges.

So I called up Fudenberg and gave him my advice, which was that he should not agree to give up his license and that he should defend on all fronts. I outlined my arguments. His office manager was on the phone as well. My opinion was directly contrary to the opinion of his local lawyers. He decided to follow my advice and hired me to defend him. It turned out to be the right decision.

In multiple interrelated cases, it's usually best not to fight on all fronts at the same time, if at all possible. It's like throwing a number of balls up in the air; it's hard to catch them all at the same time. But if you can throw them up at different times and different heights, catching them all is much easier.

Delaying the Criminal Case
The first thing to do was delay the criminal case. If Fudenberg was found guilty on that one, it would have immediate and irreversible repercussions on his license. Prosecutors are normally busy, and they usually have more cases than

they can handle. The criminal complaint was filed by Fudenberg's former nurse, a drug addict, who had her own problems. We did our own investigation about her and shared the information with the prosecutor. The prosecutor then did his own investigation and eventually she was indicted. But all this was taking time, which gave me time to work on the prosecutor about Fudenberg's stellar career.

There was another reason to delay the criminal case. The attorney for the medical board kept threatening to add the drug charges in the licensing case. But since the criminal action had not been resolved, nor was there even an indictment, there wasn't much the board could do. The board attorney did not want to interfere with the criminal case. Also, a conviction in the criminal case would have made a slam-dunk case for the board attorney, and he wouldn't have to do any work. He was happy to let the criminal prosecutor do the work for him.

Every Expert Has His Area of Expertise

So the first thing we did was notify the board that we were ready to continue the hearing on the FDA charges. The board prosecutor had charged Fudenberg with a variety of misconduct relating to Fudenberg's treating patients with transfer factor. All of the patients were treated when he was at MUSC and all of the patients were treated under an FDA-approved IND.

We had our second hearing in May 1995. For this hearing, we brought in a few doctors, including Byron Hyde, who was the foremost expert on chronic fatigue syndrome, having edited the most widely-cited text on the subject.

The board's expert agreed to be available by telephone conference. My idea was pretty straightforward. Since the board's expert was an allergist and not a classical immunologist (which are two completely different fields), I thought that I could get him to admit that he was not competent to treat any of the patients Fudenberg treated and who were the subject of the board's action. I also guessed that he didn't know much about transfer factor or chronic fatigue syndrome.

Every once in a while, a litigator examines a witness and things just go right. This was one of these cases. I did some research about the expert. He was not only reputable but he was also a highly skilled and well-published expert and scientist. The problem was he just wasn't an expert in the field on which he was being called to testify by the board.

I was extremely deferential toward him. I wanted the board to appreciate that he was an accomplished physician and scientist. He was perhaps the world's leading expert on slime mold and aspergillus infections. I asked him many questions about these topics. He spoke with a confidence and authority about these subjects, and I am sure that he greatly impressed the board with his knowledge. And he was probably not unhappy with me for asking him so many questions about his areas of expertise.

However, when we got to the diseases that were the subject matter of the board proceeding, he frankly admitted that he knew little about any of them, and whatever he knew was based on his recent cursory review of an allergy textbook describing these diseases. He readily admitted that he was not qualified to treat any of the patients listed in the complaint and agreed with me that it would have been virtually malpractice for him to give any medical opinion about the patients who were the subject of the board hearing. I think he didn't have a problem saying any of that because he had already established his expertise in his own field. By the end of the cross-examination, the board members didn't understand why the prosecutor had called this person as an expert in this case.

Another part of the complaint was that Fudenberg allegedly failed to obtain the informed consent of his patients. Sometimes the board prosecutors don't do their homework. In this case, the very consent forms that supposedly Dr. Fudenberg did not obtain were actually buried deep in the prosecutor's exhibit books. The disciplinary panel did not seem happy about this charge.

Finally, we had Dr. Fudenberg and our expert testify. Dr. Fudenberg's big problem was that he talked too much. That and his chronic fatigue problem with his slurred speech made Fudenberg perhaps the worst witness for our case. However, it was clear, based on his publications, accomplishments, and intellect, that he was as close to a genius as any of the people in the room would likely meet in person in their lifetime.

The three board members seemed sympathetic to him. The case came down to the difference between approved versus unapproved medicine. All the diseases Fudenberg had treated in this proceeding were incurable. He had treated people under federal Food and Drug Administration INDs. I think the board was at a loss to see why the prosecution felt Fudenberg did anything wrong.

In answer to the prosecution's claim that Fudenberg was experimenting on people, one board member said, "How else are you supposed to find out whether a treatment works on people?" It was a good day for a New York Jewish lawyer working in Texas, appearing in front of the South Carolina Board of Medical Examiners.

A month later, we received the proposal for the decision. The board recommended the dismissal of all charges against Fudenberg.

So far so good. We still had the criminal charges to tend to, as well as the possible board charges on the self-prescriptions and the small fact that Fudenberg was still not able to practice medicine because he had voluntarily surrendered his license.

It's Always Better to Settle, but If You Can't, You Can't

On the criminal front, the prosecutor, Max Cauthen, was a decent guy. The case investigator was tougher and wanted felony pleas to all three charges. He also wanted the surrender of Fudenberg's license. That was not going to happen.

For almost a year, I kept working on Max, sending him information about Fudenberg, arguing that Fudenberg had done a great service to humanity in his research. That he deserved better than to be tossed out of practice because of the fact that he wrote some prescription for himself on two occasions and, unbeknownst to him, he had a Demerol addict working for him.

The problem with any deal with the prosecution was that the results would be immediately forwarded to the medical board, which in turn could take action based on the criminal deal. So I decided to try to resolve the medical board problem relating to the prescription issue before finishing the criminal case.

However, the board attorney was taking a very tough position. He wanted Fudenberg's license revoked. I didn't think that was justified in this case, so I took a chance. We entered into a stipulation about the facts underlying the self-prescription matter, and we agreed that Fudenberg's conduct warranted some sanction by the medical board. The prosecutor would ask for license revocation. We would ask for a lesser sanction. This is not the way things are normally done. Typically, unless there is a deal as to the disposition or sanction, a doctor should not agree to anything.

But I didn't want a hearing on the charges. Fudenberg's former nurse, the Demerol addict, was waiting to testify against him at the medical board hearing. As she was herself facing criminal charges, initiated by us, she had some ill will against him. Who knew what she would say. So as not to take that chance, we stipulated to the facts about what he did, thereby taking the issue out of the case. The only topic of the hearing would be the sanction.

So I hopped into my trusty plane (a Bellanca Turbo Viking, for the pilots out there) and flew to South Carolina for the hearing before the full board on the self-prescribing charges. We caught a break at the hearing. The board's vice president told everyone at the hearing that his wife had chronic fatigue syndrome. She also had difficulties in her job, but she was functional when on medications, including mild sleeping pills. I took this as a very good omen. (Here, as always, it's better to be lucky than good.)

In general, in court I tell the truth and make a reasonable request. On behalf of Fudenberg, I admitted that what he did was wrong and that there should be some sanction, a period of probation and monitoring. I argued that revocation or even an active suspension was not warranted, so long as a doctor was willing to certify that Fudenberg was fit to practice.

The prosecutor took a harsh view and vehemently argued that only license revocation was a sufficient punishment. My impression was that the board was not buying the prosecutor's argument. After all, this was a world-class scientist who had an illness (shared by the board vice president's wife). Even though the prosecutor was a good ol' South Carolina boy and spoke with the right twang, he seemed to be missing the target. We were humble (which was not hard given all the circumstances of the case) and tried to tap into the board members' sense of justice and respect.

A month later, we got our decision. It basically adopted my recommended sanction. Fudenberg was then seen by a physician and got a clean bill of health. He agreed to be monitored, paid a small fine, and got his license back.

We eventually settled the criminal case on an adjournment in contemplation of dismissal. This is a common disposition used around the country for first-time offenders. The case gets adjourned for six months to a year, and as long as the defendant stays out of trouble, the case is dismissed. Fudenberg went on probation and had no subsequent problems, so the criminal case was dismissed.

Of all the medical boards that I have ever appeared before, the South Carolina Board of Medical Examiners showed the most compassion and understanding. Maybe it was because Fudenberg was such an accomplished physician and researcher. Many of my other clients are considered mavericks or worse. If so, then it is surely much easier representing a doctor before a medical board who is one of their own.

Postscript

I had not heard from Hugh for over ten years when out of the blue, he recently called me. He had some more trouble with the board. I didn't get the whole story, but on the advice of legal counsel, he voluntarily surrendered his medical license. Now he wants to practice medicine again, but the board won't give him his license back. Here we go again!

CHAPTER SIX

New Jersey Chiropractors Fight Back

Chiropractors are like the Rodney Dangerfield of the health care field; they get no respect. Some in the medical establishment—and a portion of the general population—view chiropractic as unproven, if not dangerous.[37]

It All Starts with One Patient

Chiropractic started in the United States in the late nineteenth century, and the entire system originated from the treatment of one person, Harvey Lillard. He was born with normal hearing but became progressively deaf as the result of a traumatic event. He came into contact with D. D. Palmer. Palmer palpated Lillard's spine and noticed an abnormality. He applied directed force and the lump disappeared. Almost by magic, Lillard's hearing returned, and so chiropractic was born. Based on that initial treatment success, D. D., his son

---

37   The allusion to Rodney may even be more accurate since in reality, he was a highly respected and successful comedian. Chiropractic is now the second largest health care profession in the world and the largest nonsurgical drugless profession. Many hospitals have chiropractors on staff and more and more occupational medicine sources are recognizing the value of chiropractic for low back pain that does not involve injury to the disc or spinal cord.

B. J. Palmer, and then B. J.'s son David developed the philosophy and practice of chiropractic.

Over a relatively few decades, the chiropractic movement spread throughout the country. During the early to the middle part of the twentieth century, chiropractors increased their numbers and organized. But the single most important thing they did was to make friends with the state legislatures. That paid off big time. By the1970s, chiropractors were licensed and had their own little practice niche in every state.

Despite licensure, chiropractors still did not get much respect from the orthodox medical establishment, but chiropractors were smart and tough, and they did not like being bad-mouthed by the medical establishment.

So in the 1970s, the main chiropractic professional association filed a massive class-action lawsuit against the medical establishment claiming that the AMA (American Medical Association) was guilty of an antitrust conspiracy against them. And they were right. Under the AMA's ethical guidelines, it was unethical for a medical doctor to refer a patient to a chiropractor. There was also a secret AMA committee that had targeted chiropractic for elimination.

After many years and millions of dollars, the chiropractors were vindicated in court. A Chicago federal district court judge agreed with them. The lawsuit didn't solve all of their problems, but it did show the medical establishment that chiropractors wouldn't be pushed around.

In essence, chiropractors believe that many medical conditions are caused by misalignments of the spine, which chiropractors call "vertebral subluxations." The basic chiropractic treatment technique is the chiropractic "adjustment," which is the manipulation or application of sudden force to the vertebrae. All practicing chiropractors adjust patients.

The "Straights" Versus the "Mixers"

Over time, chiropractic evolved into two major philosophical camps. The "straights" are the purists and limit their therapy to chiropractic adjustments. Straight chiropractors treat all kinds of lifestyle back injuries and auto accident victims and work-related injuries. The straights will normally only take a few x-rays and then just do chiropractic adjustments to correct the subluxations.[38]

The large majority of chiropractors and most of the chiropractic colleges are "mixers." (Most chiropractors hate this term, but I use it because it is descriptive.) Although the mixers do adjustments, they also use a wide variety of modern techniques and modalities such as hot and cold packs, traction, directed exercise, and other physical therapy modalities.

In the last few years, many mixers have added another big component to their practice: nutritional counseling. There is no conceptual connection between subluxations of the spine and nutrition, but philosophically, chiropractors have a "drugless" approach to healing. And most chiropractors are oriented toward a healthy lifestyle, so the move into nutrition counseling is understandable.[39]

The mixers also use a much broader array of testing, whereas the straights and super-straights only use x-rays. This is where a few chiropractors get into trouble. Many in the medical (and chiropractic) establishment argue that repeatedly using expensive testing like MRIs and nerve conduction tests on a patient for relatively mild back issues is unnecessary and is just a way to extract extra money from insurance companies.

There may be some truth to that. Almost all chiropractors see cash patients (i.e., patients who are not covered by any kind of insurance and pay cash). For the chiropractors who use expensive tests, it is rare that cash patients will get the full array of testing. These chiropractors make analogies like there is Cadillac care and there is Ford Fiesta care. Maybe so, but the people with Ford Fiesta care seem to get better as fast as people who have

---

38   Another group is the "super-straights" who will not treat any medical condition or physical symptom. Super-straights only correct vertebral subluxations, whether or not the subluxation is associated with a physical condition like pain. They view chiropractic as well-ness care. Most chiropractors consider them to be on the fringe. The super-straights seem to have a belief system similar to the Chinese concept of chi or energy, which uses acupuncture and acupressure to balance the energy flows. Like the other groups, the super-straights have a passionate following of chiropractors and patients.

39   This can be called "scope of practice creep," when a profession expands its scope of practice into other health care areas. There are far worse offenders than the chiropractors. (See Chapter 8, "Food Fights: Who Should Control the Nutrition Field?," to see how the dietitians have attempted to take over the entire nutrition field.)

their insurance companies pay for Cadillac care.

However, it is a complicated issue because insurance companies often require objective evidence in the form of testing to support further chiropractic care. My view is that beyond whatever initial testing is necessary to rule out a serious condition, repeated expensive tests like MRIs and nerve conduction should only be performed if the results will likely change the treatment, or if required by an insurance company.

Even Homer Simpson Goes to a Chiropractor

The medical establishment has two big problems with chiropractic. First, it does not think there is any hard science behind the subluxation theory as the cause of disease. Maybe not, but there are hundreds of articles in the best sense of "evidence-based medicine" and "controlled trials" that demonstrate the effectiveness of chiropractic on soft tissue (e.g., muscle and ligament) injury. In my opinion, chiropractic has much more science and better results than a wide range of medical interventions like the laminectomies and fusions performed by back surgeons.[40] There is a double standard here, because the majority of medical therapeutics are not supported by controlled clinical trials which are the gold standard of medical science. (See Chapter 8 for more about this.)

But the bigger complaint the medical and especially the insurance establishment has against chiropractors is over treatment. This idea has even made it into pop culture. There is an episode of *The Simpsons* where Homer goes to a chiropractor who tells Homer he has to come for treatment three times a week for the rest of his life. Over the years, the insurance industry and the federal government have come up with a variety of approaches to stop the alleged over treatment of patients by chiropractors.

Early on, many insurance companies put limitations on the number of chiropractic visits they would pay for. But remember, the chiropractors are

---

40   See, for example, Fritzell P, Olle Hägg, Wessberg P, Nordwall A, *SPINE* 2001; 26:2521–2532, which shows that surgical back fusions actually worsen some conditions over time and are less effective than chiropractic in conjunction with other nonsurgical modes of intervention.

tough and do not just roll over and take it. In response, the chiropractors organized efforts in many states to have what they called an "insurance equality law" passed. Under the law, a chiropractor was allowed to provide as much treatment as any other practitioner, like a rehab doctor or physical therapist.

But that was not a completely effective solution. A state law cannot trump or limit Medicare, which is a federal program. Also, many people have health care insurance from their employer. Employment health care plans are governed by federal *ERISA* law. Here as well, a state chiropractic insurance equality law would have no effect on an *ERISA* health plan limitation on chiropractic coverage.

Chiropractors Find a Niche or Two

Because Medicare and many private health insurance plans have put severe limitations on the amount of chiropractic treatment patients can receive, many chiropractors have moved into other areas of health care, most notably injuries from auto accidents and work-related injuries, which are usually covered by some form of state-run workers' compensation system.

In the auto accident field, chiropractors often get referrals from attorneys who represent the auto accident victims. Attorneys take these auto accident cases on a contingency fee basis. Historically, the value of an auto accident case is directly related to the amount of injuries suffered by the victim. The assumption was that the greater the injuries, the more medical care was needed. So, medical care, and in particular the medical bills, were originally considered a good proxy for the value of a case. According to the insurance companies, this led doctors, chiropractors, and attorneys to collude to provide unnecessary care to auto accident victims in order to extract more money from the poor and helpless automobile insurance companies. So the insurance companies in some states had laws or regulations passed that limited the amount of chiropractic care for auto accident cases. And on and on it goes.

Sometimes the insurance industry and the states are overzealous in trying to stop the fraud and over treatment. And when they are the chiropractors aggressively fight back, like they did in New Jersey in the mid-1990s.

Heil Florio!

A chiropractor by the name of Mike Harvey came up to me after one of my seminar lectures. Mike was short, with a big gut and a hawk-like nose. He was articulate, intense, and pugnacious. There was something odd about him, an intensity and nervousness that seemed strange and abnormal.

Mike was the head of an advocacy organization called the Chiropractic Alliance of New Jersey (CANJ). Through this organization, Mike tried to right the wrongs inflicted on chiropractors by the government. He also sporadically published a newspaper called the *Chiropractic Lampoon*. He had a copy of a recent edition and it got my attention.

It had a picture of then New Jersey Governor Jim Florio with an inked-in half-mustache, superimposed onto a body dressed in a Nazi uniform, making him look like Hitler's first cousin. The caption read "Heil Florio!" It was funny but wacko.

Mike had heard about my work for Dr. Burzynski and told me that New Jersey needed a fighter like me to help beat off the Nazis.

I thanked him and we parted, never thinking I would ever hear from him again and frankly not really wanting to because I thought he was nuts. But a few weeks later, he called me and we started talking about the problems facing chiropractors in New Jersey.

Throughout the next few months, I continued to be in contact with him. It turned out he was very thoughtful, even if he was way out there. The other guy involved in the group was Gary Pomeroy. Gary had a business which provided equipment for chiropractors. I thought Gary was smart, had boundless enthusiasm, and he was completely earthbound, unlike Mike Harvey.

They Can't Really Be Doing That

During my conversations with Mike and Gary, they mentioned that a number of New Jersey chiropractors had received letters from the fraud division of the New Jersey department of insurance demanding money. That was not unusual. The government always seems to be requesting money from people for one reason or another. But the New Jersey government seemed to have taken this normal government activity to a higher and more ominous level.

In these letters, fraud division investigators accused the doctor of committing insurance fraud. But they did not say what the fraud was, nor did they identify the patient or defrauded insurance company. The letters just demanded a payment of five thousand dollars (or more) and stated that if the chiropractor made the payment, the fraudulent conduct would not be reported to the New Jersey Board of Chiropractic Examiners.

I also heard that when the chiropractors would call up and ask for information about their alleged fraud, the fraud investigators wouldn't tell them. They just demanded payment. Frankly, I thought they were exaggerating. No government agency would do that, let alone put it in writing.

I was wrong. I received a copy of one of the letters, and that is exactly what they were saying: Pay and we will go away; don't pay and you will have trouble.

It didn't make any sense. There had to be some reasonable explanation. I asked Mike and his supporters to have as many of the doctors as they could find contact me. I wanted to hear their stories firsthand.

I spoke to several dozen chiropractors and other health practitioners over the course of the next few weeks. I learned that the investigators would threaten the doctors that unless the fine was paid, the matter would be turned over to the attorney general's office for possible criminal prosecution. I also heard that fraud investigators would tell them that if the money was not paid, the investigator would obtain patient names and conduct a more extensive investigation. Once an investigation started, word would leak out to the local newspapers about the "insurance fraud investigation." The investigators said it was not unusual for a doctor's reputation to be harmed and their practice to be severely affected once a full investigation was commenced. On the other hand, they said the matter could be easily and quietly resolved by the payment of a fine.

You don't have to be a lawyer to know that this sounds like extortion. The more I looked into it, the more I heard the same story from many chiropractors from all over New Jersey. Most of the targets of these fraud investigations didn't know each other. So when you hear the same basic fact pattern from dozens of different, unrelated sources, it starts to have the ring of truth.

The practitioners fell into two categories. Most had paid the fines. From what I could tell from telephone interviews, there were no cases of overt fraud, but there were a few cases of insurance gamesmanship, like what happens when your doctor writes a diagnosis on a medical visit so that it will be a covered visit. Most of the people who paid, however, did not engage in anything close to insurance fraud. Rather, the cases appeared to be more like clerical errors or interpretation issues concerning whether one code or another is more appropriate. This didn't seem like insurance fraud and I didn't think the fraud division had any business demanding money from these people.

Other practitioners, however, refused to sign the consent agreements or pay the fine. Now here was the strange thing, none of these practitioners had been prosecuted criminally or sued civilly for insurance fraud. Not a single one of them. All of them had been accused of fraud by the fraud division. Most had received follow-up calls from the fraud investigators making the usual threats. But I did not find a single case where any further action was taken after the practitioner said they were not paying. How could that be?

Part of the answer is that the fraud division didn't have the authority under the statute to criminally prosecute or sue anyone. That was the job of the New Jersey attorney general's office. But still, if these practitioners had really committed insurance fraud, why didn't the attorney general's office go after them? The answer was obvious. The attorney general's office didn't pursue these cases because there was nothing to pursue; they did not involve insurance fraud.

If the attorney general was not pursuing these cases, obviously the fraud division knew it. That might explain the heavy-handed tactics they were using. They knew this was their only shot. If they couldn't extract money out of the practitioners, no further action would be taken. Great, these fraud investigators were not only running an extortion scheme, but it was also a scam, or so it seemed to me.

So I had this theory about the facts of the case, but there were still many assumptions. It was like trying to guess that an animal is an elephant by touching his back leg and left ear. You can have a pretty good idea of what you are dealing with, but you can't know for sure until you spend some quality time with its trunk. But in this type of litigation, you rarely get to touch the trunk until you file a lawsuit and do discovery.

This was a tough situation. On the one hand, what these investigators were doing was wrong, if not criminal. On the other hand, New Jersey has the highest insurance rates in the country. In the late 1980s, New Jersey passed one of the most far-reaching insurance reform bills in the country. It was this reform bill that created the fraud division in the department of insurance, and the same bill specifically provided that the fraud division could settle cases for monetary fines instead of filing criminal or civil lawsuits.

How do you sue state government employees for following a state statute? And what about suing on behalf of chiropractors who do not have the best reputation because they are viewed by some as on the fringe of health care and are also sometimes blamed for driving up insurance costs?

New Jersey was the first state to try this approach to insurance fraud, and I could not find any precedent for suing government employees for threatening to enforce a statute, even if they used strong-arm tactics. It looked like we would have to make it up as we went along.

We Sue the Bastards and Give Them a Taste of Their Own Medicine
In law and in life, half measures usually get you nothing. We filed a federal racketeering action against the head of the fraud division, some of the investigators, and their supervisors. We also sued for civil rights violations.

The federal racketeering statute (the *Racketeer Influenced and Corrupt Organization Act* or "*RICO*") was enacted in order to give the federal government a strong weapon against organized crime. It made it illegal for any group to operate a business or enterprise that violated some specified federal statutes or state laws (called "predicate acts"). Among the many criminal laws that can be predicate acts are mail and wire fraud, which is any scheme to defraud that uses the U.S. mail or a telephone.

Federal or state extortion can also be predicate acts. So the complaint alleged that the fraud investigators were all committing extortion. Under New Jersey law, extortion is the taking of property by threat, or the threat of taking property without justification, including the threat of criminal prosecution.

It sounded like that was exactly what these officials were doing. Lawyers are often employed to collect money from people. However, every lawyer knows that it is unethical and improper for an attorney to threaten someone with criminal prosecution to obtain a monetary debt. That precept is embodied in the law of extortion in every state.

The *RICO* statute is not only used by federal prosecutors in criminal cases, but it is also available to civil litigants. This has caused a great deal of litigation and confusion in the federal courts. Lawyers have tried to use *RICO* for standard business disputes, because it sounds impressive to clients and also because the statute provides for treble damages and attorneys fees, which are usually not recoverable in a civil lawsuit.

The lower federal courts have attempted to stop the proliferation of civil *RICO* cases. However, the U.S. Supreme Court has repeatedly rejected these attempts to limit *RICO*. The result is that the lower federal courts continue to look very suspiciously at civil *RICO* claims filed by private litigants. No matter how many times the Supreme Court tries to stop this, the lower courts continue to come up with a variety of tactics to dissuade lawyers from using the statute in civil litigation.

I had recent experience with *RICO* in my battles for Burzynski and even made some law on the subject, so I was not intimidated by all the judicial attempts to restrict the statute. Moreover, what the investigators were doing smelled bad and seemed like extortion, which is what *RICO* was enacted to redress. The only problem was that we were accusing a state administrative agency of engaging in racketeering activity by collecting fines pursuant to a state statute. Oh well, we'd worry about that later.

To file a lawsuit, you need a plaintiff. Typically, a plaintiff is a person who is injured by the actions complained of by the defendant. Although every chiropractor I contacted was outraged and encouraged me to file the lawsuit, none of them would agree to be a plaintiff. They were all afraid of retaliation by the fraud division. That was understandable. The investigators were already threatening them. What would they do after we filed suit? Since this was a civil lawsuit and I was a private attorney, there was no witness protection or immunity. The chiropractors who paid the fines even though they did not commit insurance fraud did so for peace of mind. Being a plaintiff in this kind of lawsuit would just paint a target on their backs, and none were enthusiastic.

Besides, almost no one thought one private attorney from Texas could successfully take on the state of New Jersey. So their reluctance to formally join the lawsuit was understandable.

Because we had no other choice, Mike and Gary's organization, Chiropractic Alliance of New Jersey, became the plaintiff. This presented additional problems, since the organization itself had not been injured.

In cases like this, publicity is an important weapon, so the complaint was written like a mafia shakedown story. The filing of the action received widespread state media coverage.

After you file a lawsuit, there is nothing to do but wait until the other side files an answer. After a few extensions, the state finally answered.

The lead attorney for the defendants was Herb Stern. At the time (mid-1990s), Herb was the most prominent attorney in New Jersey. He was formerly the U.S. attorney for New Jersey, and then he was a federal district court judge. Herb had received quite a bit of publicity himself as a trial judge in a rape case involving American soldiers in Berlin, Germany. They eventually made a movie about the case called *Judgment in Berlin,* and Martin Sheen (of *West Wing* fame) played Herb. Herb was also a prominent lecturer and is regarded as one of the best trial advocates in the country.

I later learned that some of the judges and practitioners in New Jersey didn't like him and thought he was imperious and supercilious—though the description I heard was more anatomical in nature. He also had a reputation for mistreating federal magistrates when he had been a judge. Nonetheless, he was a superlative trial advocate.

Eventually, Stern's firm filed papers attempting to dismiss the case for a variety of reasons. First, they argued that the federal court should "abstain" and dismiss the case because it was a matter of state law, and the federal court shouldn't get involved.

The abstention doctrine is well recognized in federal law. Federal courts try to avoid dealing with state law matters unless there is some extreme reason to do so, like some patent illegality or unconstitutionality of the law. There are various fact patterns in which the doctrine is raised. But here it was a reasonable argument since the state of New Jersey had a strong interest in protecting against insurance fraud, and federal courts are reluctant to interfere with a state's attempts to fix a problem like high insurance costs.

The fraud division's lawyers also challenged the standing of the Chiropractic Alliance primarily on the grounds that it was not injured, but rather its members were supposedly injured. This wasn't a bad argument either. Ultimately, because of this argument, we had to give up our damage claim. The state asserted two other technical legal defenses that were not persuasive.

The Judge Lets Us Proceed, So Maybe We're Not So Crazy After All

We submitted opposition papers. The judge, Stanley Brotman, called the case for oral argument. Judge Brotman was on senior status, which means he was over sixty-five and was technically retired and could choose his own cases. He had been on the bench for a long time and was extremely well regarded. His opinions were very thoughtful, often cited, and rarely reversed. Having Brotman assigned to the case was a big advantage. It would take a very smart and independent judge to allow us to get to a jury on our claim that New Jersey state government employees were guilty of racketeering. Judge Brotman had previously written opinions that exhibited a great deal of independence in the face of large, commercial plaintiffs as well as the state government. So at least we would get a fair shake.

Oral argument was the first time that I met Herb Stern. He was short, sixty-ish, and very dapper. He looked like an older version of a Ken doll. But one characteristic stood out beyond all others—how impressed he was with himself. He walked in the courtroom like he owned it, waving and saying hello to the clerks and the bailiffs as if he had just left the bench. This guy really looked like the big-time lawyer he was.

Since it was the defendants' motion, Herb got to speak first. He was mesmerizing. His voice, his tone, and his command of the English language were simply breathtaking. It was like poetry in motion. He was a magnificent orator, probably the best I have ever heard in my life. It was actually a pleasurable experience listening to him speak. But after being spellbound (like I'm sure everyone else in the courtroom was), I started to get nervous. How was I going to respond to this guy?

But when I started to filter out the melodious voice, the cadence, the eloquent language, and the grand theatrical gestures and just focused on the substantive points, I realized that he wasn't saying too much. He spoke in vague generalities about the role of the federal courts and how they should operate. Then I realized that once you got past the oratory, he didn't even seem overly prepared. At one point, the judge asked him about a recent case that was cited in his own brief, and after some more oratory, he admitted he hadn't read it. No matter how brilliant or famous or what a great orator you are, if you don't know the facts and the law, none of the other stuff matters. Herb was wonderful to listen to, but ultimately he didn't help the judge decide the case in his clients' favor.

Then it was my turn. I was told that I was very good and much different. No one was going to accuse me of great oratory, but I knew the facts and law, and I gave simple and direct answers to the judge's hard questions or so I hoped. I had an easier time than Herb did. I researched everything myself, and I wrote every word of the brief. Writing the brief is when the lawyer really gets to know the case. It was my lawsuit, so I had spent much time thinking about it, and because of that, I sounded like I knew what I was talking about.

Judge Brotman seemed intrigued by the lawsuit, even though it was unusual. My take on it was that he was not inclined to dismiss the case but wanted to see what facts I could develop on discovery. He was, however, concerned with the standing issue. The judge seemed to accept the argument propounded in Stern's brief that the Chiropractic Alliance might not be a proper party. An association could sue on behalf of its members but only if it was seeking general relief as opposed to individual relief for each particular member. The theory is that an association cannot sue for damages sustained by its individual members.

Stern's strategy on this point was effective because it put us in a difficult position. According to the judge, we would have to present individuals who could make specific claims for damages if we were really seeking damages. Unfortunately, at that time we had no individual plaintiffs. The only alternative was to jettison the damage claims. Judge Brotman skillfully pressed me on this point at oral argument. He was also worried about turning his federal court into a refund processing center, which would also have to adjudicate the merits of every investigation of every doctor who paid money and sought it back.

I felt we could close the deal and have him keep the case if I abandoned this messy, but potentially valuable, part of the case. So I conceded on oral argument that what we were really seeking was to stop these illegal practices. This turned out to be a necessary but costly admission.

Within a few months, Judge Brotman issued a written decision. Miracle of miracles, we had won the motion.[41] The judge did not dismiss the case as requested by the defendants. This was a big victory. It was risky to sue state employees for racketeering for basically doing their job, but at least the federal court decision suggested that the case was not completely without merit. It was a good start.

Slogging through Discovery While the Magistrate Thinks We're Frivolous

After preliminary motions are decided, civil lawsuits go through the discovery phase, which is often the longest, most extensive, and most expensive part of a lawsuit. During discovery, each side gets to find out about the facts behind the other side's case or defense. This is done through a variety of procedures but mostly through depositions of the fact witnesses.

A deposition is where witnesses give testimony under oath before a court reporter. Depositions lock in testimony. Any variance from deposition testimony is usually grounds for impeachment by the adversary attorney during trial. We did depositions of the fraud investigators and their supervisors for many months. The defendants deposed Mike Harvey, Gary Pomeroy, and many of the victims of the scheme, namely the chiropractors who paid the fines.

After we won the motion before Judge Brotman, it became easier to find chiropractors to come forward, at least in agreeing to be listed as witness/ victims. Maybe ten doctors came forward. Our thinking was that if they weren't actually plaintiffs, they might not be subject to retaliation. We also felt

---

41   The decision is *Chiropractic Alliance of New Jersey v. Parisi*, 854 F. Supp. 299 (D. N.J. 1994).

that anyone who came forward as a victim would have a practical immunity from further harassment. We didn't think that the fraud division would harass someone who had surfaced as a victim of harassment in a lawsuit against them for extortion and harassment. We were right; none of the doctors who came forward were ever bothered by the fraud division.

In most federal civil lawsuits, judicial supervision is divided between a district court judge and federal magistrate judge. In most districts, every two district judges have a magistrate assigned to assist them. The purpose of magistrates in civil cases is to oversee the discovery process and resolve any discovery disputes that arise. On the criminal side, the magistrate judge primarily hears bail applications and related proceedings.

The magistrate in our case was Joel Rosen. Joel was a former state attorney general, which caused me concern since we were going against a state agency. I was even more nervous after the first telephone conference with Rosen, which preceded Judge Brotman's decision denying the state's motion to dismiss. Three times during that call, Rosen said that the lawsuit was frivolous and that the plaintiff and its attorney should be sanctioned—that is to be forced to pay the defendants for filing the lawsuit. This was not a good start.

For the next year, during subsequent conferences, Rosen repeatedly reiterated that he thought this was a frivolous case and that we should be sanctioned. But we were committed to the case, and we were not going to back down, not even in the face of direct threats by a federal magistrate.

What bothered Rosen was that the New Jersey statute specifically permitted the fraud division to obtain (or as I would phrase it, "extract") civil fines from health practitioners without making a referral for criminal prosecution. Rosen's problem was that how could it be improper, let alone a racketeering activity, for fraud investigators to do what the statute said they were allowed to do.

The fact that the investigators advised the practitioners they could be prosecuted under a criminal statute was, according to Rosen, perfectly legitimate. Rosen also thought it was fair to tell them they would not be prosecuted if they paid the fine. Sometimes no matter how hard you try, you just can't convince a judge of your position. Fortunately, Rosen was only the magistrate and not the trial judge, and, initially, there wasn't much for Rosen to do because discovery went smoothly.

The Sergeant Shultz Defense: "I Know Nothing; I See Nothing"

I spent many days deposing the defendants. They all took the party line: none of them had ever threatened anyone with criminal prosecution because that would be wrong (even if Rosen thought it was proper). They all denied there were any quotas for fines. None of them personally threatened any health practitioner or knew of anyone who made such threats. Not one had ever threatened a doctor with public exposure or financial ruin. And none of them had ever heard of such a thing happening at the fraud division.

To listen to them, they were just a bunch of happy, friendly and helpful guys trying to stamp out insurance fraud in the state of New Jersey. But I had them. For each investigator who testified under oath that he never threatened anyone with anything, I had at least two victims to testify that the threats were made. (I only sued the investigators for whom I had witnesses who would testify about the tactics.)

Lou Parisi: The Character in Chief

Most of the investigators in the department were former state troopers, probably because Lou Parisi, the head of the department, was himself a former state trooper. Lou became head of the department one year after its creation. When he started, there were only two or three investigators, but after a few years under his direction, there were over 120 investigators. During the years he headed the fraud division, it collected millions of dollars from consent agreements it coerced people into signing.

The agency's finances were unusual. At the end of the year, the fraud division's expenses would be added up and all of the auto insurance companies that did business in the state of New Jersey would be sent a pro-rata bill based on their volume of business. The money the fraud division collected would indirectly go to the same insurance companies, via paying down the enormous debt the state of New Jersey incurred to a joint car insurance pool. So the fraud division was created as a state agency, but its expenses were paid by the insurance companies and the money it collected would ultimately go back to the insurance companies. To me it sounded like the state of New Jersey was just renting out its name to a bunch of insurance companies.

Parisi was a publicity hound and was constantly in the local and national press because of his high-profile sting operations. I have to admit, some of the tactics he used were funny and effective. One classic Parisi sting was the phony bus accident. He had an empty bus fake a small accident in a poor neighborhood. The bus driver would then open the bus doors, a video camera would capture the people jumping on the bus after the accident and claim to be injured. The "victims" would hire attorneys, see doctors, and make claims against the city or state. The videotapes of these accidents made for good TV copy, and Lou was the darling of the media because of these and other flamboyant antics.

He was also a tireless advocate for exporting his methods of fraud prevention to other states. As a result of the media attention and the fact that he had collected so much money supposedly from insurance cheats, other states viewed New Jersey as on the forefront of fraud prevention. Many states were contemplating similar fraud programs. But the other states did not know that the program was largely based on the use of intimidation to extract fines out of people or for making honest mistakes.

Not all of his publicity was good. *The Trentonian* ran a story on its front page concerning so-called insurance rate evaders (i.e., people who lived in other states who used New Jersey addresses for the purposes of obtaining car insurance). The article had several inside sources who claimed they used harassing tactics, threatened criminal prosecution, and had quotas. This was such a good article that I attached it to my complaint. I decided I would help Parisi in his attempt to be exposed to the public but not necessarily in the most flattering light. It would turn out that I would only be partially successful in this endeavor.

One benefit of winning the motion to dismiss before Judge Brotman was that it made the case more credible. We got some publicity from the decision because it set precedent. This was the first lawsuit against ongoing employees of a state government under a federal racketeering statute, and the suit had withstood a motion for dismissal.

Two Brave Souls Finally Come Forward

Because of our initial success and the good press we received, we finally managed to convince two health practitioners to come forward as party plaintiffs.

Although most of the practitioners we found were chiropractors, there were other types of practitioners who were targeted.

Jeff Susman was a dentist who worked in the Bronx but lived in New Jersey. Jeff was one brave fellow. His story is exemplary, and he was the ideal lead plaintiff. Here is how the fraud division got to him.

He put a crown in a patient. As everyone except the fraud division knows, a patient needs two office visits to get a crown. During the first visit, the dentist grinds the tooth down, takes an impression of all the teeth, and puts in a temporary crown. The impression is then sent to the lab where the permanent crown is fabricated. During the second visit, the crown is installed.

One of his patients who was insured by a New Jersey company had her first visit in late March. The second visit was in early April. The rub was that on April 1, the patient's health carrier was changed. Jeff's office initially filed the claim with the date of the second office visit. The insurance company rejected the claim because coverage had expired. Jeff's office called up the insurance company and explained the situation. The insurance company advised them to re-submit the claim with the March date, thus making the claim payable because the plan had not expired as of the date of the first visit. His office complied with the request.

Unbeknownst to Jeff or the claims department of the insurance company, the special investigations unit at this insurance company noticed the two claims for the same patient for the same amount but for different dates of service. For some reason, they forwarded the matter to the fraud division for investigation.

The case was assigned to a senior investigator at the fraud division. (It seemed that all the investigators were "senior investigators.") As was typical, the investigator performed no investigation. He sent out the fraud division's standard demand letter with the consent agreement. Jeff called the senior investigator and attempted to explain the situation. The investigator cut him off, saying he was not interested in any of the facts of the case because he already knew this was a clear case of insurance fraud. He said the situation looked very bad for him, but he should not worry because the matter could be completely resolved by the payment of the five thousand-dollar fine. If the fine was paid, then there would be no reporting to the state of New York or the New Jersey Dental Board, and there would be no further repercussions.

Jeff attempted to explain that he didn't do anything wrong and insisted that there could not be any evidence of insurance fraud. However, the investigator was adamant that they had him cold, and his only way of avoiding further problems was by payment of the five thousand-dollar fine. The investigator said that if he didn't pay the fine, he could be prosecuted criminally in both New York and New Jersey, and he would also face licensing actions in both states.

Jeff was outraged. He called the investigator's supervisor. The supervisor backed the fraud investigator and told him to pay up or face the consequences.

Jeff refused to knuckle under and wrote a letter to his state representative. He received no satisfaction, but after six months, the fraud division finally decided there was no basis to proceed and closed the case.

Of course, had Jeff paid the money initially as demanded by the investigator, the case would have also been over, and the state would have been five thousand dollars richer. This was a good case for us and clearly showed some of the tactics of which we were complaining.

Sometimes you get lucky in discovery, and we did in this case. We obtained the investigator's notes, which documented his conversations. The notes revealed that he had actually called the insurance company, and he was told there was no insurance fraud and that the special investigations unit had mistakenly sent Jeff's file to the fraud division. What did the investigator do once he was told there was no insurance fraud? He called Jeff and left a message that it had all been worked out, and that he only had to pay one thousand dollars, which he could pay over time. I asked the investigator about this at his deposition. He came up with some tortured interpretation about the money being a donation or some other ridiculous thing. Now we had them. This case showed the fraud division was seeking fines from people they knew did not engage in insurance fraud. This was not insurance fraud prevention; it was a criminal shakedown using the mantle of a state agency.

The other plaintiff was a chiropractor in South Jersey named Sam Soriero. Soriero's case was more complicated. He had been treating a patient for chronic pain. At some point, the patient was in a car accident and had a different injury. When treating two different injuries, a chiropractor is required, to the extent possible, to separate the treatments and bill each insurance company separately. Typically, auto accidents are covered by an insurance company that is different from a person's health insurance policy. Soriero attempted to do this and created bills to the two companies for the same days of service.

Of course, problems may come up. Chiropractors are notoriously poor record keepers. Typically, all they do is list the procedures on a "travel card" (a card that travels with the patient as he or she goes around the office to see different office personnel) and send a bill. Soriero's notes were not the best.

So he sent out bills to both insurance companies. Sam never received double payments, but one insurance company found out about the other and sent the case to the fraud division for investigation.

A senior investigator contacted him and demanded five thousand dollars. Soriero hired a lawyer, who had the number reduced to four thousand dollars. The investigator said that as long as Soriero paid the fine, there would be no further repercussions in terms of licensing or criminal prosecution. He lied. Immediately after Sam paid the fine, the investigator sent the case over to the attorney general's office for criminal prosecution. After investigating the case for a year, the attorney general's office declined to prosecute.

Subsequently, Soriero had some unrelated problems before the licensing board. The government attorney used his consent decree against him in a licensing case, even though they were not supposed to. Soriero was outraged by all this and agreed to become a plaintiff, after we won the initial round before Judge Brotman.

On our end, we produced for deposition a number of victims, all who had more or less the same type of interaction with the fraud division. First, they received the demand letter. The fraud investigators would then call up and tell the doctor that if they didn't pay they could be sued civilly, prosecuted criminally, and/or have their practices ruined by adverse publicity. Many of these doctors hired local attorneys to represent them. However, the attorneys were general practitioners who did not know much about health fraud. More importantly, they did not know the fraud investigators didn't really investigate; they just collected money based on referrals of suspicious conduct from the insurance carriers.

The lawyers advised their clients that it was cheaper to settle than to fight. As a result, many of the victims we identified simply paid the fraud division rather than risk the downside of a lawsuit. Virtually all of the victims at most had clerical mistakes or legitimate interpretations of claim forms. None of these guys committed insurance fraud.

We Finally Find the Gun, and It's Still Smoking

As we continued to depose investigators, it became clear that the fraud division seemed to have its own problems with the New Jersey attorney general's office, which was the New Jersey state agency that would pursue these doctors, civilly or criminally. Apparently, since there is so little investigation by the fraud division, the attorney general's office was disinclined to pursue these cases, which is why none of these so-called investigations ever turned into lawsuits or prosecutions.

Although we had some cases, we were just speculating that this was all a scam and that it was their normal practice not to investigate the cases before sending out the demand letters. But from the files I obtained from the investigators through discovery and my discussions with the providers, it seemed like a pretty good hunch.

And then we found the "smoking gun." From the beginning, I felt there had to be something big out there but I didn't have any idea of what it was. I talked to hundreds of folks in New Jersey about the case. The plan was to seek out individuals who had a friend or relative who worked for the state that could provide us with inside information.

The first whiff of the smoking gun came a year into the case. I was speaking with a well-placed local attorney who had some state government background. He mentioned that he knew someone in the attorney general's office, and there was a rumor they had conducted their own investigation of the fraud division and came to the same conclusion I had. He said the primary author of the report, who was head of one of the main divisions of the attorney general's office, had been demoted after he submitted his report and was now processing state licenses in the New Jersey backwaters.

I called up one of the sources. Because I am not adept at pretending, I identified who I was, what I had heard, and what I was looking for. The individual was not completely helpful, but he was an honest person. Through some arguably skillful questioning, and based on what the person refused to deny, I surmised that there was one or more memos about the investigation and that some of the conclusions I reached were not totally dissimilar to the conclusions in the reports. The investigation and report had been completed several years previously, so the attorney general's office obviously hadn't taken any corrective measures, except banishing those involved in producing the investigative report.

This could break open the whole case. If the fraud division had been investigated by the attorney general's office, and if it had determined that the fraud division engaged in misconduct, then all kinds of good things were likely to happen. That the fraud division was still engaged in this activity meant that someone pretty high up in the attorney general's office had disregarded the conclusions of its own investigation. The smoking gun was starting to smell like a cover-up of criminal activity.

Does Anyone Have Handcuffs?

At the time, the New Jersey attorney general was Deborah Poritz, who, I was told, was a friend of then Governor Christie Whitman. Who knew how high this could lead? I was really exited about the case now.

The next day, I subpoenaed the attorney general's office for the memos. I put enough details in the subpoena to make them understand that I knew the documents existed and what was in them. I didn't expect an eighteen-month battle to get these memos, but that's what I got.

In due course, the attorney general refused to produce the memos, citing a variety of privileges. Basically, the general rule in discovery is that any document that is not privileged and reasonably calculated to lead to the production of relevant information is discoverable and must be turned over to the other side if requested. There are many kinds of privileges that limit production of documents. Perhaps the most important privilege is the attorney-client privilege. Essentially, a party cannot be compelled to turn over documents between it and his attorney, with some rare exceptions. Medical records are another example of a privilege.

Another important privilege relates to executive or government functions. Oftentimes government officials are exempt from producing documents that are crucial to the running of government. The biggest case involving executive privilege of documents involved the Watergate tapes. Nixon argued that there was a privilege protecting him from producing the tapes of White House conversations. He lost.

The attorney general argued all kinds of privileges and filed a motion for a protective order to quash my subpoena. As is required, their motion was in writing and cited a variety of legal authority. We responded and argued that none of these privileges applied.

The motion was returnable before Magistrate Rosen. Despite his not-so-veiled threats against me, I thought Rosen was very smart and a fair person. Since I knew I was right on the law, I was hopeful and expecting him to rule in our favor. The attorney general submitted copies of the memoranda to the magistrate judge so that he could determine whether any privilege applied. Because it was an important motion, the magistrate scheduled oral argument on the case. At oral argument, Rosen said some of the memos were directly relevant to the lawsuit. He also seemed skeptical about the application of the privileges in this case; as well he should have been, since they really did not apply. After a couple of weeks, he rendered his decision. Lo and behold, he denied the motion to quash. The magistrate wrote a good decision.

The attorney general sought an immediate stay of the decision and Magistrate Rosen granted the request. The attorney general then appealed to District Judge Brotman. Judge Brotman had previously denied Herb Stern's motion to dismiss the case and was familiar with the lawsuit.

We did more briefs for Judge Brotman. He took six months to decide the motion, because he was tied up on other matters. He affirmed Magistrate Rosen and also ordered that the memos be produced to me.

The attorney general's office then went back to Magistrate Rosen to get a stay so they could appeal to the Third Circuit Court of Appeals. Over my objections, Magistrate Rosen granted the stay, and so we were still denied access to the memos even though two judges had ordered them produced. Thereafter, the attorney general filed further briefs with the court of appeals. I filed answering briefs, and we had oral argument before a three-judge panel of the Third Circuit.

All three judges seemed skeptical that the documents were privileged. Things went my way during oral argument. Indeed, these judges didn't even think the attorney general had a right to appeal at this stage in the case, because there was no "final order." Appellate courts do not like to make decisions piecemeal. They told the deputy attorney general arguing the case that they could only hear the merits of the appeal if Deborah Poritz refused to turn over the documents. Then she would be held in contempt, and the contempt order would be reviewable by them as a final order. But until that happened, they would not deal with the merits of the application. That's what they said at oral argument, and that's the way the decision came down several weeks later. The attorney general's appeal was dismissed on what is called jurisdictional grounds.

By this time, we had gone through three different levels of courts, and all three had ordered the attorney general's office to produce these memos. We waited for a week to see what they would do. Attorney General Poritz blinked and turned over the memos. They were worth waiting for.

Turns Out It's a Smoking Nuclear Bomb

One of the memos specifically criticized the activities of the fraud division and found that they were more interested in collecting fines than identifying insurance fraud. The memos also indicated that the attorney general's investigation uncovered that there was, in fact, a quota on fines, a fact denied by every investigator I deposed under oath.

It is fair to say that these memos were a bombshell. We received them just before Christmas. It was a good Christmas present. The case was set for trial in early February. These documents made our case.

All this time, I was talking to various print and TV media about the case. NBC's *Dateline* was interested in doing something about this case or Parisi or both. Various New Jersey newspapers were interested. Unfortunately, there was a protective order on the memos, so I couldn't release them. Eventually, one newspaper, the *Asbury Park Press*, filed a motion to obtain the memos. Of course, the attorney general's office objected because they were embarrassing to the state and the attorney general, who was obviously letting the fraud division continue in its unethical, if not illegal activities. The paper's attorneys were first-rate, and they won the right to obtain the memos. The memos were published and widely reported in the New Jersey press. It no doubt caused the attorney general's office embarrassment. They disavowed the reports and took the state party line that the actions of the investigators were proper and comported with state law.

Through December and January, we prepared for trial. Our witnesses were reluctant to come forward, especially since there would be no money for them because I had waived the right to sue for damages. At their request, I attempted to revive my damage claim by submitting a jury charge instruction on monetary damages.

We Go to Trial, but All We Get Is a Surprise Surrender

We went to Camden, New Jersey, for the trial. *Dateline* and some of the local media were outside the building, since cameras are not allowed inside a federal court building.

We found out that there were two other cases scheduled for trial that same day. Apparently Judge Brotman usually schedules several cases overlapping and then attempts to settle all or most of them.

We met Judge Brotman for a pretrial conference. I was deathly ill at the time and could barely speak. The first thing the judge wanted to know was whether I was trying to revive my damage claim. He told me he was very disturbed about that because he had kept this lawsuit, in large part, because he thought I had agreed that we wouldn't be seeking monetary damages, thus turning his courtroom into a fraud division refund department. He was right. He threatened to dismiss the whole case right then and there. I started to backpedal full speed, again abandoned the damage claim, and assured him that we were only seeking injunctive and declaratory relief. After letting me grovel for a suitable length of time, he decided not to dismiss the case.

But defense counsel also had a surprise for me. A few months prior to the trial date, I had sent them a settlement proposal. It was a reasonable proposal, one that would protect health practitioners and make sure these types of tactics would not be employed in the future. I didn't expect the state to accept it and they didn't, at least not six months before. But during our time with Judge Brotman, defense counsel announced that the state of New Jersey would agree to almost everything I had asked for in my proposal. They blindsided me! I certainly didn't want to settle the case on the day of trial. I wanted to drag these investigators over hot coals, expose them to the public as criminals and scam artists, and give Parisi and his bunch a black eye before the whole state.

But when an adversary says his client is willing to settle for what you asked for, what can you do? I mumbled something about it being too late and let's take testimony, but based on defense counsel's offer, Judge Brotman decided to immediately send the case down to Magistrate Rosen to act as a mediator to try to settle the case. Given the fact that there were two other cases set for trial the same day, it wouldn't have surprised me if everyone but me already knew the state was going to fold.

The Fraud Division Gets a Bigger Taste of Its Own Medicine

We spent the better part of a day negotiating the terms and wording of the settlement. I wanted these tactics to stop. We agreed that the fraud division would enter into a consent agreement. With some intended irony, the consent agreement was similar to the ones the fraud division forced the chiropractors and other health practitioners to sign. Under the agreement, the fraud division did not admit to any wrongdoing (just like the health practitioners did not have to admit to wrongdoing), but they agreed that they would no longer do the things they were not admitting they had ever done, like threaten health practitioners with criminal prosecution or any of the other nasty things we alleged.

In addition, they agreed to provide all health practitioners with a letter attached to the consent agreements that explained their rights. It was similar to a taxpayer's notice of rights that is sent with tax information. They also agreed to provide an eight-hundred number and to submit to monitoring and oversight from the attorney general's office to ensure these tactics would no longer be employed.

As part of the settlement, Judge Brotman would retain jurisdiction over the case for three years. This was not an insubstantial sword over the fraud division's head. They knew that if I heard of any complaints from health practitioners in the future, I would be back before Brotman in a heartbeat.

Most happily for me, the fraud division also agreed to pay a substantial part of my unpaid legal fees. So, like the practitioners they had extorted, the fraud division also had to pay a fine. The documents were prepared and approved by the parties and the case was over.

Dateline did do a story on our case, sort of. A settlement is not nearly as juicy as a jury verdict, and Parisi and his crew were not found liable. So *Dateline*'s angle was how Parisi was attacking insurance fraud in New Jersey, but it mentioned that he did have critics and that there was even a lawsuit against him that ironically resulted in the same type of consent agreement he had forced health practitioners to sign. The story was not bad, but because of the consent agreement, it was not the story we had originally hoped for.

The resolution of the case by way of a consent agreement had a satisfying irony. We didn't get our pound of flesh, but we got a fair result and an end to the illegal government activity. Sometimes the government comes up with crazy schemes that are improper and even illegal. And sometimes you can fight city hall and win, or at least get the government to back down.

Postscript

If Mike Harvey wasn't crazy when I first met him, he went completely off the deep end after this case. Although married with children, he became seriously involved with a chiropractor's assistant he met at the same seminar where I met him. He left his wife, but asked her to run his chiropractic business. She took care of the business and him too. He had put most of his money in an offshore trust that supposedly was beyond the taxing authority of the U.S. government. It was, but only because it was a scam and he lost every penny he invested. But the government didn't see it that way and the feds (and his ex-wife) went looking for their share of the money he invested.

Mike got hit with a very large divorce property settlement award, far beyond what he could pay. Being the creative and fun-loving guy that he was, he used his computer to print up hundreds of thousands of "Harvey Bucks" with his picture on the bills. He sent the amount due his ex-wife and her lawyer in "Harvey Bucks." They were not amused.

Mike is now wanted by the federal government on counterfeiting charges. He is living in a beach resort somewhere in the Caribbean, giving chiropractic adjustments to guests and employees. He has no plans to return to the United States.

After this case, Gary Pomeroy started an advocacy organization for chiropractors called "Chiropractic America." Gary and I took on the department of insurance in another case, and we put on a few seminars for New Jersey chiropractors.

Gary also developed the first national marketing program for chiropractors. He really enjoyed creating the marketing ads, which usually showed a partially dressed beautiful woman extolling the virtues of chiropractic. He personally chose the models after a rigorous selection process. As his attorney, I advised him that it was necessary for me to be involved. I even offered my services *pro bono* (for free), but he rejected my offer.

My good friend Gary Pomeroy died in late 2006 of adrenal cancer at the age of 49. A partner Gary took on before he died is continuing Gary's advocacy and marketing work.

Parisi left the fraud division several months after the case concluded. Some say our case forced him out. Others say that he would have been fired long before but New Jersey waited until our case was over. In any event, he landed on his feet, taking a job with a large New York insurance company as its fraud prevention director. I hear he's up to his same antics in New York. I always got a kick out of the way Parisi scammed the insurance scammers. He just went a little too far this time.

Deborah Poritz, who was the attorney general of New Jersey during the case, was promoted by Christie Whitman to the New Jersey Supreme Court. She served as chief justice until her retirement in late 2006.

As far as I know, the assistant attorney general who supervised the investigation of the fraud division and wrote the smoking gun memos is still processing state license applications somewhere in the farmlands of New Jersey.

Perhaps in part because of the problems we uncovered with the fraud division, the New Jersey legislature passed the *Automobile Insurance Cost Reduction Act of 1998 (AICRA)* which created the Office of the Insurance Fraud Prosecutor, which now oversees insurance fraud investigations.

CHAPTER SEVEN

Naturopathic Skirmishes

If you consider naturopathy in its broadest sense—as the use of natural remedies to cure the body's dysfunctions and maladies—then it is by far the oldest, most established and successful treatment regime on this planet. There have been millions and perhaps billions of successful treatments for a wide variety of medical conditions over millions of years. How can this be? It's a trick statement: I didn't say that all of those treated were *Homo sapiens*.

Zoopharmacognosy is the process by which animals use plants, soils, and even insects to treat diseases. It is naturopathy in the animal kingdom. This is a relatively new field of study, but the phenomenon that animals self medicate with plants and other materials is an established fact.[42]

The formal study started when scientists noticed that sick chimpanzees would go to a specific type of tree or plant, meticulously extract one part of the plant material, eat it and their symptoms would then resolve. From these

---

[42]   See Benyus, Janine M., *Biomicry: Innovation Inspired by Nature* (New York: Quill, 1998) Chapter 4; see also "Really Wild Remedies: Medicinal Plants Used by Animals" in *Zoogoer*, Smithsonian National Park Zoological Park, January/February 1998 and on the web at http://nationalzoo.si.edu/publications/zoogoer/1998/1/reallywildremedies.cfm.

original observations, it has been documented that chimps, apes and other animals ingest leaves and other plant material to rid themselves of tapeworms and other parasites. Other monkeys were observed to eat dirt from specific places which was high in a certain mineral.

Navajo Indians believe that many of their herbal medicines were given to them by bears. They may have observed bears rubbing up against tree bark which had specific medicinal properties. So the antecedents of naturopathy have been around for a long, long time.

Returning to our species, the earliest recorded use of herbal remedies comes from the Sumerians more than five thousand years ago. The Chinese documented the use of over three hundred herbal remedies in the second millennium B.C. The Indians have used their herbal Ayurvedic medical system for almost as long. The Egyptians were also into herbal remedies. And let's not forget the Indians in South America who have a long tradition of using plants for medicinal purposes.[43] Even the Europeans used herbs and other type of natural remedies.[44]

The point is that the use of herbs and other natural materials to treat diseases and medical conditions is not a new idea. Before the advent of synthetic chemical medicine, what little effective medicines there were came from herbs, like willow bark (aspirin) and cinchona bark (quinine for malaria). And to this day, some of the most successful drugs are either derived from plants or are chemically synthesized based on the active ingredients of plants.[45]

Though having its antecedents in herbal medicine and natural cures, naturopathy as a distinct medical discipline was started in America by a German immigrant, Benjamin Lust. In 1902, he founded the American School of Naturopathy.

---

43   Chris Kilham, a self-described "medical hunter," has written an excellent book on the subject: *Tales from the Medical Trail: Tracking down the health secrets of shamans, herbalists, mystics, yogis and other healers* (New York: Rodale Press, 2000).

44   *Heal Thyself: Nicholas Culpeper and the Seventeenth-Century Struggle to Bring Medicine to the People* (New York: HarperCollins, 2004), by Benjamin Woolley, tells the story of an outsider who brought herbal medical knowledge to laymen and in doing so paints a detailed picture of the state of medical knowledge in seventeenth century England.

45   The cancer chemotherapy drug Taxol was originally isolated from the bark of the Pacific yew tree. The statin drug Mevacor (Lovistatin) is a fungus produced by rice, *monascus purpureus*, or as it is called in the supplement industry, red yeast rice.

Naturopathy's main guiding principle is that disease is a corruption of the body's ability to heal itself. Naturopaths use various modalities, such as herbs, supplements, Chinese medicine, homeopathic remedies, and various forms of manipulation, to put the body in a position where it can heal itself. Among the core values in naturopathy are disease prevention, treating the whole person rather than the symptom, and the Hippocratic Oath to first do no harm.

I believe naturopathy and other benign, patient-friendly medical systems like homeopathy developed and initially prospered in large part as a reaction to the ineffective, toxic, and dangerous modalities of allopathic (i.e., conventional) medicine like bleeding and caustics, which were used before the advent of antibiotics and other modern medical therapeutics.

By the mid-1930s, naturopathy was popular enough in America to find its way into the federal employment dictionary of professions. In the early- to mid-twentieth century, many states had some form of recognition and regulation of naturopaths.

However, the popularity of the profession diminished, probably for two reasons. The elders of the church of medical orthodoxy succeeded in having the naturopathic licensing boards eliminated, which made naturopathic practitioners unlicensed and unable to "practice medicine." But in fairness, by the 1940s and 50s, conventional medicine started to develop effective technologies and pharmaceutical products for some conditions, thereby reducing enthusiasm for naturopathy.

However, in the last few decades, naturopathy has experienced a resurgence. Fourteen states now license naturopathic physicians.[46] Naturopathy's increasing popularity may be a direct result of conventional medicine's dismal results in treating many chronic diseases. People want solutions, and if their allopathic doctors can't cure these conditions with drugs, people will try herbs and non-Western remedies.

---

46   Alaska, Arizona, California, Connecticut, Hawaii, Idaho, Kansas, Maine, Montana, New Hampshire, Oregon, Utah, Vermont, and Washington, plus the District of Columbia and a few U.S. territories.

Naturopaths Circle the Wagons and Shoot at Each Other

There are two kinds of naturopaths: the naturopathic medical school graduates and the correspondence school graduates.

There are only a few residential naturopathic medical colleges in North America.[47] Like traditional medical schools, it takes four years to obtain a degree. The graduates of these schools call themselves "naturopathic physicians." They learn all of the traditional naturopathic remedies but also learn some allopathic medicine. Naturopathic physicians are trained to perform minor surgery, learn to deliver babies, and administer IVs. The states that license naturopaths will only give a license to a graduate of one of these naturopathic medical colleges. In these states, licensed practitioners can be called "doctor."

It is rare for naturopathic physicians to get into legal trouble, but when they do, it's usually big trouble involving serious patient harm or death.[48] This can happen when a practitioner employs naturopathic remedies for acute or life-threatening conditions when there is a safe and effective allopathic (traditional or conventional) remedy available.

Most of the naturopaths practicing in the United States today have not attended a residential naturopathic medical college. They are the correspondence (or distance-learning) naturopaths. Some correspondence schools are well-regarded in the alternative health community. The largest correspondence school is the Clayton College of Natural Health. Over the years, I have run into a number of Clayton graduates. For the most part, they seem to be

---

47　Bastyr University, College of Naturopathic Medicine (Bothel, WA), National College of Naturopathic Medicine (Portland, OR), Southwest College of Naturopathic Medicine (Phoenix, AZ), The University of Bridgeport, College of Naturopathic Medicine (Bridge-port, CT), Canadian College of Naturopathic Medicine (Toronto, Ontario, Canada), and Boucher Institute of Naturopathic Medicine (New Westminster, BC, Canada).

48　See, for example, http://www.seattleweekly.com/2005-06-08/news/death-by-natural-causes.php, http://www.wweek.com/editorial/3329/9039, http://www.oxfordpress.com/news/content/shared/news/nation/stories/2006/01/BOTOX_MCCOMB_0126_COX.html.

committed and reasonable people.[49]

But none of these schools are recognized by an accrediting agency recognized by the U. S. Department of Education, though some schools have accreditation from a naturopathic accrediting board.[50] There are no federal or state training or certification requirements for schools for unlicensed practitioners. Some of the smaller correspondence schools are little more than diploma mills.

Correspondence-school graduates are not trained to perform invasive procedures, like IVs. They study traditional naturopathic remedies like herbs, homeopathics, aromatherapy, iridology, and other forms of unconventional diagnostics and therapeutics. Traditional or correspondence-schooled naturopaths usually do not present themselves to the public as primary care providers. People tend to go to traditional naturopaths for chronic or lifestyle-impairing, non-life-threatening conditions. As a result, when traditional naturopaths get into trouble, it usually does not involve death or serious patient injury.

The two types of naturopaths are bitterly at odds, and each group has its own national naturopathic organizations.[51] The four-year graduates want to put the correspondence-school graduates out of business, usually by proposing state licensure, which requires a four-year degree. The four-year graduates claim the correspondence schools do not give their "graduates" sufficient knowledge to care for patients or clients.

The correspondence-school graduates simply want to be left alone to practice, but they are skeptical of the four-year graduates' desire to be "physicians."

---

49 Another well established school is the Trinity College of Natural Health run by Wendell Whitman. Wendell also runs the "Heath Freedom Expo" which is a traveling convention showcasing the latest and greatest health remedies. At these conventions, there are also speakers who advocate "health freedom," which means that unlicensed practitioners should be able to treat patients.

50 The entire accreditation issue is one of the subjects of dispute between the two groups. The correspondence school graduates claim that the four-year programs are no more accredited than the correspondence schools (see http://www.anma.com/facts.html).

51 The American Association of Naturopathic Physicians (www.naturopathic.org) is the four-year school group. The American Naturopathic Medical Association (www.anma.com) is open to all naturopaths but mostly serves the interests of the naturopaths who have not graduated from the four-year programs.

They make a hard distinction between allopathic medicine and naturopathy. They believe that by having one foot in each camp, the naturopathic physician does neither system justice. Some of the correspondence-school graduates have training in nutrition, homeopathy, or various types of body work. There are quite a few chiropractors who also have traditional naturopathic credentials.

There are surely many decent and highly effective traditional correspondence-school naturopaths. However, a naturopath only finds me if there is a problem, so my experience is necessarily skewed. Still, of all the unlicensed alternative health practitioners practicing, the correspondence-school naturopaths seem to have the most problems with state prosecutors.

How Trouble Finds the Correspondence School "Naturopathic Doctors"

Most criminal cases against correspondence-school naturopaths involve the same scenario. First, the naturopath calls himself or herself a "Naturopathic Medical Doctor" or a "Naturopathic Doctor" and will use the moniker "NMD" or "ND," which is usually stitched on to the naturopath's white medical lab coat. For some reason, and it is probably just ego, many naturopaths are not satisfied with referring to themselves as simply "naturopaths." They have to be called "doctor." Maybe they all had Jewish mothers.

In many states, it is a crime for anyone to use the title "doctor" unless the person has a degree from an accredited school. Most prosecutors feel it is inherently misleading for a person who has a correspondence-school certificate to refer to himself as any kind of doctor. Many naturopaths say they call themselves "doctor" in the original sense of the word, which was "teacher." I understand that naturopathy views the naturopath as an educator, but I agree with the prosecutors on this one. If the correspondence schools were smart, they would stop giving out the "Naturopathic Doctor" degree, but I wouldn't count on that happening any time soon because of marketing and business reasons. They can probably get more people to enroll and pay for a doctorate than a certification.

A few of these naturopaths have too much confidence in their ability to treat serious diseases and life-threatening conditions. End-stage cancer patients often look for life-saving alternative treatment after they are pronounced terminal by conventional doctors.

Enter the bold, unlicensed "Naturopathic Medical Doctor" who will tell the patient there are simple cures for all forms of cancer, and if they just follow the naturopath's herb and supplement regime, the body will cure the cancer "naturally." If the patient dies while under the naturopath's care, the authorities may try to blame the unlicensed practitioner, even if the patient was close to death before seeing the naturopath.

Common Machines, Unusual Uses

The other area where trouble finds the correspondence-school naturopaths is the sale of supplements to remedy "tendencies" to serious medical conditions like cancer or diabetes. How do the correspondence naturopaths know what tendencies their clients have? They use an expensive device, which may have started as a basic FDA-approved biofeedback machine. Here is how the whole thing works, but some background first.

A biofeedback device is an instrument that provides a visual or auditory signal corresponding to the status of one or more of a patient's physiological parameters such as skin temperature, muscle activity, or brain wave activity. These devices are approved by the FDA.[52] But they are only approved for relaxation training and muscle re-education. While practitioners can use these devices for any purpose, manufacturers cannot sell them for anything other than these approved purposes. More to the point, any modification to the device that changes its operation or function would turn it into an unapproved (or technically, an "unregistered") medical device.

A German doctor by the name of Reinhold Voll discovered that the energy flowing through the acupuncture meridians could be read using a skin galvanometer, and he created a device that supposedly could relate important diagnostic information from this energy flow. He called the system "EAV" (electro-acupuncture by Voll). The first computerized system was the Dermatron, followed by the Computron, the Entero, and the latest and greatest is called the QXCI.

---

52   For the legally curious, biofeedback devices are regulated under 21 CFR (Code of Federal Regulations) Section 882.5050.

There are two analytic parts to the machine. A galvanic skin measurement device is coupled to a software program which takes the physiological data from the subject and correlates the data to all kinds of things like sensitivities to substances, medical conditions such as cancer and hepatitis C, stress imbalances in the body, or just the energy levels based on the acupuncture meridians.

Sometimes it is explained that the correlations of the data are based on the notion that all living things generate vibrations or energy patterns. These patterns can be identified and analyzed in order to determine the health of an individual and tell what organ or body system is either not working correctly or has a tendency to disease.

Where do these correlations come from? There are many sources. As indicated, it started from acupuncture research, but there are other influences as well; sources like Royal Rife, inventor of the Rife machine, which treated cancer and other diseases based on the frequencies tumors broadcast.[53] There are more contemporary sources as well.[54]

Some practitioners take these devices a step further (or one step further into la-la land, according to conventional authorities). They ask the person hooked up to the machine questions about sensitivities to foods or other things and the readings change, which supposedly shows additional sensitivities. This may not be as crazy as it seems. Remember, these are basically biofeedback devices, so there could be some significance to a person having a

---

53   For more on Rife and his machine see *The Cancer Cure that Worked: 50 Years of Suppression* by Barry Lyne.

54   Although I am skeptical of the machines in use today, I believe that the underlying theory will prove out. I predict that in the not-too-distant future, it will be accepted that portions of medicine can be reduced to noninvasive physics; diseases will be diagnosed and treated by conventional doctors with nonharmful electromagnetic fields based on the theory that all objects generate and reflect electromagnetic waves or energy and are part of a field of energy. These ideas are a part of a powerful new paradigm called "field theory" which could be the answer to the physicists' holy grail, the search for a grand unified theory. Field theory also provides a theoretical basis for controversial phenomena like homeopathy, the amazing properties of water, ESP, past life regression, the secret life of plants, and the power on intentionality. For a comprehensive and highly readable account of this new theory, see Lynne McTaggart's book, *The Field* (New York: Quill Press, 2003).

reaction to certain words.

Is there anything to all this? Modern allopathic medicine thinks not—which, to many in the alternative health field, is a sure sign that these machines are effective.

The FDA considers all of these EAV machines to be illegal since the software that creates the correlations turns the underlying biofeedback device into a new and unregistered medical device. Whenever the FDA finds out about a company marketing one of these devices, it sends a "warning letter" and asks what corrective action the company will take. Usually the corrective action taken is that the entrepreneur will close down the operation and reopen it under a different name with a different mailing address. The FDA is ineffective in policing these unregistered medical devices.

My problem with these devices is that it is impossible to prove that they don't work. If the device finds a "tendency" to colon cancer, who is to say that the tendency does not exist? The "tendency" is not recognized by science, and there is no accepted scientific test to prove or disprove such a tendency. Only these modified biofeedback devices can establish these tendencies. And the machine (or the practitioner using it) does not claim that there is a medically detectable cancer, just that the cancer is in some incipient state which could take years or decades to turn into actual cancer.[55]

Philosophy of science involves the attempt to differentiate science from pseudoscience. Karl Popper, one of the most respected and most prolific thinkers in the field, would say in effect, if it can't be refuted, it ain't science. The essence of science is the creation of a hypothesis about some part of the world and testing it out to see if the world agrees. If a theory or hypothesis can explain any result and there is no fact that can refute the theory, it ain't science.

And that's my problem with these machines. There is no way to verify, prove, or disprove any of the claimed tendencies to a disease. Popper would call these machines pseudoscience, and I would agree, at least until there is

---

55 Some chiropractors and a number of unconventional medical doctors also use these machines.

some way to show that the machines can be wrong.[56]

Another device popular with the correspondence-schooled naturopaths is the dark field microscope. This is a just a garden-variety microscope with a computer or video screen in addition to a standard eye-piece. The naturopath will stick the patient's finger to get a drop of blood, put it between two slides, and then put the slide under the microscope and display the blood on the video screen.[57]

The naturopath looks to see if the blood cells stick together (which is bad) or flow freely (which is good). Conventional medicine does not accept this test as diagnostic of anything.

Some naturopaths use the dark field microscope to diagnose real medical conditions (as opposed to tendencies to diseases). One of the main diagnostic techniques is the Enderlein method, created by a German alternative health care practitioner.

Dr. Gunther Enderlein believed a person's medical problems were visible in a blood sample. How? Because the blood contains tiny pictographs of medical conditions. If a woman is pregnant, the Enderlein practitioner will be able to tell because there will be pictographs of a placenta. If someone has stomach cancer, their blood will have a picture of a little-bitty stomach. It doesn't matter where you take the blood from, because every drop of blood will have a picture of all of the medical conditions of each individual.

Among other problems with the use of these machines, and especially the biofeedback-based machines, is that patients hear what they want to hear. Regardless of how many times the practitioner explains that the machine just determines "tendencies to a disease," the patient hears, "You have cancer."

Then the practitioner explains that the client can eliminate the tendency to cancer or eliminate the cancer shown in the dark field microscope by buying supplements that a naturopath will sell them.

---

56   According to quack-buster Stephen Barrett, what little scientific testing there is on these machines does not support efficacy claims for things like allergies. See http://www.quackwatch.com/01QuackeryRelatedTopics/electro.html. However, people in the alternative health community do not consider Barrett to be fair or reliable, to say the least.

57   Most states consider sticking a person with a pin or needle "practicing medicine." Hence it is technically illegal for an unlicensed naturopath to perform this test.

The patient goes back home and tells his family that he has cancer and shows family members the five hundred to one thousand dollars worth of supplements that will resolve the cancer before it is big enough to show up in conventional medical tests.

Not all members of the patient's family are as favorably disposed (or gullible) as the patient. Sometimes an unhappy relative will contact the medical board or the local district attorney and tell them that there is a guy (or gal) claiming to be a doctor who diagnosed cancer with a biofeedback machine.

The D.A. will start an investigation. Usually an undercover sting follows. A male and female cop will pose as a husband and wife. One of them will have some vague complaint about feeling tired and generally unwell. You can bet that the undercover cop is in excellent physical health and probably competes in Iron Man marathons.

The bold "naturopathic medical doctor" will then hook up the cop to the diagnostic machine which will show that he has a tendency toward a number of things, including some form of latent, incipient, or otherwise undetectable cancer. Our hero will try to explain that this is not full-blown cancer but just a tendency to get the disease, which will turn into cancer unless the client takes care of the problem now.

The cop will usually ask other incriminating questions about the results of the tests and also about the practitioner's credentials. Many correspondence-schooled naturopaths have a wall full of framed certificates in their office.

The undercover cop will then buy all of the supplements recommended by the naturopath. After the sale is completed, the naturopath will be arrested for practicing medicine without a license and fraud.

But I Am "Federally Certified"

Unethical or ignorant practitioners will tell their patients they are "federally certified." However, there is no such thing as "federal certification" for naturopaths. They could mean that the Department of Labor recognized naturopathy in the 1930s in its Dictionary of Professions.

They may also mean that they have a certificate acknowledging they are registered as a naturopath in the District of Columbia. Since the home of the federal government is in the District of Columbia, some naturopaths may mistakenly believe that they are thus "federally certified."

There is not much to District of Columbia certification. I know because it was used against me in a case. A police detective applied for and received a District of Columbia naturopathic certification, pursuant to which he was entitled to call himself a naturopath registered in the District of Columbia. He also received one of those shiny certificates, suitable for framing.[58]

The correspondence-schooled naturopaths do have a national certifying organization that confers a board specialty credential.[59] There are reputable membership organizations associated with traditional naturopathy. They encourage naturopaths not to call themselves "doctor." These organizations argue that practitioners should practice traditional naturopathy and know and respect the limitations of their schooling. Naturopaths who follow the advice of these groups typically do not have any problems with the authorities.

Chutzpah and Filmmakers

Over the years, some of my most colorful clients have been naturopaths facing criminal charges. One naturopath I represented practiced as a surgeon for many years in a foreign country, but he never actually attended medical school. He just invented medical school credentials. By all accounts, he was a pretty good surgeon. His lack of formal education didn't stop him from publicly complaining that correspondence naturopaths were insufficiently

---

58   My annoyance with naturopaths exaggerating their credentials once got the better of me. At a hearing on a criminal case against a naturopath, the practitioner's credentials came up. I vehemently defended the validity of the correspondence "naturopathic medical doctor" credential.

    After I sat down, my client congratulated me on my passionate defense. I told him I felt strongly about it because I had never actually attended "law school." I had only taken a correspondence course from some paralegal in California who gave me a "doctor of law" certificate. My client's jaw dropped; he turned ashen, and I could see the fear forming in his eyes. Then I grinned. He was not amused.

59   It is called the American Naturopathic Medical Accreditation Board, www.anmab.org. This board also accredits distance learning naturopathic schools, but the board is not directly or indirectly recognized by the U.S. Department of Education. But none of the boards of any of the alternative medicine specialties are so recognized, so lack of recognition has little meaning in the alternative health field.

trained to safely practice naturopathy. I guess they call that "chutzpah."

This naturopath taught me about the credentials some naturopaths obtain to give the appearance of legitimacy. There are many certificates available to anyone who requests them and pays a small fee. This naturopath was also adept at making his own certificates. I suspect he is not the only naturopath with this skill.

The good news about criminal cases involving correspondence-school naturopaths is that they usually do not involve harm to patients. Most of the supplements and remedies naturopaths provide are nontoxic and relatively harmless. As a result, these cases are about technical violations of the "practicing medicine without a license" statute and some overselling of remedies, with a touch of fraud, based on the cancer-tendency diagnosing devices.

Most of these criminal cases are pled out. Of course, once the practitioner is discovered and is above the radar screen, it is time for him or her to move on and do business somewhere else. The authorities usually confiscate the machines.

Recently, I represented a naturopath who tried to protect himself against prosecution by having three different names: his real name and a professional name for each of his two professions.

He was or claimed to be a naturopath (and basically anyone can claim to be one) and sold supplements and equipment to people. He considered himself to be an educator, not a practitioner. He got into trouble for selling a water treatment machine, which supposedly helps treat terminal cancer, and a supplement (cesium) to an advanced cancer patient.

The client became violently ill from the cesium and had to be hospitalized. He called the naturopath from the hospital. The naturopath "educated" him to leave the hospital and restart the cesium. The client complied, got violently sick again, and was readmitted to the hospital.

The client eventually died of his disease and a friend contacted the police. The police started an investigation, did the obligatory sting, and executed a search warrant on the naturopath's apartment.

And that's where his two professional worlds collided. In searching for evidence that the naturopath was practicing medicine without a license, the police found several fully automatic assault weapons, thousands of rounds of ammunition, and a few hand grenades.

No, the naturopath was not a terrorist or militant white supremacist. Turns out his first love and his other profession was a more creative, but probably less socially useful, endeavor. He was a movie producer and director with a special niche. His movies were in the genre of "biker porn," which is very big in some places.

He sent me a few of his movies. I have as much of an "artistic" appreciation of pornography as any normal middle-aged guy, but this stuff was too much. Call me old-fashioned, but a girl chained to a bike performing sex acts on three old, fat, mustached, bald guys in leather pants and leather vests (no shirts) doesn't do it for me.

The guns, ammunition, and fake grenades were all props for his movies. Unfortunately, the guns were not registered. The police also discovered a couple of driver's licenses with the naturopath's picture but with his different names. It took the authorities some time until they figured out who he really was.

The naturopath was arrested and charged with practicing medicine without a license, fraud in the sale of the equipment, numerous weapons-related charges, and possession of fictitious and forged identity documents.

The case came in through a health activist. There was some talk about making this the poster case for the health freedom movement. I told the activist to find another poster child.

Sometimes the police make mistakes. In this case, I thought the police had no right to search and find assault weapons since the scope of their search was limited to objects related to the illegal practice of medicine. So we made a motion to suppress the weapons and the illegal identity documents.

A good time to get rid of a case is when a defense motion is pending, especially before the prosecutors have to do a response. This saves them time and gives them an added incentive to plead the case out.

Fortunately, the prosecutors were not out for blood. No one died. I gave my standard speech about alternative health and freedom of choice and whatnot. The prosecutors probably thought that I was a Martian. But it seemed to me that they simply wanted to get rid of the case, because they had a very large docket and could not try even a small percentage of all the criminal cases they had filed.

The case took place in a large urban setting where, because of overcrowding, they were releasing prisoners after serving a small fraction of their sentences. After some back-and-forth, we agreed that the naturopath would plead guilty to a felony or two and have a couple years of state jail time imposed (looks good to the voters) but have the state time probated, so long as the naturopath didn't violate the terms of his probation. Instead of the written multi-year state prison time, the naturopath would actually receive 180 days in county jail. But the naturopath had already spent almost eleven days in custody after he was arrested (and before I was retained). Because of overcrowding, it looked like he would spend less than a week in jail. It seemed like a good deal.

The prosecutor wanted the naturopath to stop practicing naturopathy. This was not a problem since the naturopath had been planning on closing his naturopathic consultant business and going full time into his first love, the biker porn/humiliation/violence movie business.

The naturopath spent less than one day in jail because of overcrowding. The field has lost the services of one naturopath, but the porn industry gained the services of a full-time producer/director.

I only had one case with a correspondence-school naturopath that did not work out. But it was the only case I ever had where there were multiple serious and credible allegations of harm to patients. Unlike most correspondence-school naturopaths, this fellow used invasive procedures in which he had no formal or legitimate training. That case still gives me nightmares, in large part because the practitioner received a lengthy prison term.

Naturopathy Works, but Be Careful

Naturopaths provide valuable services and can give helpful advice about a wide variety of conditions, but traditional naturopaths are not doctors, and some of them are not adequately trained. A few of them seem to work miracles. For one recent criminal case, I had several dozen people provide letters attesting to amazing cures for conditions like Ménière's disease, which is incurable by conventional means. Based on all my work in the field and the voluminous scientific evidence supporting herbal remedies, I am a believer in naturopathy.[60] But even so:

If a naturopath tries to hook you up to a machine to tell you about your "tendencies to diseases," if one tells you that your blood has little pictures of your organs, or if a naturopath wears a white coat and insists on being called "doctor" (but did not graduate from one of the few accredited schools), then watch out, be skeptical, and hold on to your wallet.

---

60   See for example: *The Scientific Validation of Herbal Medicine*, by Daniel B. Mowrey, PhD, published in 1986. There is something close to the *PDR* (*Physicians Desk Reference* for drugs) published by a German Commission which is approved by the German equivalent to the FDA. This German Commission publishes monographs listing 191 herbs thought to have sufficient clinical research to be used by physicians. Mark Blumenthal, who runs the American Botanical Council, (www.herbalgram.org) has published several versions of the monographs. See for example, *Herbal Medicine: Expanded Commission E Monographs*. Another valuable source is the *PDR for Herbal Medicine*, 4th ed., edited by Guenwald, Brendler, and Jaenicke, which discusses over six hundred herbs and other natural remedies. (All of these books are available on Amazon.)

CHAPTER EIGHT

Food Fights: Who Should Control the Nutrition Field?

What, if any, vitamins and nutritional products should you take to supplement your diet, prevent cancer and heart disease, or help treat common medical conditions? What kind of practitioner should you seek out to get answers to these questions? What kind of training and credentials should a person have to charge you for advice about these things? The answers to these questions depend on who you ask.

Arguably, the most important aspect of public health, and certainly the part which affects each and every one of us on a daily basis, is the food supply, diet and nutrition.

In America today, obesity is a growing epidemic. We are getting fatter because we are taking in more calories, while obtaining fewer nutrients. The obesity problem is also a sign of the failure of the American food industry and our food culture.

But beyond the obesity epidemic, there is a growing chorus of voices warning of serious health dangers from our food supply, the food industry and our eating habits.[61] Modern food technology has created what one author has termed "edible food-like substances,"[62] which are overly dependent on corn syrup or other unhealthful corn products.

Exacerbating the health consequences of poor nutrition is our inclination to seek painless cures to what ails us, rather than focusing on more difficult things like disease prevention and behavioral modification.[63] We look for simple remedies to counteract unhealthy lifestyle choices like smoking, drinking, and an over-reliance on animal fats and on highly processed foods to fulfill our dietary needs. We'd rather take a pill than change our habits. Who wouldn't?

Conventional medicine has been slow to recognize these dietary problems and even slower to propose solutions, in part because historically, medical schools have provided almost no education about nutrition. I also believe that there are forces at play which propose "continued scientific study" as a means

---

61   One of the clearest and most articulate voices raising this alarm is Michael Pollan, who has authored a beautifully written, persuasive book called *The Omnivore's Dilemma* (New York: Penguin Press, 2006). Pollan argues that we are now "the people of corn."

62   See Michael Pollan's article, "Unhappy Meals," published in *The New York Times Magazine*, Sunday, January 28, 2007, available on the web at http://www.nytimes. com/2007/01/28/magazine/28nutritionism.t.html?ei=5090&. I believe this article is the basis of Pollan's new book, *In Defense of Food* (New York: Penguin Press, 2008) which has just been released.

63   For decades, the most powerful voice advocating cancer prevention and the toxic and disease causing properties of products has been Samuel S. Epstein. He has written many excellent books. He is surely one of the most important health mavericks in the country. I had a meal with Sam many years ago. He is a very impressive fellow. His books are listed at: http://books.google.com/books?as_auth=Samuel+S+Epstein&ots=UWpIIzoMhZ&sa=X &oi=print&ct=title&cad=author-navigational&hl=en.

of forestalling solutions.[64]

For many decades, registered dietitians have acted as the authoritative voice about diet and nutrition. In my judgment, they are part of the problem, not the solution, and they have been a willing accomplice to the food industry's efforts to substitute "edible food-like substances" for food with real nutritional value. Follow the money, or just go to a dietitians' national convention and see which companies are the sponsors and exhibitors in the trade exhibition booths and you will see my point.[65]

On the other hand, for decades, the alternative health field has recognized the public health problems with the food supply and nutritional deficits caused by modern food technology. The alternative health community has proposed solutions, as evidenced by the organic food and dietary supplement industries, and the professionals (other than the dietitians) engaged in providing nutritional advice. Based on the explosive growth of these industries, it appears that the alternative health solutions are resonating with consumers.

But because our diet and nutrition problems and the proposed solutions are so important to public health, the government has stepped up and tries to regulate the field.

---

64   There are many examples of this in recent history. For decades, the tobacco industry called for more research on the connection between smoking and lung cancer. The American Medical Association and the American Cancer Society were willing participants (or co-conspirators). In 1964, the Surgeon General's office finally publicly linked smoking to lung cancer. Did the AMA endorse it? Nope, the church elders in the AMA called for more studies. It was all about the money which the tobacco industry gave to the AMA.

Sometimes trade protectionism is the reason why innovations are suppressed or delayed. The fight between surgeons and gynecologists about who was qualified to perform and read pap smears cost the lives of thousands of women in the middle part of the twentieth century. See the recently published *The Secret History of the War on Cancer* (New York: Basic Books, 2007) by epidemiologist Devra Davis for a detailed discussion of these and other examples. Devra is a health maverick in that she talks about things which are against the interests of the church of medical orthodoxy. Because of her recent book, I wouldn't be surprised if the church elders try to make her life more difficult.

65   Someday someone will write an exposé of the dietitians and their relationship to the fast food and food processing industry like the way Devra Davis has exposed the past financial relationship between the American Cancer Society, the AMA, and big tobacco in *The Secret History of the War on Cancer*.

The FDA Tries to Control Supplements but Fails (So Far)

For the past forty years, there has been an ongoing battle over the FDA's authority to regulate dietary supplements. In the mid- to late-1960s, the FDA proposed onerous restrictions on the manufacture and use of dietary supplements. It tried to impose premarketing approval requirements, similar to but slightly less stringent than the regulations governing the approval of drugs.

In reaction to the FDA's efforts, in 1974 Congress passed legislation (the Proxmire amendment) which essentially prohibited the FDA from imposing its onerous regulatory burdens on dietary supplements.

In the early 1990s, it was claimed that the FDA intentionally misinterpreted a recently enacted nutritional labeling act ("*NLEA*" or the *Nutritional Labeling and Education Act of 1992*) to usurp sweeping new powers to restrict access to dietary supplements. The FDA's actions created an uproar in the country (or as anti-alternative health people say, amongst the dietary supplement industry).

As a backlash, in 1994, Congress, spearheaded by Senators Orrin Hatch, alternative health's good friend Tom Harkin, and then New Mexico Congressman Bill Richardson, passed a dietary supplement-friendly bill called *DSHEA* (the *Dietary Supplement Health and Education Act*).

In a nutshell, *DSHEA* regulates dietary supplements as foods rather than as drugs. Hence, unlike the FDA's regulation of drugs, there is no requirement that the safety and efficacy of a supplement be proven to the FDA's satisfaction.

DSHEA also defines the difference between a dietary supplement and a drug. The difference is essentially functional, that is, related to the intended use of the product. A drug is any article that is intended to diagnose, cure, or mitigate a disease.

A dietary supplement is an ingredient taken by mouth which the manufacturer intends to improve health, but which is not intended to diagnose or treat any specific medical disease or condition. Thus, a product can be either a dietary supplement or a drug depending on the manufacturer's claims about the product. If the product claims to cure a disease, it is a drug; if it just claims to generally improve health or the "structure or function" of a bodily system, then it is a dietary supplement.

As a result of *DSHEA*, for now, Americans have almost complete freedom to purchase and use dietary supplements.[66] However, since *DSHEA* was enacted, the FDA and its congressional supporters, led by Congressman Henry Waxman and Senator Dick Durbin, have been trying to repeal or water down *DSHEA* and give the FDA essentially the same control it has over drugs. But that probably won't happen, at least as long as Sir Tom Harkin and the Right Honorable Orrin Hatch are still in the Senate (and may they live long and prosper).

How Consumers Obtain Dietary Supplements

Consumers purchase dietary supplements in three different ways: in health food and other retail and online stores, as MLS (multilevel sales) customers, and as clients or patients of clinical nutritionists, chiropractors, and other complementary medical providers. Many health food stores have knowledgeable clerks who can provide general information about products. However, people who buy supplements in stores often know what they want, and these purchases are usually not meant to treat any ongoing, serious medical issues. The same is generally true with multilevel sales.

Enter the Nutritionists

What if you want to resolve a specific medical or dietary problem, or you don't even know exactly what your problem is but you want to know whether a supplement or herb might help? That is where the clinical nutritionists (and specially trained chiropractors and medical doctors) enter the picture.

There are several different organizations that train clinical nutritionists. Each provides its own certification, and each has its own trademarked name. The largest and most influential groups in the country are the CNSs (Certified Nutrition Specialists), the CCNs (Certified Clinical Nutritionists), the

---

66   Many parts of the world have much more onerous dietary supplement regulations. There is an international movement afoot to pass highly restrictive supplement regulations and standards called CODEX which would limit the potency and access to dietary supplements. The CODEX battleground is currently in Europe, but many ardent supporters of dietary supplements fear that CODEX will come to America.

CNs (Certified Nutritionists) and the CNHPs (Certified Natural Health Practitioners).

All clinical or certified nutritionists believe in the healing powers of specific foods, vitamins, supplements and herbal remedies. They are all opposed to an over-reliance on processed or highly refined foods (such as canned foods, frozen dinners, fast food, etc.) to meet dietary needs.

Almost all nutritionists believe that a healthy diet consists mostly of vegetables, legumes, fruits, nuts, some types of fish, chicken (free range if possible), and occasionally, lean cuts of beef, if you can't live without it. However, even with a relatively healthy diet, most nutritionists believe that dietary supplementation is necessary for almost all people because of the poor state of the food supply, the American diet, air and water pollution, and poor farming practices. Many nutritionists provide highly individualized counseling based on a variety of assessments and testing.

Basically, the stock-in-trade of nutritionists is the recommendation of foods and the sale of professional-grade supplements to correct nutritional deficits and resolve medical problems.[67] And that is the biggest bone of contention between nutritionists and the registered dietitians.

The Battle Is Joined

The registered dietitians (RDs) are the largest, most organized, and best funded food/nutrition professional group in the country. The RDs believe that only supplements which have been proven to be effective by randomized

---

67   Many nutritionists believe that some of the supplements available in supermarkets lack adequate quality control and may be less effective than therapeutic grade supplements which are only available through nutrition professionals. They claim that professional-grade supplements have higher quality control and better potency. There are two technical bases for the nutritionists' concerns: the binding agents and the proper form of a vitamin or mineral. Some fillers or glues used in some supplements cannot be broken down by the body, and hence the material would not be available to the body or could be toxic. There are many different forms of minerals and vitamins, but not all forms of a basic mineral or vitamin can be recognized or absorbed by the body. The least useful forms of these materials are often less costly to manufacture. Sometimes the cheapest vitamins or minerals are not effective at all or much less effective than higher quality products. Most consumer supplement manufacturers acknowledge this but insist they use high-quality ingredients.

controlled clinical studies that have been published in a few mainstream medical journals should be recommended to people.

The dietitians believe that at the current time, there are only approximately three supplements that have met this standard: calcium for people with osteoporosis, folic acid for pregnant women, and maybe vitamin D for people with calcium or vitamin D deficiencies. The recommendation by nutrition practitioners of any other supplement for any other condition is considered by the dietitians to be unethical quackery.

This is complete and utter nonsense and a short digression is needed to explain why.

A Digression: Just How "Scientific" Is Conventional Medicine?

For hundreds of years, conventional doctors have been complaining about quacks and charlatans who use unproven remedies. It is ironic that when the proven and established medical therapies were leeches, bleeding, and forcing patients to ingest caustics like mercury, the medical establishment was calling other people quacks, including nonmedical school trained people who were giving citizens herbs and other folk remedies to treat medical conditions.[68] Does any of this sound familiar?

Fast forward to 1978. The Congressional Office of Technology Assessment, aided by an advisory board composed of leading medical and university school faculty, published a report entitled "Assessing the Efficacy and Safety of Medical Technologies." The report estimated that only between ten and twenty percent of all conventional medical therapies have been proven by scientific evidence.[69]

The OTA report caused much hand-wringing among the medical church elders. In response, they invented a new paradigm called "evidence based medicine" and called for "outcomes research" to justify medical therapeutics.

---

68   For an interesting history of so-called quackery see *Quacks: Fakers and Charlatans in English Medicine* (London: Tempus, 2000), by Roy Porter.

69   U.S. Congress, Office of Technology Assessment. *Assessing the efficacy and safety of medical technologies*. Washington: U.S. Government Printing Office; 1978. Report No.: OTA-H-75.

Under the new paradigm, medical interventions were supposed to be based on scientific evidence, and if possible, on the gold standard, which is the randomized, controlled clinical trial.

Since that time there have been a number of studies showing that there are varying degrees of scientific support for a much larger percentage of therapies than the OTA's estimate.[70] However, it seems clear that the majority of medical therapeutics are not supported by primary (as opposed to meta-analyzed) randomized controlled clinical trials, and there are many other kinds of evidence that medical practitioners rely on daily in making therapeutic decisions.[71] The dietitians' insistence on controlled clinical trials as a prerequisite to recommending a supplement is simply not consistent with the therapeutic practices of contemporary medicine.[72] The dietitians are attempting to hold the nutrition field to a higher standard than the standard primarily used in medical therapeutics.[73]

All the professional nutritionist groups and the entire supplement and health food community believe that the scientific and clinical evidence (the same type and quality of evidence relied upon by doctors every day in their therapeutic practices) is very strong for the use of nutritional supplements and herbs for many conditions.[74] They also believe that much of the

---

70   See, for example "The Impact of Evidence on Physicians' Inpatient Treatment Decisions" by Brian Lucas et. al. in *J. Gen Intern Med.* 2004 May; 19(5 Pt 1): 402–409.

71   See the table of types of scientific evidence supporting medical therapies listed by medical specialty at http://www.shef.ac.uk/scharr/ir/percent.html. The conclusion in the article referenced in the previous footnote is consistent with this table.

72   There is also a debate as to whether this new "evidence based medicine" paradigm should be the only game in town. Historically, there have always been questions about whether medicine is or should be an art or science or both. To some thinkers in the field (called medical epistemology which is "the systematic study of medical knowledge to discover its nature, basis and the conditions, possibilities and limitations of its application in practice") the answer is not clear cut. For more information about this subject see *The Journal of Evaluation of Clinical Practice*, Volume 13 Issue, August 2007 which reviews the development of the "evidence based medicine" paradigm.

73   An excellent book which makes the same point by showing how diseases are treated in America compared to three modern European countries is *Medicine and Culture* (New York: Penguin Books, 1988) by Lynn Payer.

74   For books referencing the scientific evidence supporting supplements see the "Diet and Nutrition" part in the "For Further Reading" section of this book.

negative scientific information about supplements is a result of bias and faulty science.[75]

The dietitians think that any nutritionist who sells supplements instead of just giving advice will go straight to hell because of the conflict of interest in both giving advice and selling a product as a result of that advice. (By that logic, any surgeon who actually cuts someone open, rather than just advising surgery, would have the same conflict of interest.)

The nutritionist groups and the alternative health community believe that dietitians are only experts in food technology and that they are unqualified to provide sophisticated, clinical nutritional advice unless they obtain training beyond the dietetics curriculum.

Most ominously, the dietitians believe that only a registered dietitian should be permitted to give advice about nutrition.

During the beginning of a recent Texas legislative session that dealt with the fight between the dietitians and the nutritionists, a legislator was overheard to say, "Here we go again, the food fights." Let's look closer at one small part of the food fights and two of its participants.

The Dietitians Try to Take Over the World of Nutrition (and Mostly Succeed)

The field of dietetics started to organize in the early part of the twentieth century, following the establishment of the medical boards. The original purpose of the profession was to provide food service management (i.e., kitchen management) and dietary planning in medical-related institutions, such as hospitals and nursing homes.

Dietetic education originated as a home economics program and its programs continued to be accredited by the American Home Economics Association until the 1970s. Most dietitians work in institutions like hospitals, schools, and prisons. Very few of them work in a full-time clinical practice,

---

75   One of the most visible scientists talking about the bias and other methodological flaws in the negative clinical trials and reports about supplements is Jeffrey B. Blumberg, PhD, who is a professor of nutrition at Tufts University. Read anything he writes or any interview he has given to get a handle on these problems, including: http://www.google.com/search?hl=en&ie=ISO-8859-1&q=jeffrey+blumberg+and+clinical+trials and http://lpi.oregonstate.edu/ss02/blumberg.html.

advising individuals in a noninstitutional setting, unless they have specialty clinical training beyond the basic dietetics curriculum.

Up until the1970s, the dietitians were pluralistic and practiced a "live and let live" philosophy. They believed that many different kinds of professionals were competent to provide nutritional advice.

But that philosophy changed, and during the past twenty years, the American Dietetics Association (ADA) has implemented a national strategy of creating a monopoly for dietitians. The organization now believes and powerfully promotes that only a registered dietitian should be able to provide advice about nutrition. Begrudgingly, they say that other licensed health care professionals, such as medical doctors, can provide some nutritional counseling, as long the advice is just an incidental or small part of that licensed practitioner's practice.[76]

The ADA strategy had been implemented through their affiliate state dietetic chapters. The state chapters made friends with the key state legislators and had bills introduced that prohibit nondietitians from providing nutritional advice for a fee. And in perfect Orwellian Newspeak, their legislation also usually defines a dietitian as a dietitian/nutritionist, and allows all dietitians to counsel people outside of an institutional setting.[77]

The dietitians have been wildly successful in their legislative efforts. Approximately thirty states have enacted legislation granting dietitians a monopoly to engage in nutrition counseling. Most of the other states give title protection or registration to dietitians.[78]

---

76   For example, the *Minnesota Dietetics Act* (Section 148.632 (3) for the legally inclined or the disbelievers) provides that a licensed practitioner, such as a medical doctor, can provide nutritional counseling if the nutrition practice is "incidental" to the other profession, so long as the doctor does not claim to be a dietitian or nutritionist.

77   If they could get away with it, the dietitians would also try to have the legislation prohibit anyone from speaking about nutrition in public unless they were a licensed dietitian. But that went too far for most legislatures.

78   A title or registration act creates a legislatively recognized title or right to use a particular title. If a state has such an act, anyone who wants to use the title has to meet certain requirements and register. However, if a state only has a dietitian title act, as opposed to a restrictive licensure act, nutritionists who are not dietitians can work; they just cannot call themselves "dietitians."

The Dietitians Take Texas (Almost)

One of the states that has a dietitians' title act is Texas. However, for the past twenty years, the Texas dietitians have been trying to turn their title act into a restrictive licensure act. A small group of nutritionists and others have stopped them, at least for now.

The CCNs (Certified Clinical Nutritionists) are a national group of nutritionists with their offices in the Dallas suburbs. They are the only nutritionist group headquartered in Texas, so the CCNs view Texas as their home turf.

The CCNs originated as a state nutrition group in Florida. In the late 1980s, the group approached a popular Texas nutritionist by the name of Winna Henry to run the group. She took the job and over the ensuing years made the CCNs into a national, well-respected membership organization. Among its members are leading voices in the nutrition field, and some of its members have health care credentials in medicine and chiropractic.[79] The group also developed a clinical nutrition certification program for health care professionals (overseen by the CCN sister organization, the Clinical Nutrition Certification Board). There are even a number of dietitians who have obtained certification as a CCN and are actively involved in the organization.

The Texas legislature goes into session from early January through early June every other year, on odd years. Like in many states, elected legislators work part time and are otherwise employed. Most are them are businesspeople or attorneys. The staff of the legislators works full time, even when the legislature is not in session.

In 1999, the Texas dietitians sneaked a restrictive licensure bill through both houses of the Texas legislature over the Memorial Day weekend, without any hearings before either of the Texas legislative houses. The CCNs started the holiday weekend with a future, but when they came back to their offices on the Tuesday after Memorial Day, under the dietitians' bill, most would have to close their practices by September 1999.

---

79   See the "For Further Reading" section at the end of the book for a sample of books written by practitioners with the CCN credential.

The CCNs immediately organized a last-ditch effort to have the bill vetoed by then Governor Bush. They contacted the bill's sponsor. It turned out that the dietitians forgot to tell him that that the bill would eliminate all the other providers of nutrition counseling in the state of Texas. The bill's sponsor was so concerned that he wrote to Bush and asked him to veto his own bill.

The other thing the CCNs did was hire the best lobbyist in Austin they could find—Stan Schlueter. Behind the scenes, Stan lobbied hard and effectively. In the final hours of the legislative session, Schlueter convinced the Bush office to veto the dietitian bill. The bill died on Governor Bush's desk.

That the dietitians almost put the CCNs out of business in their home state made a deep and disturbing impression on them, and especially Winna. Stan and others said the best way to protect the CCNs was to pass their own bill that would protect their title or create a license which would formally recognize the CCNs' right to practice in Texas.

The Legislature Tells the Groups to Make Nice and Work Together

During the 2001 legislative session, the dietitians again sought exclusive licensure. This time, the CCNs introduced a title act to protect their right to practice. Under their proposed bill, anyone else could still provide nutrition advice for a fee. Their bill also created a nutritionist board, similar to the medical, dental, and dietetics boards.

Both the dietitians' licensure bill and the CCNs' title bill were sent to the same Texas Senate Committee on Health and Human Services. The legislators felt that since the two groups were providing the same service to the same people, there should only be one board and one bill.

That attitude frustrated both groups, since each basically thought the other group were charlatans. Both groups made noises about trying to work together, but it was impossible.

The dietitians repudiated the idea of selling supplements in addition to just giving advice about the food groups. The CCNs were extremely mistrustful of the dietitians. They had previously worked with the dietitians to pass a joint bill in Florida, but it turned out badly. Despite the joint bill, the CCNs were prohibited from practicing in Florida. The CCNs also hadn't forgotten that at the previous Texas legislative session, the dietitians almost put them and everyone else out of business.

As a result of the mutual distrust and disrespect, the groups did not reach an agreement. The senators on the committee and their staffs thought it was a ridiculous fight between two groups that do the same thing. They didn't want any part of it, so neither bill got out of the committee in 2001. The status quo was preserved. The dietitians continued to have their title act, while the CCNs had no state recognition but at least they and the other nutritionists were allowed to practice.

2003 and It's the "Same Ol' Same Ol'"

Both groups came back for the 2003 Texas legislative session, and it was the "same ol' same ol." By then, I was the CCNs' legal counsel. Stan Schlueter, the lobbyist who helped kill the dietitians' bill in 1999, continued to work as the group's lobbyist.

The guy on the other side of the table was the Texas dietitians' long-time lobbyist/attorney, Greg Hoosier. Greg is middle-aged, smooth as silk and extremely knowledgeable about Texas politics. It was hard to say who was more rabidly anti-nutritionist, Hoosier or his dietitian clients. But that's what made him a good lobbyist.

In 2003, nothing had changed. The dietitians thought that all nutritionists were uneducated, unethical charlatans and the CCNs thought the dietitians were paternalistic, if not fascist. The CCNs were even more appalled by the dietitians' lack of training or understanding of clinical nutrition issues and held them responsible for green Jell-O in hospitals and soft drinks in schools. Most nutritionists also feel that the dietitians are not providing adequate nutritional support for immunocompromised patients, such as cancer patients taking chemotherapy.

There was a hearing before the House health committee on both bills. Hearings are held on days when the Legislature is in session conducting business and voting on bills. Between breaks in the voting and adjournments, the representatives attend their committees and hold hearings. The days with votes and hearings are extremely hectic for the legislators and their staffs. There are hundreds of bills before the many legislative committees. Each bill is important to some group and may be opposed by other groups. As a result, committee hearings can take many, many hours and can deal with dozens of bills.

Perhaps reflecting the legislators' view of the "food fights," we finally had our hearing around 1:00 a.m., thirteen hours after we were told to be ready to speak. By then, a few of the members of the committee were in the back room, probably sleeping. But I have to give the committee members credit, they plodded on, hour after hour patiently listening to testimony for all kinds of bills, some fairly important, but some pretty ridiculous.

One of the bills which was heard before ours was for a law to add a warning on five gallon buckets that they may be dangerous to infants. The citizen speaking for this bill did a demonstration. He put a bucket on the table. He then took a child's baby doll, stood it up, walked it up to the bucket, had it climb up the side and then he threw the doll into the bucket, head first. Then he started screaming in a high-pitched baby voice, "Help me! Help me!" I am as much in favor of child safety as anyone, but this is why we waited thirteen hours?

Eventually, it was our turn to speak. Practitioners from both sides testified. Some of the CCNs told very compelling stories of the clients they helped who had been unsuccessfully treated by other health care practitioners. The dietitians told their stories about their training and how they only recommended things which have been scientifically proven (like Jell-O and canned fruit cocktail). My job at the hearing was to answer some of the technical questions about the CCNs, set out the dietitians' national monopoly agenda and argue that Texas was now in their crosshairs.

But none of that mattered. Because the parties could not reach an agreement, both bills died in the committee. The status quo remained once again. The dietitians had their title act and the nutritionists had nothing but their right to practice, for the next two years anyway.

For 2005, We Try Something Different: We Attack

This was getting old, so for the 2005 session, we tried something different. A licensing or title statute is passed for a finite period of time, usually ten years. At the end of that period of time, the statute and the board created by the title or licensure act come up for "sunset review," which is the process by which the legislature reviews the board and determines whether to renew it and the legislation for another fixed period. Normally, sunset review is just a formality, and boards are renewed as a matter of course. In 2005, the dietitians' title act was coming up for sunset review.

Because I am a litigator, I felt it was time for the CCNs to go on the attack. That's what litigators do. We argued to the sunset review committee that the dietitian board should be disbanded and that their title act should not be renewed. It was a long shot, but why not. It was a good start to putting the dietitians back in their rightful place of institution food management and food technology, since they were doing such a wonderful job in those areas.

The CCNs and a few other smaller groups came to the dietitians' sunset review hearing and testified against them. We also went after them for having a scope of practice in their statute that exceeded their training. We argued that since they work mostly in hospitals and other institutions and don't work alone, there was no need for a separate board.

For some reason, our arguments upset the dietitians. Too bad. They had steamrolled their opposition in most other states, but it was not going to happen in Texas, at least not in this session.

The dietitians vehemently defended their right to practice, their need for a board, their training, the benefits of their work, and in general how they were responsible for the good health of Americans. They also defended their right to counsel individual patients (about the food groups, the food pyramid, and the three supplements they recommended to patients). They brought with them literally a handcart full of multicolored books on nutrition, which presumably every single dietitian in Texas had read and used as they worked their magic in Texas hospitals and other institutions.

As expected, despite the objections of the CCNs, the dietitians' board was renewed.

Under the CCNs' new executive director, Kevin Henry, at the 2005 legislative session, the CCNs filed a licensure bill instead of a title act. Many of the CCNs opposed licensure or even a title act since many were libertarians or were otherwise mistrustful of government control over natural health care. Some CCNs feared that any bill would infringe on their right to practice. But the lesson of the 1999 dietitians' bill passage was still deep in the group's psyche, so the CCNs were certainly going to ask the legislature for some protection.

The group's leadership decided that it was time to bring some standards to the field. The CCNs' proposed licensure bill had several levels of licensees depending on the practitioners' education and training. We thought the bill would protect pretty much all of the state's practitioners from the dietitians, and thus satisfy the groups who opposed licensure. We were dead wrong.

Back Together Once Again

Both licensure bills were referred back to the Senate health committee to work on a joint bill and board. Once again, the dietitians and the nutritionists met. This time, just for grins, I agreed to essentially everything the dietitians asked for. The more I agreed, the faster Hoosier (the dietitians' lobbyist) backpedaled. He couldn't commit to any of the concessions he had extracted from me.

I had enough contact with the Texas dietitians to know that they were never going to agree to a joint bill. They preferred the status quo rather than having clinical nutritionists on their board. And frankly so did I. So for me, it was all about running out the clock and getting to the end of the session without an agreement. I am sure Hoosier felt the same way. However, we received some unexpected help from the alternative health community.

Wherein the Dietitians and CCNs Are Blown Out of Austin and Never Saw It Coming

Unbeknownst to us, in the alternative health community, rumors started circulating that the dietitians and the CCNs were close to making a deal on a joint exclusionary licensure bill. We weren't, but that's the nature of rumors. And we never saw it coming.

It started slowly at first, dribs and drabs—and then more and more, and then it was a tidal wave of faxes sent to every Texas legislator. By some estimates, there were as many as three hundred thousand faxes, all saying the same thing: "Don't let the dietitians and the CCNs monopolize the nutrition field." The legislators were overwhelmed, and the people on the health committee were annoyed because the dietitians and the CCNs had forgotten to mention all these groups who would be adversely affected by the joint bill and who were opposed to any kind of licensure bill. Oops!

During our last meeting in Austin, the staff counsel for the Senate health committee, Ann Kimbol, looked at me, and in a poignant understatement said that maybe before the next session I should find out who all these groups were and what they wanted so the fax machines could have a rest.

The 2005 legislative session ended, and the CCNs (and everyone else) would still be able to practice their profession, and the dietitians still only had a title act. And that was fine with me.

A few months prior to the start of the 2007 legislative session, I sent Ann Kimbol an e-mail asking how it looked for a dietitians/nutritionist bill in the upcoming session. She quickly responded by asking me the position of all the other groups who did the fax blitz at the end of the previous session. Oops again. Time to figure something out. I needed a big idea.

Who Was That Masked Man?

I made some calls to find out who had blown the CCNs and dietitians out of Austin. There were many groups and individuals involved, and I talked to a few of them, but the name I kept hearing was Clinton Miller.

I had run across Clinton a few times in the past. Clinton is the most venerable health-freedom lobbyist in the country. He had been working in the field since the early 1960s, and his trademark and specialty was mass-targeted communication for the purpose of defeating legislation. He was involved in every big alternative health legislative project for the last forty years, and he had an impressive track record. The CCNs and dietitians were just one of his more recent and smaller victims. I didn't know him well, but I decided to give him a call.

Clinton was very gracious and almost apologetic as he said he didn't know I was involved with the CCNs. We immediately hit it off and traded war stories. (For him it was literal. He flew a B-17 out of England during World War II.)

As soon as I told him my idea, he agreed and said he would participate in person, no small concession for an eighty-five-year-old man with an infirm wife.

We All Meet and Come Together

I was proposing something that had never happened in Texas, or perhaps in any other state. I was calling a meeting of all of the diverse health groups (except the dietitians) to discuss common interests and a joint legislative response to common problems (read, the dietitians). Clinton loved it and agreed to allow me to use his highly regarded name to make it happen. And it did happen.

In early November 2006, all of the major players in the Texas complementary health industry met in my conference room. Most of the people who came had never met one another, as they represented different and competing sections of the alternative health community.

There were professional organizations like the homeopaths, the naturopaths, and several different nutritionist organizations. The trade organization for the health food stores and health supplement manufacturers was there, as were prominent supplement manufacturers. We even had some of the bigger multi-level organizations attend.

The common denominator was that they all either manufactured, distributed, sold, or advised about the use of complementary and alternative health care products. While they mostly competed against each other for the hearts and money of consumers, their views on regulation were similar.

But we quickly realized that we had another thing in common: a common enemy, the dietitians, because if the dietitians had their way in Texas, all of these folks (or the people they represented) would be out of business. The meeting lasted all day. There were many differences voiced, but the focus was on the common issues. By the end of the day, the group decided to form a formal coalition to oppose the dietitians and to ensure that freedom of choice would survive in Texas.

The coalition also decided to introduce a "health freedom bill." Six states already had this type of law on their books. A health freedom bill gives unlicensed practitioners the right to provide health care services to clients, so long as they do not "practice medicine," which means so long as they do not diagnose or claim to cure a disease. In the ensuing weeks, a draft of the bill was circulated and approved by the coalition.[80]

The last task was to find someone to run this coalition. I had originated the idea of the meeting, organized and ran it. (I even ordered and served lunch.) But I am a guerrilla fighter, not an organization man. The group needed someone who had the time to lead a broad coalition over an extended period of time.

Enter the Colonel

Peter McCarthy is a retired Air Force colonel. He flew B-52 bombers, was a Pentagon planning officer, and later commanded a squadron that deployed crews for the first Iraqi war. After retiring from the military, he became a pilot for a major U.S. carrier. But apparently he wanted more out of life, so he became a naturopath.

Peter was head of the Texas Health Freedom Coalition, one of many Texas organizations advocating for consumer health freedoms. The group had been a part of the 2005 anti-dietitian/CCN fax campaign. Peter was initially skeptical of my desire to bring all of the organizations together, but he eventually came around.

Peter, more than anybody else, stepped up to champion the goals of the assembled group during the initial meeting. He had obvious organizational

---

80   I was on the committee which drafted the bill, but the bill was written by Patrick Jackson who was uniquely qualified since he is both a naturopath and an attorney. His job was made easier since the other member of the committee was Diane Miller, Esq., who heads the National Health Freedom Coalition (www.nationalhealthfreedom.org). Diane is one of the country's preeminent thinkers and organizers in the health freedom movement. I don't always agree with what she says, but I listen very carefully to her, for among other reasons, she has been involved in just about every state health freedom legislative battle.

skills. So Peter assumed the leadership mantle, and I faded back into the jungle (like the good little guerrilla fighter I try to be).

Bombs Away at the 2007 Legislative Session

Peter did a terrific job. He found James Jonas, a very influential lobbyist, to represent the group in Austin. Peter and Radhia Gleis, the Texas CCN Chapter President, and a few other members of the coalition's executive committee pushed the Texas Health Freedom Bill.

Peter's efforts also resulted in other health-related groups joining the coalition. Peter did all this while flying a full schedule for his airline job and working as a naturopath. Many people were responsible for whatever positive results the Texas Health Freedom Coalition had, but Peter is at the head of the list and Radhia Gleis is right up there with him.

During the 2007 legislative session, once again the dietitians submitted a restrictive licensure or practice act, and the CCNs submitted a title act. There would be no meetings between the CCNs and the dietitians this time. We were now ensconced in a coalition, and we were going to stay there. (Having been beaten senseless by Clinton Miller and the others in 2005 made it an easy decision.)

The dietitians hired two other high-powered lobbyists to help Hoosier. They decided not to go back to the Senate Health Committee, which had already rejected their bill the previous three sessions. This time they put their bill before a House government committee. But they didn't get any better treatment there.

Peter and Radhia organized the coalition's opposition to the dietitians' bill. I helped organize our witnesses who would testify in opposition to the dietitians. Radhia acted as the chief interrogator preparing the witnesses. She was tougher than most attorneys I know. Like many CCNs, she was extremely passionate about the subject.

But apart from her general passion, she had some personal motivation as well. For many years, Radhia had taught a nutrition course at a franchise weight loss clinic, but she had been fired due to pressure from the dietitians that the clinics only use licensed dietitians as instructors. She was mad as hell about that.[81]

The dietitians' bill eventually went to a hearing, but the entire alternative health community was there to beat the bill down. Even the medical doctors opposed the dietitians, which may have been the unkindest cut of all. Hoosier must have known he was in trouble because he never got up to speak for his own bill, and he had spoken at every previous hearing for the dietitians' bill.

Dead or Not, a Litigator's Got to Do What He's Got to Do

Right before I was to speak to the committee at the hearing on the dietitians' bill, one of committee members let it quietly be known that the dietitians' bill was dead and buried, and there was no need for further testimony. But, dead or not, I just couldn't resist the urge to stick it to them, in part for making me listen to all their condescending, self-righteous nonsense during the previous sessions. And I did say that I am a litigator, and litigators attack. I went after them hard; such is my nature. I am sure my testimony did not make a bit of difference, except to me and a couple of people on our side, and maybe Hoosier.

"We'll Be Back"

After the committee hearing, all the dietitians walked out of the meeting, sullen faced. As he walked past, Hoosier turned to me and said "We'll be back." Hoosier was no Arnold Schwarzenegger, and the cyborg-dietitians had once again failed to take over the world of nutrition—in Texas anyway.

To the regret and dismay of the dietitians, and to the joy of the Texas alternative health care community, Texas consumers would still have access to complementary practitioners providing nutritional advice, at least until the next legislative session.[82] No doubt, the dietitians will be back, but so will we.

---

81   Ironically, since Radhia had a master's degree in nutrition education, she could teach nutrition to dietitians in a college level course, but she could no longer teach nutrition to people trying to lose weight.

82   The CCNs' bill never made it to a hearing. The Texas Health Freedom Bill made it to a hearing but died in committee along with the dietitians' licensure bill.

On the Front Lines of Public Health

Because I think diet and nutrition are the most important determining factors for the future health of Americans, I believe that the nutritionists (along with the chiropractors and medical doctors trained as nutritionists) are the most important health practitioners in our country today. They are on the front lines of public health, educating and moving the public towards a healthier diet, and battling health problems created by the food industry, while conventional medicine and the registered dietitians do little but pander to the food processors.

Slowly, the public is starting to demand changes from the food industry. To the extent the mainstream food industry doesn't adequately respond, then our old economic friend "demand" (of the "supply and demand" duo) will continue to fuel the explosive growth of the organic food and dietary supplement industries.

The title of this chapter posed the question "Who should control the field of nutrition?" My answer is that no one group should control the flow of information about diet and nutrition. The field is too big, the health implications too great, and there are too many unanswered questions for any one group or philosophy to be anointed as the guardian of truth.

Therefore, I don't have any problem with the dietitians promoting their ideas about the food groups, the food pyramid, or the health benefits of white bread, refined sugar and "edible food-like substances." That is their right. But I have a huge problem with them trying to outlaw competing groups with different ideas and control the flow of information about nutrition, and so should you.

CHAPTER NINE

What If There Were Magical Cells?

Stem Cells 101

What if there were magical cells that would repair cell damage caused by aging or diseases such as cancer and multiple sclerosis (MS) and could also heal traumatic spinal injuries like what happened to Christopher Reeve? What if these cells didn't need a program or guide to find the damaged cells? Suppose they just automatically knew the location of the damage, went straight there, and rebuilt or replaced the damaged cells? Pretty neat, you'd say; maybe too far-fetched. Well, that's the promise and hype of stem cells.

Actually, stem cells are a large part of human biology. Although scientists have trouble defining with precision what a stem cell is, most agree that it is a cell that can divide into an identical daughter cell and a specialized cell (or technically a precursor of a specialized cell like a liver cell or neuron). And, here's the kicker; it can do both at the same time. One daughter cell can be a stem cell (itself capable of producing a specialized cell) while the other daughter can be a precursor to a specialized cell. Biologists say this is a pretty nifty trick. In a literal sense, a fertilized egg is the ultimate stem cell. That one cell continuously divides into cells that can divide and become specialized cells.

Stem cells come in two basic flavors: embryonic and adult. An embryonic stem cell is a stem cell that is derived from an embryo, which is the period of cell development from the fertilized egg until eight weeks. Embryonic stem cells are taken from the inner cell mass of an early-stage embryo known as a blastocyst. Human embryos reach the blastocyst stage four to five days after fertilization.

Once there is a biologically recognizable fetus, any stem cell would technically be considered an adult stem cell. There are two practical sources of adult stem cells: umbilical cord blood (and placental material) and live humans of any age.

Everyone has stem cells in their bodies. The major source of stem cells is the bone marrow. But there are other places where stem cells are found, like in the intestines and skin. Usually, the more prone to death a cell is, the more likely there are to be stem cells, because the stem cells are the biological mechanism by which the dead cells are replaced.

The ability of a stem cell to form a different type of cell is referred to as its potency. An embryonic stem cell is considered "omnipotent" or "totipotent," meaning it can form any cell in the body.[83] Adult stem cells from umbilical cord blood are considered "pluipotent," meaning they can form many different kinds of cells. Adult stem cells from live human cells are less potent, or so the current thinking is.

Until recently, it was thought that an adult blood stem cell from the bone marrow could only become a blood cell, an intestinal stem cell could only become an intestine cell, and so forth. But recent experiments are changing the way scientists think about adult stem cells. Adult stem cells seem to have some potency or plasticity beyond turning into the type of cell in their defined germ line. But it is too early to tell how potent full-blown adult stem cells are or can become.

At the present time, there is relatively little lab work on embryonic stem cells sponsored by the federal government because of President George W.

---

83   I am told that technically only a blastomere, which can make an entire conceptus, is considered truly totipotent. Embryonic stem cells can make any tissue in the body except the amniotic sac and the umbilical cord.

Bush's limitations on embryonic cell lines. That will hopefully change once he leaves office. But as a result of his policies, U.S. embryonic stem cell research does not dominate the field the way U.S. research dominates many medical/scientific research fields.

In the near term, any clinical applications of stem cells in the United States are likely to come from adult stem cells and specifically from umbilical cord stem cells, because of Bush's embryonic stem cell policies.

Mitch Ghen Falls in Love with Stem Cells

Which brings us to Dr. Mitchell Ghen and how he managed to get in trouble with the federal government. The first thing you notice about Mitch is that he is short. But after a couple minutes, he seems to get bigger. Maybe it is his deep baritone voice or perhaps it is his wit or energy. And of course, like many maverick doctors, Mitch has a healthy ego.

Mitch always had a lot of questions. After he became a medical doctor, he had spiritual questions, so he decided to find answers. He became an ordained orthodox rabbi along the path to finding his answers. Mitch had what many of the better alternative practitioners had—an insatiable curiosity coupled with drive and a prodigious intellect.

I also met Mitch's wife. She spent much of her pre-Mitch adult days in what she describes as the biker culture (as in motorcycles). Rabbi and Rebbitzin Ghen were quite the pair.

Mitch had knocked around in private practice in different parts of the country. He became curious about the aging problem and possible solutions. So he started looking into it, and because Mitch is Mitch, he ended up editing one of the principal textbooks in the anti-aging field.

Fortuity brought Mitch to stem cells. One of Mitch's patients had a daughter who had a boyfriend who was interested in opening up a clinic utilizing novel treatments including possibly stem cells. Mitch met the couple, did some research, and concluded that stem cells could benefit patients with neurological conditions. Although there were no clinical studies showing efficacy, there were good theoretical reasons for thinking the treatment might at least help patients with their symptoms. So Mitch and the couple decided to go into business together and opened a clinic in Atlanta, Georgia.

Prior to going into business, they consulted with an Atlanta law firm to see whether they could legally provide experimental treatments like stem cells. The law firm opined that as long as the stem cells and other treatments were extracted, processed, and delivered in Georgia, it would be legal to use them on patients in Georgia.

Their thinking was that if everything took place in Georgia, the federal government, and in particular the Food and Drug Administration, would not have jurisdiction over the practice, since there would be no interstate commerce. They also felt that it would be legal under Georgia law to provide the non-FDA-approved treatment since Georgia had what is called an "access to medical treatment act" that allowed doctors some freedom to provide unconventional or unapproved treatment to patients in Georgia.[84]

With the green light from the lawyers, the clinic opened for business. It lasted only a few months due to a falling out between Mitch and his two business partners. Mitch and his partners decided to go their separate ways.

Mitch opened up his own clinic in Atlanta specializing in treating patients with neurological conditions. He treated all his patients with umbilical cord blood, which was rich in stem cells. He developed a special process to preserve the cells, which he also felt would lessen the effects of graft-versus-host disease. (The disease is what it sounds like.) He opened for business in the fall of 2002.

This would not be a full-time business for Mitch, not yet anyway. He was still running three clinics in North and South Carolina that he had purchased

---

84   The reason Georgia had an access law was because the president of the Georgia senate, Ed Gochenour, developed terminal brain cancer. His doctors gave him a few months to live. Like many other terminal brain cancer patients, he went to Houston to be treated at the Burzynski clinic. Ed went into complete remission as a result of Burzynski's treatment. He was treated during the time of the federal prosecution against Burzynski, and Ed's treatment was threatened. He, like some other Burzynski patients, appeared before Congress on Dr. Burzynski's behalf. The federal prosecution of Burzynski so rattled him that almost single-handedly, he pushed an access bill through the Georgia legislature, to the benefit of many Georgia residents. Unfortunately, Ed's brain cancer recurred and he subsequently died. I met Ed at the Burzynski congressional hearings and at the clinic. He was a good man.

from another alternative health practitioner. He would treat his Atlanta stem cell patients on the weekends. He hired some staff and farmed out most of the patient interaction work and the marketing. The clinic had offices in Atlanta, but the initial contact person worked out of a home office in the upper peninsula of Michigan.

Prior to starting his new venture, Mitch consulted with a large, well-regarded Washington law firm to check the legality of providing cord blood to patients. In contrast to the prior venture, Mitch was going to obtain the umbilical cord blood from an out-of-state cord blood bank, so there was going to be interstate commerce, which meant the FDA would definitely have jurisdiction. The law firm advised him that he could treat any patient he wanted with cord blood because it was an "off-label" use of an approved substance.[85]

So Mitch opened up a clinic in Atlanta in late 2002 to give patients cord blood. By early February 2003, Mitch had treated about forty patients, most of whom had ALS (amyotrophic lateral sclerosis), commonly known as Lou Gehrig's disease. The physicist Stephen Hawking is a prominent victim of the disease. ALS is incurable and usually fatal. Most victims end up in a wheelchair unable to control their bodies. ALS patients suffer horrible deaths. They slowly lose muscle control and they usually suffocate to death because they cannot breathe. There is no generally recognized treatment that is either curative or has a proven substantial beneficial effect on the disease.

Mitch's results were interesting and maybe promising, but for the most part, they were unspectacular. Some patients showed some benefit in terms of increased mobility. Some appeared to be stable for awhile, which in a horribly degenerative disease is not bad. One of the patients even got up from a wheelchair, but the treatment was not a cure. To Mitch's and his staff's credit,

---

85   In the United States, only drugs that have been approved by the federal Food and Drug Administration can be legally used on humans. However, most drugs are only approved for one specific use. After a drug is approved for that one use, it is often found to be effective in other conditions. The use of an approved drug for a condition not approved of by the FDA is called an "off-label use" (of an approved drug). Physicians have discretion to use any approved drug for basically any condition whether that condition has been approved by the FDA. However, the drug manufacturer is not supposed to market or actively promote off-label uses of a drug.

it was not marketed as one.

Some patients received no benefit from the treatment. The transplant procedure was expensive, twenty-five thousand dollars. The blood product alone cost around fifteen thousand dollars. Because it was an experimental procedure, it was not covered by health insurance.

Rabbi Mitch Meets FDA Bob under Unpleasant Circumstances

Someone wasn't happy with what Mitch was doing, because a complaint was filed with the Georgia and federal authorities.[86] The complaint was sent to the FDA's Office of Criminal Investigations in Atlanta where it landed on the desk of FDA special agent Robert Kurkyndal. Bob had been a criminal investigator in the postal inspector's office for a number of years, but he had just transferred to the FDA. During his years as a postal inspector, he encountered just about every kind of fraudulent scheme imaginable. That turned him into a pretty jaded fellow.

Bob was told that umbilical cord blood was an unapproved new drug and that there was no evidence it helped ALS or any other kind of neurological condition. So Bob approached this case like any other mail or wire fraud investigation he had conducted over his long career. Most of the people he investigated were scam artists. He never cut them any slack. And because of this background, he was not going to cut Mitch any slack either. This was going to be his first big investigation with his new department, and maybe he wanted to show everyone in the Atlanta federal office that there was a new sheriff in town and he meant business.

So the first thing Bob did was to organize a raid on Mitch's clinic. Because he wanted to spread around the fun, he also invited the medical board to join in the festivities.

To put it in legal parlance and procedure, Bob sought a search warrant to seize evidence at Mitch's clinic. Usually the case agent or the assistant U.S. attorney prepares an affidavit that explains there is reason to believe (or "probable cause" in legal jargon) that a federal crime has been committed.

---

86   Because patient complaints are confidential, we never found out who filed the complaint. Mitch suspects it was a drug company.

In his affidavit, Bob stated that Mitch was giving umbilical cord blood to ALS patients and that was a federal crime. He enlisted assistant U.S. attorney Randy Chartash to help, and they presented the information to a federal magistrate. The magistrate's job is to make sure that the government really has probable cause, but you do not often hear about a magistrate not giving the government a search warrant. (The reason for that would depend on who you ask.)

There would be no initial friendly discussions between the government and the doctor in this case. The first thing Mitch, his staff, and his patients heard from the federal government was when government agents barged into the clinic on February 6, 2003, with a search warrant allowing them to seize all the patient records. (Because of my job and proclivities, I am not a fan of government raids in heath care cases.)[87]

Mitch called me within a few days of the raid, and I flew out to meet him and talk to some of his staff. The first question that needed to be resolved was whether he should continue treating patients with cord blood. He had at least a half dozen patients in the pipeline scheduled to receive the treatment in the coming weeks. They were all desperate and desperately ill.

I reviewed the two prior legal opinions. I didn't think either of them accurately analyzed the law. On the other hand, I was very impressed by an e-mail the FDA had sent to a prospective patient. The FDA's e-mail said that as long as it was "not more than minimally manipulated," umbilical cord blood could be given to a patient for any condition.

Frankly, I was not convinced that this particular e-mail from the FDA public information office was consistent with the FDA's own regulations, but who was I to argue with the FDA's department of public communications? After all, it was their job to communicate with the public.

---

87   Recently, Bob informed me that in order not to scare the patients, or Mitch's kids who were at the clinic, he left most of his agents out in the clinic's driveway, and only went in with the medical board investigator; bless his heart.

Keep the Doors Open

Based on this e-mail, and the pressing need these patients had for this potentially helpful treatment, I told Mitch to keep treating patients. Also, I felt that whether he treated forty or sixty patients would not likely affect the outcome of the case, especially in light of the legal opinions and the FDA e-mail. I figured there would be enough confusion to negate any adverse effects from his continuing to treat patients after the FDA raid. So during the two weekends following the raid, Mitch treated several other patients.

Hang Together or Hang Separately

But while this was happening, FDA Bob was not just sitting on his thumbs. He started to call previously treated patients to see if he could generate more complaints against Mitch. As is normal in these kinds of criminal investigations, the government also tries to intimidate employees of the target of the investigation. Based on his wealth of experience at the postal inspector's office, Bob was very good at scaring people. Some of the employees were rattled. But I spoke to them and calmed them down and explained that harassment by government agents was part of their SOP (standard operating procedure).

It is also standard practice in these investigations to do an undercover sting operation. Prior to obtaining a search warrant, Bob pretended he was a patient with ALS and telephoned the clinic to obtain information about Mitch and the treatment. The person handling telephone calls from prospective patients was Ed Beck, the guy living on some small island in the upper Michigan peninsula. All of the calls were routed to him, and he forwarded the information to people who worked at the Atlanta clinic.

By the time Bob made his undercover call, the clinic had treated several dozen patients, some of whom had promising, albeit interim, results. Ed read to Bob an excerpt from one of the positive letters. The patient had gotten up from his wheelchair and started walking with a walker after being injected with the cord blood.

Ed also told undercover Bob that eighty percent of the patients had benefited from the treatment and twenty percent had not. Bob and the assistant U.S. attorney made a big deal about how these statements were fraudulent and misleading people into taking the treatment. However, I was not concerned. I had seen much worse. Mitch's clinic was telling all comers that the treatment was experimental, which by definition means it had not been proven to be effective for any condition. I don't have a problem with alternative practitioners relating "anecdotal evidence" about their past experience with the treatment, so long as the information is accurate and the patients are clearly advised that these modalities have not been proven to the satisfaction of the FDA or conventional medical practitioners.

One of the biggest problems that occurs after the feds or any state agency raids a medical clinic (or in technical parlance, executes a search warrant) is the fear and confusion experienced by the staff and patients. The feds try to exploit this to move its investigation forward. By that I mean they try to scare everyone involved into thinking they will all spend many years in jail unless they immediately spill their guts, plead guilty, and then thank the feds for their mercy. (I am a defense lawyer. Deal with it.)

The job of a criminal defense lawyer for a target is just the opposite, namely to slow things down, quiet things down, take control of the situation, and make sure nobody cooperates with the authorities. This is sometimes a daunting task because no one, not even a criminal defense attorney, can impede a federal investigation. That would be obstruction of justice or witness tampering. A lawyer cannot tell a company employee not to talk to the authorities. However, a lawyer can investigate the facts of the case, which in this case meant interviewing all of the employees of Mitch's clinic who had relevant information to the investigation. A lawyer can also give his or her opinion about the legality or appropriateness of an employee's conduct. The lawyer can also advise a potential witness as to his or her rights and obligations to speak to or cooperate with state or federal authorities and the consequences of such action. In short, it is a very delicate process.

Fortunately, after interviewing all of the clinic employees who were potential witnesses in the case, they all realized that despite all the bluster from the feds, there really was nothing to the criminal case. As a result, none of the employees implicated or inculpated Mitch or any of the other people in the clinic.

We also called most of the previously treated patients, and almost without exception, they were supportive of the treatment and wished Mitch and the clinic no harm. Eliminating clinic employees and previously treated patients as adverse witnesses took the steam out of the criminal investigation.

But FDA Bob Closes the Doors and Locks Them Tight

But the feds just don't roll over and die; FDA Bob had a few other tricks up his sleeve. He found out that the clinic was continuing to treat patients. Bob decided to put a stop to that.

Mitch had been getting his cord blood from a cord blood bank in Florida. There was little demand for cord blood. Mitch was the blood bank's biggest customer. They were charging Mitch almost fifteen thousand dollars for each patient treated, just for cord blood, so after treating forty patients, the blood bank was making good money.

From the documents he seized, Bob found out who was supplying Mitch with the blood. Bob telephoned the head of the blood bank. There is some dispute as to what Bob told him. The executive understood Bob to threaten to prosecute him and his company as co-conspirators unless he immediately stopped shipping the blood to Mitch.

Bob's recollection was different. He said that he would never threaten anyone with criminal prosecution, but he does recall asking the executive whether he and his company wanted to be involved in an ongoing criminal conspiracy. You've got to love these guys.

Whatever was said, the company got the message. The cord blood bank immediately notified Mitch that it would no longer be shipping product to him. Such are the powers of the federal government. There had been no trial and not even an indictment. The feds were just conducting an investigation. Yet they managed to stop the treatment by the application of fear and pressure. Like I said, you just have to love these guys. I know I do.

Bob's actions created a big problem for Mitch. There were at least a dozen patients who were scheduled to receive the treatment and who had already paid for it in advance or at least paid a deposit. These patients were not coming in for cosmetic surgery. They were all terminally ill with a horribly debilitating disease that would surely kill them. All of these patients had decided it was worth their time, money, and hope to try the treatment. Although the clinic looked around for other sources of cord blood, they could not find any source in the United States.

We only had two options. The first was to file an injunction action against the FDA on behalf of the clinic and its patients to force the FDA to allow them to continue the treatment. I had previously filed a case or two like that and surprisingly, I had some success. However, here, it was not the FDA that was preventing the people from being treated. Rather, it was the clinic's inability to obtain cord blood. Of course, FDA Bob certainly moved the blood bank in that direction. But the company's reluctance to provide cord blood meant that we would have to name the blood bank as a defendant as well. Somehow I did not see a federal judge ordering a private blood bank to provide its product to a clinic that was the subject of a federal criminal investigation for illegally using its product. Call me skeptical. Even though I had previously forced the FDA and M. D. Anderson to reinstate the antiferritin clinical trial, I didn't think it would work in this case.

Also, I was not excited about forcing a federal judge to decide whether using cord blood in MS and ALS patients was legal. It was one thing to wave around the legal opinions about the treatment, and I had a lot of fun waving the FDA's own e-mail in FDA Bob's face, but I was not convinced that any of these opinions were correct. So the last thing I wanted was a smart federal judge looking too closely at these opinions. I would feel much more comfortable waving them before a jury in a criminal trial to show that Mitch did not have any criminal intent and acted in the good-faith belief that it was legal to give the treatment to patients in Georgia.

The only other alternative was to advise the patients waiting on the treatment that it would not be available. And that is what we did. I decided to take the heat, and so I sent the letter as the attorney for the clinic. I didn't like explaining to these people that their only hope to extend their lives was being taken away from them, since I had spent much of the past twenty years helping people in this very type of situation. But that was the only practical option. Mitch refunded all of the money he had received from the untreated patients.

As might be expected, many of these folks and their spouses and caretakers were upset, but they understood that the fault lay with the federal government and not with the clinic. Some of the family members became quite vocal in expressing their hostility and antagonism toward the FDA and FDA Bob.

The most vocal of the group was Jerry Hoggatt. His wife Fran was a fifty-eight-year-old woman recently diagnosed with ALS. She was already in a wheelchair and was rapidly deteriorating. Jerry wrote dozens of letters to the federal government, congressmen, state officials, the news media, and anybody else who would listen to him. Several print and TV news organizations did stories on Fran and her desire to get stem cell treatment. But ultimately none of it did any good. The FDA continued its criminal investigation and did not rescind its threat against the cord blood bank (or the non-threatening questions, according to FDA Bob).

File an IND, Yeah Right!

We explored other ways to deliver the treatment to the patients. The normal way experimental drugs are given to patients is through filing an IND (Investigational New Drug application) with the FDA. Some of Mitch's supporters and friends of friends thought an IND could be fast-tracked given the patient population. I was skeptical, but it didn't hurt to investigate the option.

So I contacted several FDA officials and also checked with an FDA consultant. I was not surprised when the consultant told me it would take at least one hundred thousand dollars and a minimum of six months to prepare an IND application that had any chance of being approved. The FDA officials were cordial and helpful, but they simply had no concept of how full-time clinical practitioners operated. It just was not feasible for a one doctor operation like Mitch's to hire the technical support staff to put together the documentation necessary to file an IND, even one that would be fast tracked.

And therein lies the problem with the drug development process in the United States. Only drug companies have the money to push drugs through the approval process. Individual or even small groups of medical practitioners simply do not have the time or financial wherewithal to even get permission from the FDA to test a drug or promising treatment. The IND route was a nonstarter for Mitch.

"You Have to Know When to Hold 'Em and Know When to Fold 'Em"

Aside from these fruitless discussions about an IND, I spent much time talking to treated and untreated patients, the clinic's employees, FDA Bob, and the assistant U.S. attorney. The government wanted Mitch to plead guilty to a felony, but they would recommend leniency, just because they were nice guys.

I didn't think much of their case. No clinic employees would testify against Mitch. His patients and their family members were generally supportive. I thought Mitch's Web site and his informed consent form were informative and accurate. And of course, I had the two legal opinions and the FDA's e-mail stating that what Mitch was doing was legal. There were always risks. But I didn't see this as a criminal case. So we respectfully declined the government's generous offer for a felony plea and leniency.

The investigation continued, month after month, and we continued to resist all attempts for Mitch to take any kind of plea, even a misdemeanor. I talked myself blue in the face to Bob and the government lawyer about how the legal opinions proved Mitch acted in good faith and how much fun we would all have at the trial listening to the FDA explain that its own communications department was advising patients that the treatment was perfectly legal.

Over ninety percent of federal criminal cases result in plea agreements. Nonetheless, like Kenny Rogers sang, "You have to know when to hold 'em and know when to fold 'em." The government gave us one last chance to plead the case out, but based on my advice, Mitch said no.

We didn't hear much from the federales for some time. But even the feds eventually understand when it is time to fold. I guess they decided that there were bigger and more important criminals in need of prosecution.

By the end of 2003, we heard less and less from the feds. That could be either good or bad. It could mean that they were losing interest in the case or it could mean that they were putting the case together for an indictment. And you can't expect these guys to tell you which of the alternatives they are pursuing.

You just have to wait it out. Indeed, most of the time, the feds don't even tell you that you are off the hook. They simply go away and stop bothering the target and the witnesses. And they certainly do not make any statements to the media acknowledging that an investigation is closed or that they made a mistake in pursuing the matter.

Eventually Bob begrudgingly admitted to me that there would be no indictment against Mitch or any of his employees, but he still thought they were all guilty. He hinted that they decided to go in a different direction, whatever that meant. Several years later, I would find out in great detail what he meant by that. But the important thing was that because of circumstance, luck, and some skill, the feds backed off and closed their investigation of Dr. Mitchell Ghen. Of course the feds got something too. They put Mitch's Atlanta stem cell clinic out of business.

Mitch Chases His Newfound Love and Becomes the Traveling Man

By this time, Mitch was bitten by the stem cell bug. Unfortunately, there was no way he could treat patients with stem cells from umbilical cord blood in this country. A group of promoters/businessmen/con-men approached him about opening up a clinic in Mexico. As this was his only option to continue with his research and treat his untreated patients, Mitch quickly agreed and moved his family to some part of the hinterlands of Mexico. But promises made were not kept, and the endeavor fell apart within a few months.

The only good news was that most of the patients who were in the pipeline in Atlanta when the cord blood supply was cut off were eventually treated in Mexico. It was, however, too little and too late for Fran Hoggatt. Her disease rapidly progressed and by the time she could get to Mexico, she was already close to death. She died within a month or two of receiving the treatment.

After the deal in Mexico fell through, Mitch came back to America and worked part-time at a clinic in Florida. Then he found another group who had contacts with government officials in Gabon, Africa.

So Mitch worked in Gabon doing research, refining his techniques, and treating patients. After a few years, he decided to move back to this hemisphere, Belize to be exact. Mitch is now the director of medical research for a private international group with offices around the world. He currently treats patients using stem cells and is now treating a variety of medical conditions including some forms of cancer, multiple sclerosis, and ALS, and the research is continuing.

Stem cells are surely the next big idea in medicine, and Rabbi Mitch is out there in front of the pack in the finest tradition of the medical mavericks. It's too bad that a guy as bright and innovative as Mitch Ghen was driven out of the United States and forced to use this cutting-edge technology in third-world countries rather than in the United States. But I guess that is the price we have to pay for health safety, or so the regulators would have us believe.

Postscript

For those concerned that your tax dollars were wasted by government employees engaging in a fruitless investigation that did not result in a federal indictment, worry not.

Although the feds moved away from Mitch and his clinic, FDA Bob and AUSA Chartash found another target close at hand. After Mitch left his original stem cell venture, his former partners opened up a stem cell clinic in Atlanta called Biomark. They treated dozens of patients, many of whom had multiple sclerosis. They took stem cells from umbilical cord blood and grew the cells in cultures.

Since he wasn't getting anywhere on Mitch's case, in late 2003, Bob raided Biomark. Not waiting to see how the story would end, and wanting to continue their stem cell business, the owners of Biomark left the country and relocated to South Africa. They continued to arrange for treatment in Europe and became famous or infamous for providing unapproved stem cell treatment. Eventually their European operation was shut down as well.

As to their American problems, they initially hired an attorney out of California. But alas, they were not as fortunate as Mitch. The two Biomark owners were indicted in 2006 on fifty-two counts of wire fraud and FDA violations. They are currently fighting extradition from South Africa. Bob and I are renewing our acquaintanceship. It will take several years to prepare the defense of that case.

Stay tuned for the sequel: *Galileo's Lawyer/Rasputin's Mouthpiece: More Tales in the Alternative Health Wars.*

CHAPTER TEN

Further Thoughts

There is no conclusion to this book because complementary and alternative practitioners will surely continue to be prosecuted, persecuted, and sued. These battles will continue to be fought so long as people have medical conditions that cannot be cured by conventional medicine—in other words, so long as there continues to be a need or demand for the services and products of complementary and alternative practitioners and manufacturers. But even though there is no conclusion, if you do something long enough, chances are you will have something to say about it, and I do have some further thoughts on the subject.

As set forth in the introduction, many of the cases in this field involve two competing interests or policies: the right of people to have control over their own bodies versus the government's role or obligation to protect the public from dangerous, questionable, or unproven remedies. Most reasonable people would agree that both interests are legitimate. So it becomes a matter of balancing these competing interests.

The clearest example of where the government overprotects people is in its irrational insistence that terminally ill cancer patients should only use

FDA-approved drugs or standard remedies and can only use experimental drugs after so called "proven remedies" have failed. Everyone in the conventional medical community knows that there are certain types of cancer for which there are no conventional curative treatments. The FDA's insistence that terminal patients take these drugs (which at best extend life a few weeks or a month or two) before experimental or unconventional treatment can be utilized makes no sense.

For over a dozen years, legislators like Senator Tom Harkin and Congressman Dan Burton have tried to fix this problem. But their legislation has gone nowhere ultimately because the medical and pharmaceutical industry do not support it, and most congress folk are not interested in protecting the average person from government in this area, or so it would seem to me. A new access bill in now circulating, and maybe this time Congress will do the right thing.

Even the courts have tried to create an exemption from the FDA act for terminally ill patient cancer patients. In the 1970s, a brave Oklahoma district court judge tried to give people the constitutional or statutory right to use unconventional medicine like laetrile, but the Supreme Court slapped him down. Just recently, a panel of the District of Columbia Federal Court of Appeals suggested that terminally ill patients may have a right to investigational drugs before their approval. However, on reargument before all the judges of the circuit, the case was reversed. So terminally ill patients are still left with only FDA-approved treatments. This just seems wrong to me. Dying patients should have the ultimate say as to what treatment they should be able to take, and their choices should include any experimental or unconventional treatment the patients can get their hands on.

But on the other hand, I don't have a problem with state governments prosecuting naturopaths or anyone else who pretend they are doctors, who vastly inflate their credentials, or who scare people into taking supplements to cure "tendencies" to cancer. And of course, above all else, information about drugs, supplements, products and devices, and testing equipment should be as accurate and complete as possible, on pain of unwanted governmental attention. There should be little tolerance for anyone, whether conventional or complementary, who misleads the public or patients, or overstates their qualifications, experience or past results.

I have a major problem with the undereducated but well-organized and well-financed dietitians who are trying to stop the dissemination of truthful information about dietary supplements and who pretend there is not a vast body of literature out there supporting the use of many supplements. This smacks of the feudal times when guilds protected the monopoly of their members by having the king enforce the guild's exclusive right to practice a trade. That an organization like the dietitians is taking control of the flow of information about nutrition is disconcerting because they are overtly hostile to dietary supplements and oppose efforts to move away from their antiquated "four food group" mentality. Hopefully the success the dietitians have had in the state legislatures will eventually be seen for what it is: a naked grab for power, thinly disguised in the mantle of consumer protection.

I also have a problem with the way drugs are tested in this country. There is too much emphasis on protecting the public, which is an abstract concept, and not enough concern by the government and the drug testing centers on the individual patients/subjects, especially those with terminal diseases.

And it seems to me that there is a fundamental flaw in the way supplements are tested here. Supplements are not drugs and supplements often work differently and more indirectly than drugs. I have seen the way alternative remedies are tested in this country, and I am very skeptical of the methodologies employed. Increasingly, legitimate scientists are starting to publish articles about the bias and methodological flaws in the testing of herbs and supplements.

Medical science is a human endeavor. That means it is necessarily infused with an inherent disorder, messiness, bias, animus, and lack of objectivity. The philosophers of science have it wrong to the extent they believe that psychology, sociology, prejudice, and even sociopathology play no role in the growth of medical knowledge (or the lack thereof).

As to the legislative and administrative process for the licensing and disciplining of health care practitioners, I think laymen do not understand how much bias, subjectivity, professional self-interest, and trade protectionism is involved in the regulation and sanctioning of health practitioners. Complementary practitioners continue to be sanctioned across the country merely because they use treatments that are not accepted by conventional medicine, even in the absence of patient harm or patient complaints. Some (but certainly not all) of these cases are the result of narrow-minded bias or worse.

Since all of these non-objective, knowledge-inhibiting, and all-too-human forces will surely continue, the future should be as interesting as the past has been.

And Finally, a Moment

The setting: the Burzynski clinic's thirtieth anniversary celebration, late 2007. Almost everyone from the clinic and Research Institute was there. So were the patients from the days of the Burzynski wars, including, of course, Mary Jo and Steve Siegel (Steve was the master of ceremonies of the event), Rita Starr, Paul Michaels and his mother, Mary Michaels, Dustin Kunnari and his parents, Marianne and Jack. Jim and Donna Navarro, and many, many others who supported Burzynski over the years were also there.

It felt like a cross between a family reunion and a meeting of war veterans. Feelings you can only have toward people with whom you have a common bond tempered by shared experiences involving great uncertainty and peril. Sort of like a *Band of Brothers*.

It was a long and emotional night, reigniting feelings and thoughts I hadn't felt or thought for ten years. Half of my family was away on a trip, but I convinced or forced my fourteen-year-old son, Daniel, to come with me. I made him wear a suit but not a tie, and as a further concession, I let him wear his skater's beanie over his almost shoulder-length hair, presumably so everyone would know that he was a "skater dude."

Daniel and I sat at the same table as Marianne, Jack, and Dustin Kunnari. Dustin had been diagnosed at age two with medulloblastoma. His parents refused conventional therapy and instead went straight to the Burzynski clinic. He was now a completely normal, healthy sixteen-year-old. He and other patients spoke and expressed their gratitude to Dr. Burzynski for saving their lives.

As the party was ending and people were starting to leave, I was still sitting with Daniel at the table, but the Kunnaris were standing and talking to some other patients. Donna Navarro, the mother of Thomas Navarro, came toward our table. She put her arms around Dustin, hugged him, and started crying. Marianne Kunnari looked at them both and also started crying.

At that moment, for me, everything else in the ballroom disappeared. It was just those three. Looking at Donna Navarro, I could almost feel her anguish and her loss. Dustin had medullloblastoma just like her son Thomas, and both kids had the same terminal prognosis. Dustin received treatment without any prior chemotherapy. It was largely based on Dustin's remission with the same disease that the Navarros tried to convince the FDA to allow Thomas to undergo Burzynski's treatment first, just like Dustin had done. But the FDA refused. They forced Thomas to take chemotherapy. It was the side effects of the chemo that eventually killed Thomas, even though his tumors were shrinking under Burzynski's treatment.

That moment, seeing Donna Navarro hug Dustin Kunnari with Marianne looking at them, the two mothers crying, brought it all back for me; the joy, hope and satisfaction as well as the anguish, heartache and frustration.

Maybe I was getting misty too, because Daniel asked me if I was okay. I mumbled something, gave him a hug, kissed him on his beanie, and said, "Thanks for coming. We're out of here."

Acknowledgements

I would like to thank my friends and colleagues who graciously agreed to review and comment on this book and offered words of encouragement. In particular, Brad Hayes, the most knowledgeable chiropractor I have ever met; William Dailey, my local and co-counsel in my California cases; Marcus A. Cohen for his valuable insights on Dr. Revici; and Lynne Ford, whose enthusiasm for the book helped keep me writing (and rewriting). Some of the people who helped me wish to remain anonymous, so to the following individuals, thank you: ██████████, ██████████, and most of all ██████████, the most talented and generous ██████████ I ever met.

As strange as it may seem, I would also like to acknowledge the many adversaries I have faced over the years. Much of what I have learned as a lawyer has come from them, especially in the early years. To Alice, Mike, and especially Harvey; to Dewey for always being a gentleman and having the humanity to know when to push hard and when not to; to Mike, George, and Amy for forcing me to dig deeper to help keep the Burzynski clinic open. Nietzsche said that what doesn't kill you makes you stronger. So I acknowledge the many adversaries who have made me stronger, even if that was not their intent.

To Trish Lambert and her Amherst writing course. I had been struggling with this book for many years. I don't know what she did, but after taking her five-session course, I completed a draft in three months. It was the best hundred bucks I've spent in a long time.

To my graphic designer, Sonja Fulbright, for her eye, taste, and her common sense advice.

To my family and especially my wife, Amy, for her support and valuable comments.

And with profound gratitude, I acknowledge the patients, those who survived, and especially those who did not. Their courage, tenacity, and spirit have inspired me professionally and personally.[88]

---

88   Pictures of Thomas Navarro, Sue Spenceley, Jimmy Hagen, and many of the other patients and their doctors mentioned in this book are posted at www.galileoslawyer.com.

Appendix: Healthcare Law 101

I could also call this section "It's a Regulatory Jungle Out There!" It may be helpful to more fully understand the stories in this book if some of the key terms in healthcare law are discussed, and a short explanation is provided about how healthcare is regulated in the United States.

Who Regulates What

The federal government and the governments of each state regulate different parts of healthcare system. The federal government (which I sometimes affectionately refer to as the "federales" or the "feds") regulates drugs, supplements, and medical devices via the FDA (Food and Drug Administration, or as people in my community call it, the "Foot Dragging Administration").

The FTC (Federal Trade Commission) regulates advertising by product and device manufacturers. (In one recent action, the FTC went after the male performance enhancer company which features "Smiling Bob" on cable commercials. After the FTC went after them, Bob is not smiling as much).

What Rights Do You Have to Take Non FDA-Approved Treatments? (Almost None)

United States citizens do not have a constitutional or a statutory right to receive any treatment they want. Only drugs which have been approved by the FDA for some use can be legally marketed and used in this country, with two exceptions.

A patient can use an experimental drug as part of a clinical trial (or under a special/compassionate use exception, if the patient does not meet all of the entry criteria to enroll in the clinical trial). In addition, there is a "personal use" exception, whereby the FDA allows patients with serious diseases to bring up to a three months supply of an unapproved drug from another country. The personal use exemption has been mostly applied to AIDS patients, but cancer patients are also usually allowed to bring into this country non FDA-approved cancer drugs.

Once a drug has been approved by the FDA or after the FDA has approved or "registered" a medical device, a licensed practitioner can use the drug or device for any medical condition and not just the use for which it was approved. This is called "off label use." However, manufacturers are not supposed to promote or advertise off label uses of drugs or devices.

The FDA Approval Process, or If You're Not Big Pharma, It Ain't Happening

Before a drug is approved by the FDA, it has to go through extensive, lengthy and extremely expensive testing to prove that the drug is safe and effective for its intended use. There are various estimates about the time and costs for a drug to be approved, but it could easily be ten years and cost between $100 million and $250 million. Many drugs are tested and abandoned during some stage of the testing and approval process.

Drug testing involves a preclinical and a clinical phase. Preclinical work involves testing a drug on cells and is called *in vitro*. Drugs which show some promise *in vitro* move on to testing in animals, which is called *in vivo*.

Initially, *in vivo* testing is done on small animals, like white mice. Drugs which show promise in these tests are then tested on larger animals, like dogs or monkeys. Testing on these larger animals usually gives scientists an idea of both the effective and lethal doses of the drug. The *in vitro* and *in vivo* stages of a drug test could take years, and many tens of millions of dollars, or more.

Testing on Humans: All It Takes Is a Few Hundred Trees and $$$$

Once all the *in vitro* and *in vivo* animal studies are completed, and if the drug shows promise in these models, the drug company submits an application to test the drug in human beings, which is called an Investigational New Drug (IND) application.[89] INDs are almost always extremely lengthy documents and usually run into the thousands or tens of thousands of pages, or more, because they must contain the complete history of drug testing, extensive information as to how the drug is manufactured, and extensive chemical analysis.

Usually IND applications are prepared by major drug companies or by smaller drug companies with the help of private FDA consultants (most of whom are former FDA employees). It is virtually impossible for a clinical practitioner to prepare an IND to test a drug. It is simply too expensive and time consuming for an individual doctor or even a small group of doctors to prepare the paperwork.

In addition to the extensive and expensive paperwork, in most FDA clinical studies, the patients are not charged for the drug. Oftentimes, many of the medical services are provided for free as well. Usually the owner of the drug pays for all this, which makes drug testing an extremely expensive proposition since hundreds of patients are usually needed to complete clinical trials.

After an IND is submitted, the FDA has 30 days to respond to the application. If it does not respond, then the clinical study can progress. If the FDA has questions about an IND application, they will put the IND on "clinical hold." The FDA and the sponsor of the study go back and forth asking and answering questions and frequently the FDA asks for more data. This can take months, or in the case of Dr. Burzynski, six years.

Normally, the first drug test under an IND is a Phase I clinical trial, which only tests the toxicity of a drug. Being one of the first patients in a Phase I clinical

---

89   The regulations for IND applications are found at 21 Code of Federal Regulations (CFR) 312.

trial is not a good thing. By definition, the early patients in such a study are the first humans to receive the drug. Drug companies cannot always predict a drug's side effects on humans based on animal studies. Testing the dosage and side effects in humans is the job of the initial patients in a Phase I clinical study.

That leads to the second problem or downside in being an early Phase I test subject. Because of the uncertainty about how the drug will affect humans, the early subjects in a Phase I study often receive less than the expected therapeutic dose of the drug. Some drugs are found to have intolerable side effects on the early test subjects even in reduced doses. So for safety reasons, early patients in a Phase I clinic trial often receive what is thought to be a sub-optimal dose of the drug.

If the drug is tolerated in the early patients, gradually the dose is increased in subsequent patients, up to what the investigators expect to be the ideal therapeutic dose.

Once the investigators establish the safe levels of the drug in humans, and if the drug still shows promise, they will continue into Phase II clinical studies. Phase II studies continue to study toxicity, but they also test for efficacy. Phase II studies are usually fairly small in terms of numbers of patients enrolled.

More Testing and More $$$$$$

If the drug is relatively safe and has achieved some beneficial therapeutic response, then it moves on to Phase III (or even sometimes Phase IV) studies. These are large-scale studies to test the efficacy and response rate of the drug, i.e., the percentage of people who have a positive result from the drug.

A Lot More Trees and More $$$$$$$$

Once a drug goes through all of these phases of clinical studies (and this process usually takes many years), the sponsor submits an application for New Drug Approval (NDA).[90] The NDA application contains extensive information

---

90   See 21 CFR 314.

about the clinical trials, the drug's chemistry, and all kinds of other information. The FDA thoroughly reviews the application. It can approve or disapprove the application, or require more testing. And that is how drug companies spend hundreds of millions of dollars getting a drug approved.

Nutritional Supplements

Nutritional supplements are treated much differently than drugs as a result of a dietary supplement act passed by Congress in 1994. Under the act (referred to as *DSHEA* and discussed on pages 224-225), a dietary supplement does not need to be approved by the FDA before it is sold. The difference between a dietary supplement and a drug is one of the most unintuitive parts of federal health law.

A drug is any chemical product which is intended for the treatment, diagnosis or mitigation of a disease or medical condition. Thus, the definition is functional. It is based on the product's intended use, not its chemical composition.

If a supplement manufacturer makes a claim that an herb, mineral, or vitamin is a cure for a disease, by FDA regulatory magic, the product is a drug and cannot be legally sold unless it has gone through the full IND and NDA drug approval process. The only claim a supplement manufacturer can make is that the product helps the structure or function of a physiological or biological system.

For example, a product which claims to cure benign prostate disease is a drug, regardless of its chemical composition, even if it is an herb. But that same herb which only claims to help good urinary flow is a supplement.

Because of the functional definition of a drug, supplement manufacturers and people who sell supplements try not to make any kind of disease claims for fear of turning their product into an unapproved new drug.

However, there are a few supplements, such as folic acid for pregnant women and calcium for women with osteoporosis, for which some limited claims can be made, because the FDA was presented with sufficient data supporting such claims. But there are very few supplements in this category, and that number is not likely to substantially increase for two reasons: the high cost to provide convincing evidence to the FDA, and the fact that these products are not patentable, so companies do not have a financial incentive to pay for testing.

So federal law, primarily through the FDA, regulates healthcare products. There are stiff civil and criminal penalties for FDA act violations. The FDA does not directly regulate health care practitioners, that job is left to the fifty states.

The States Regulate Healthcare Practitioners

Each state has its own set of laws that license various types of healthcare practitioners. All states broadly define the "practice of medicine" so as to include anything having to do with the diagnosis, treatment, or mitigation of any disease or medical condition. Unless licensed as a medical doctor (or otherwise licensed by the state to practice a healthcare profession), a practitioner cannot diagnose, cure, treat, or mitigate a disease or medical condition, or even offer to do so. The illegal practice of medicine constitutes a misdemeanor or felony depending on the circumstances and the state in which the act occurs.

All states now license chiropractors. Many states license acupuncturists. Fourteen states license naturopaths. (These states are listed on page 208, footnote 47.) Almost all states have some certification or regulation for dietitians and/or nutritionists. In approximately thirty states, in order to provide nutritional services for a fee, a dietetics/nutritionist license is required.

One of the main functions of state licensure of healthcare practitioners is to protect the public (or so it is claimed). Only if the practitioner has gone to an accredited school and has passed a state licensing examination can he or she practice his or her profession, if the profession is subject to licensure in the state. The healthcare boards supervise the admission of practitioners into state licensure.

The other way healthcare boards protect the public is by investigating and resolving disciplinary complaints against practitioners. The source of the complaint is not disclosed to the practitioner. When a complaint is made against the practitioner, there is an administrative process which the board has to follow.

This administrative law process is much more streamlined and abbreviated than criminal cases or civil lawsuits. Some people (and even some lawyers) feel that it is no real process at all.

The board can impose a variety of sanctions against the practitioner for a violation of ethics or the standards of care of the profession. The sanctions range from fines, to suspension, to the ultimate sanction, license revocation. A practitioner who loses his license has a right to appeal to state court, but most of the time, the courts defer to the decisions of the healthcare boards, especially if the case involves a standard of care issue.

Throughout the country, there are thousands of unlicensed healthcare practitioners. Most of them never run afoul of the law. The key is that they cannot claim to diagnose or treat diseases or medical conditions. They do other things, like restore the body's energy, allow the body to heal itself, and/ or provide nutritional support. They do everything but diagnose or treat diseases or medical conditions.

Class dismissed. You all passed!

For Further Reading

The Legal Aspects of Complementary and Alternative Medicine

The most prolific and leading legal scholar/author in the field is Michael H. Cohen, Esq. He has written several law review articles and many books on the subject, including *Complementary and Alternative Medicine: Legal Boundaries and Regulatory Perspectives* and *The Practice of Integrative Medicine: A Legal and Operational Guide*.

A complete list of his publications and Amazon links to his books can be found at his Web site, www.michaelhcohen.com.

See also: "Notes and Comments: Alternative Medicine's Roadmap to Mainstream," Kristen J. Josefek, Boston University School of Law, *American Journal of Law and Medicine*, 26 Am. J. L. and Med. 195 (2000); *The Shadow Health Care System: Regulation of Alternative Health Care Providers*, Lori B. Andrews, 32 Hous. L. Rev. 1273 (1996).

The Battles between CAM and Conventional Medicine

Ralph Moss has written what is probably the most comprehensive book on alternative health practitioners who have been persecuted by the medical establishment, *The Cancer Industry* (New York: Paragon House, 1989). He also has an excellent book on the failures and overuse of chemotherapy called *Questioning Chemotherapy*. More information about Ralph and his books can be found on his Web site: www.cancerdecisions.com.

For a recent book on the battle between homeopathy and conventional medicine, see *Copeland's Cure* (New York: Knopf, 2005) by Natalie Robbins.

However, the definitive treatise on the history of homeopathy and its battles with the allopaths is the multi-volume *Divided Legacy: The Schism in Medical Thought* (Berkeley: North Atlantic Books, 1973) by my late friend Harris Coulter. Harry wrote several other books on homeopathy as well as a few books on the problems with vaccinations. Most of his books are listed at http://www.homeopathic.com/code=COU-DIV3H.

An interesting study on the sociology and biases in the testing of an unconventional therapy is *Vitamin C and Cancer: Medicine and Politics* (Hong Kong: St. Martin's Press, 1991) by Evelleen Richards.

There are many books written by CAM supporters that take a harsh view of conventional medicine's attempt to suppress CAM modalities including: *Racketeering In Medicine: The Supression of Alternatives* (Norfolk: Hampton Roads, 1992) by James P. Carter, and *Dirty Medicine: Science, Big Business and the Assault on Natural Health Care* (London: Sling Shot Publications, 1993) by Martin J. Walker.

The History of American Medicine

Paul Starr's *The Social Transformation of American Medicine* (New York: Basic Books, 1983) is required reading for anyone seriously interested in under-standing how medicine evolved in this country. It is simply the best work in the field, and a few others must agree since it won the 1984 Pulitzer Prize for general nonfiction.

Complementary and Alternative Medicine in General

Bookstores have entire sections on complementary and alternative medicine. The biggest and most comprehensive book is *Alternative Medicine: The Definitive Guide,* 2nd Ed., (Berkeley: Ten Speed Press, 2002) by Burton Goldberg,

John W. Anderson and Larry Trivieri (bring someone to help you carry it home; it's heavy).

Anti-Alternative Health Resources

For those wanting to read how alternative health remedies never work, and how people are duped by these snake oil salesmen, there are many books, publications, and Web sites that debunk and criticize all things alternative.

My late "friend" Victor Herbert and Stephen Barrett wrote a classic anti-supplement book called *The Vitamin Pushers* (New York: Prometheus Books, 1994). The title says it all.

The most recent antisupplement book has the pithy and understated title: *Natural Causes: Death, Lies, and Politics in America's Vitamin and Herbal Supplement Business* (New York: Broadway Books, 2006), written by journalist Dan Hurley. The author has a very limited view of what constitutes scientific evidence. The book is well written, and I enjoyed reading it. Just don't expect fair or balanced (and that is an understatement). The dietitians should love this book since it regurgitates their view that there are only about three supplements that have proven to be effective, and anyone involved selling other supplements is an immoral quack or an unethical businessman.

For a recent book that argues that all complementary and alternative therapies work because of the placebo effect see *Snake Oil Science: The Truth About Complementary and Alternative Medicine* (Oxford: Oxford University Press, 2007) by R. Barker Bausell. The book has a really clever cover. If he is right that it's all just a placebo, then I know many cancer patients who apparently talked themselves out of terminal cancer, including many infants and very small children. And I also know numerous patients who went through multiple regimes of ineffective conventional medicine for chronic conditions only to be subsequently cured by placebos given by unconventional practitioners.

Stephen Barrett, one of the most visible quack-busters, has a popular anti-alternative health Web site called www.quackwatch.com. It covers all things alternative and natural, and is all negative, all the time.

Emanuel Revici

There is only one biography of Revici, *The Man Who Cured Cancer* (New York: Be Well Books, 1996) by Kelly Item. It is out of print but is available from a variety of sources including Amazon.

The best source for detailed information about all things Revici is Marcus A. Cohen. Marcus has published articles about Revici and his treatment in the *Townsend Letter for Doctors*. Part 1 appeared in the August–September 2004 issue and is available at http://findarticles.com/p/articles/mi_m0ISW/is_253-254/ai_n6176266/pg_1.

Stanislaw Burzynski

Dr. Burzynski and his researchers have published over two hundred articles on antineoplastons. See his Web site, www.Cancermed.com, for the list of these publications.

The only published book about Burzynski is *The Burzynski Breakthrough* (Los Angeles: GPG, 1997) by journalist Tom Elias. Half of the book consists of stories of some of the individual patients treated by Burzynski during the heyday of his problems.

What About Kids?

There is very little written specifically about this subject. Michael Horwin has written an excellent law review article on the subject, "'War on Cancer': Why Does the FDA Deny Access to Alternative Cancer Treatments?" originally published in 2001 in the *California Western Law Review*, and republished in *Albany Law Journal of Science and Technology* Summer/Fall 2003 (13 Alb. L.J. Sci. & Tech. 681). Michael has personal experience in this field, as the authorities forced his young son to take conventional therapy for a malignant brain tumor, after trying to get his son on Burzynski's treatment.

Sue Spenceley and the RIT Program

Until now, there has been almost nothing written about RIT's patients and their fight to get this treatment. The only mention I found on the subject is

a short blurb in *ScienceNewsOnline* at http://www.sciencenews.org/pages/
sn_arc97/7_19_97/bob1.htm.

H. H. Fudenberg and Transfer Factor

There are no books or publications in the lay press about Fudenberg or transfer
factor. However, Fudenberg is a very prolific author, and he has published
almost nine hundred journal articles. The best source for further information
about him and transfer factor is his Web site, www.nitf.org.

Chiropractic

There are numerous books on chiropractic. Louis Sportelli, one of the
country's most visible and politically active chiropractors, has written a short
book which I hear is very good at explaining the basics: *A Natural Method of
Health Care: Introduction to Chiropractic* (Norwalk: Practicemakers Products,
2001).

The most popular trade journal for chiropractic is *Dynamic Chiropractic*
(*DC*). It is available online at www.chiroweb.com. *DC* is readable by a layman
and contains many articles about recent trends in chiropractic and scientific
studies in the field. On occasion, I publish articles in *DC* about various legal
issues affecting chiropractic.

What I referred to in the book as the "super-straights" is a wellness based
model of chiropractic created or advocated by Terri Rondberg, who runs an
organization called the World Chiropractic Alliance. I did some legal work for
Terri and his group many years ago and found many of the group's practitioners
to be highly competent and very enthusiastic about advancing the general
health of their patients through on-going chiropractic care. More information
about this approach can be found at www.worldchiropracticalliance.org.

Naturopathy

There are many books on naturopathy and natural healing. One of the most
recent is by David Brady called *Healthy Revolution* (New York: Morgan James,
2007). David teaches at the University of Bridgeport. He is a chiropractor, has
training in naturopathy and is a certified clinical nutritionist.

There is much original information about naturopathy at www. soilandhealth.org. This Web site contains an online library of old and mostly out-of-print books, many of which are downloadable. Particularly recommended are the works of Henry Lindlahr and James Thomson. However, many others are worth exploring. The site offers blurbs for most of their books.

Nature Doctors, by Kirchfeld and Boyle, is available in used copies through Amazon and new from https://ncnm.edu/bookstore/ (the book store at National College of Naturopathic Medicine which is now the publisher). This book recounts the history of naturopathy.

Diet and Nutrition

There are dozens if not hundreds of books on nutrition and diets. Throughout the years, as an attorney in the field, I have attended numerous alternative health conferences and have heard lectures from some very smart people, many of whom have written books. Here are some of the people I have been most impressed by and some of the books they have written. (All of these authors have Web sites where you can obtain more information.)

Russell L. Blaylock, MD, CCN. *Health and Nutrition Secrets That Can Save Your Life* (Albuquerque: Health Press, 2002). *Excitotoxins, The Taste That Kills* (Santa Fe: Health Press, 1997). Russell was a neurosurgeon before he started focusing on nutrition issues. He publishes a terrific monthly newsletter called *Blaylock Wellness Report.* Definitely go to his Web site at www.russellblaylock. com.

James B. LaValle, RPh, ND, CCN. *Smart Medicine For Healthier Living* (Garden City: Avery Publishing, 1999); *Cracking The Metabolic Code: 9 Keys To Optimal Health* (North Bergen: Basic Health Publications, 2004).

Ross Pelton, RPh, CCN. *The Nutritional Cost of Prescription Drugs* (Englewood: Morton, 2004). *Mind Food and Smart Pills* (New York: Doubleday, 1989).

Fred Pescatore, MD, CCN. *The Allergy and Asthma Cure: A Complete 8-Step Nutritional Program* (Hoboken: John Wiley & Sons, 2003).

Elizabeth Lipski, PhD, CCN. *Digestive Wellness* (New Canaan: Keats Publishing, 1996).

Theresa Dale, PhD, ND, CCN. *Revitalize Your Hormones: Dr. Dale's 7 Steps To a Happier, Healthier & Sexier You* (Hoboken: John Wiley & Sons, 2005).

Michael A. Schmidt, PhD, CCN. *Brain Building Nutrition: How Dietary Fats & Oils Affect Mental, Physical and Emotional Intelligence* (Berkeley: North Atlantic Books, 2006); *Beyond Antibiotics, Healthier Options for Families* (Berkeley: North Atlantic Books, 1993); *Childhood Ear Infections* (Berkeley: North Atlantic Books, 1990)

Carol N. Simontacchi, MS, CCN. *The Crazy Makers: How The Food Industry Is Destroying Our Brains & Harming Our Children* (New York: Putnam Books, 2007).

I would also recommend any book written by Patrick Quillin, including his most recent book, *Beating Cancer with Nutrition* (Carlsbad: Nutrition Times Press, 2001). Patrick is a registered dietitian (too bad they don't listen to him) and has a certification in clinical nutrition. He is one of the most thoughtful and knowledgeable people in the field. Go to his Web site for more information about his books: http://www.patrickquillin.com/.

Another popular author who has been around a long time is Gary Null. There is not enough space here to list all of his books. Best to go to his Web site for a complete list. www.garynull.com. Gary does it all. He has DVDs, sells vitamins and has hosted a popular radio show, at least as long as I've been in the field (and that's almost twenty-five years). Gary is a good friend to alternative health practitioners, and he is one of the most passionate and knowledgeable spokesmen for good nutrition and alternative remedies out there. I have been a guest on his show several times for the Revici, Burzynski and other of my cases.

As indicated in the "Food Fights" chapter, Jeffrey B. Blumberg, PhD, is one of the leading scientists talking about bias and other problems with the studies on supplements and nutrients. Among his many articles and interviews are: "Why Clinical Trials of Vitamin E and Cardiovascular Diseases May Be Fatally Flawed. Commentary on 'The Relationship between Dose of Vitamin E and Suppression of Oxidative Stress in Humans'" published in *Free Radical Biology and Medicine* 43, no. 10 (2007): 1374–76; *Unraveling the Conflicting Studies on Vitamin E and Heart Disease* at http://lpi.oregonstate.edu/ss02/blumberg.html.

For more information about the noble and selfless efforts of the American Dietetics Association, see its Web site, www.eatright.org. (People who are really in the nutrition and health field get a big laugh out of the name of the ADA's site.)

For more information on the CCN certification see the Clinical Nutrition Certification Board at www.cncb.org. For more information about the CCNs (the International and American Association of Clinical Nutritionists) see its Web site, www.iaacn.org.

For more information about the Texas Health Freedom Coalition, go to www.texashealthfreedom.com.

Stem Cells

Mitch Ghen has published a review of the work in the field, "Potential Clinical Applications Using Stem Cells Derived from Human Umbilical Cord" published in *Reproductive Biomedicine Online* (www.rbmonline. com/article/2372), July 18, 2006.

Currently the only book on umbilical cord stem cells is *Umbilical Cord Stem Cells* (Laguna Beach: Basic Health, 2006) by David Steenblock, DO, and Anthony Payne, PhD.

The longest and most comprehensive book on the history of stem cell research for layman is *Cell of Cells: The Global Race to Capture and Control the Stem Cell* (New York: Norton, 2007) by Cynthia Fox. The book has a very good exposition of the South Korean stem cell fraud case. Another worthwhile book on the subject is *Stem Cells Now: From the Experiment that Shook the World to the New Politics of Life* (New York: Pi Press, 2006) by Thomas Scott.

Index